Sierra's Journey

Lee Anne M. Sgambati

NEWMAN SPRINGS PUBLISHING
320 Broad Street
Red Bank, NJ 07701

First originally published by Newman Springs Publishing 2023

ISBN 978-1-68498-625-5 (Paperback)
ISBN 978-1-68498-626-2 (Digital)

Printed in the United States of America

This book is dedicated to the biggest fighter I know, my baby girl, Sierra. To all of the people who have incurred TBIs and have fought for their lives back; and to my husband, Jeff, who never got the chance to read the finished product of *Sierra's Journey*.

On August 24, 2017, as I was eating dinner with my boyfriend and my roommate, I received a phone call from Coach Lucas. "Lee Anne, do you know where Sierra is?" he said.

"Yes, she is on her way to Las Cruces. She should be here any minute," I said.

Then the most terrifying words came out of his mouth. "No! She's been in an accident and airlifted to Albuquerque."

I asked him what happened. How did he get this information? I couldn't comprehend what he was saying. I told him that he must be wrong, that I was just texting her a little while ago and she was on her way home. He assured me that he had the correct information, that she and a couple of her teammates, along with Sierra's boyfriend, were in an accident. Her teammates' parents were already on their way to Socorro where the accident happened, and Sierra had to be airlifted to Albuquerque because she was in very bad condition.

All of a sudden, my world fell apart. I grabbed my driver's license, put my shoes on, and headed out the door. I grabbed my keys, and my boyfriend stopped me and told me, "No way you are driving!" He insisted on taking me, and I didn't have time to argue with him, so we jumped in the car and started the three-hour drive to Albuquerque. I immediately called Sierra's dad, Art, and told him what I knew, which wasn't much. He asked what happened to her. "Is she okay? Who was she with? How did it happen?" I had no answers to any of his questions. When we got on the road, the only information we had was that she was airlifted to Albuquerque from Socorro where the accident occurred.

We didn't know what her injuries were or what her prognosis was. My heart was pounding out of my chest. I had so much anxiety I felt like I was going to explode. When we got on the road, I started getting phone calls. I was told there were four people in the car; two of her teammates, her boyfriend, and our baby girl. Our nineteen-year-old who worked so hard her whole life to earn the full ride that put her in that car that fateful day. We learned that the car rolled seven times and that our daughter and her boyfriend were ejected from the vehicle.

My first thought was, *Ejected? She always wears her seat belt!* Maybe they were mistaken? We had just had a talk about that the week prior when she went back to school for her second year of college. She assured me that she always wore her seat belt on the highway because she had lost a friend of hers in high school. She didn't always wear it in the city, but she knew how important it was to wear it on the highway. The helplessness was overwhelming.

My roommate, who was present when I got the call that changed our lives, told me that he would call my big sister and our family. We were about an hour into the 225-mile trip when my sister called me and informed me that my son, Anthony, was on his way to Albuquerque. Until that point, I tried to convince myself that it wasn't that bad, that it was Sierra. Sierra overcame every obstacle that was put in her way and kicked its butt. Nothing ever held her down. Now my son was on his way to Albuquerque because his sister was airlifted.

It was at that point the realization that our baby girl could die set in. I started telling Jeff, "If she doesn't make it, neither will I." There is no way I could do this again. I could not survive the death of another child. I started praying to God, for him to please spare my child, telling him that he knew I wouldn't survive if he took her. I told Jeff again, "Please understand what I'm feeling. I can't do this again."

He tried to soothe me, and I tried to make him understand that I know what it takes to survive the death of my child, and there was no way I could do it again. All the feelings of losing one of my twin boys came rushing in. The helplessness, the hopeless feeling in which no words can ease the pain. That conversation was interrupted by many phone calls. Calls from the state police, informing me that she had incurred a severe brain injury, also that she was ejected from the vehicle and was found in some bushes. Her pelvis was probably broken, and then he asked if she was sexually active. I asked him why he would ask me that when she was in a car accident. He explained to me it was because there was indication that she had been raped.

I knew this was not a possibility; she had a wonderful boyfriend who loved her very much. I would find out the answer to that question when I got to the hospital. Besides the state police, I received several calls from doctors, trying to get permission to administer the surgeries and procedures she desperately needed to stay alive.

Her dad got on the road as soon as I called him to tell him about the accident. He had so many questions to which I had no answers. We caught up to him around Hatch, New Mexico. I called him and told him that he needed to call Sierra's boyfriend Morke's parents and give them the information we had. They lived in Panama and didn't speak English, so it became his job to keep them informed. Although he only knew what I knew, which wasn't much, they called about every fifteen minutes to get any kind of update they could.

The details were very cloudy until we got to the hospital. But this was their son, and they were a day's worth of traveling away. I felt such deep pain for them as well. I knew we were only three hours away, and the ride was grueling. It was the longest ride of my life. It was very tough on us. I couldn't imagine the feelings they were experiencing. So as I was taking phone calls from doctors and police officers, getting as much information as I could, I would then call her dad, and he would call Morke's parents so we could keep them in the loop as much as possible. We also learned that Leslie, the driver; Andrea, the passenger; and Leslie and Andrea's family were on their way to the Socorro hospital where the other three were transported. This was good news for them because if they were in Socorro, their injuries were not life-threatening.

Our daughter received the worst injuries by far. She was fighting for her life, and the prognosis didn't look good. The phone calls from the doctors only proved to bring more feelings of anxiety and helplessness. They could not or would not tell me she would live. They just said, "We're doing everything we can." I begged them to keep her alive, to please not let her die.

During one of my many phone calls from the state police, I asked them if they could give us a clear path for us to get there at a high rate of speed, so he told us to get past Truth or Consequences, and we had free reign. At that point, we were already close to T or C, so once we passed it, we got up to speeds of 140 mph so we could get there as soon as possible. We arrived at the hospital in about two hours where she was still in surgery.

As we waited in the hall for her to come out of surgery, more and more people kept showing up. Before I knew it, there were about fifteen of us waiting in the hallway outside the operating room. It seemed like hours that we had to wait when, finally, a large medical staff came out of the operating room, wheeling someone out. I looked at this person and asked if this was my child. They asked me what her name was. I told them, "Sierra Gonzalez."

"Yes!"

This was the scariest answer I have ever received. Yes, it was my child, our baby girl. I just didn't recognize her. I broke down and cried. I cried from my chest and from my stomach; I couldn't catch my breath; I couldn't think of anything except, *Oh my god! Please, Lord, please protect our baby!* They wheeled her into Neurosciences ICU where I began my bedside vigil, at least as much as she would let me.

The doctors came in and explained to us the extent of her injuries; she had traumatic brain injury, diffused axonal injury (which meant the two hemispheres of her brain shifted), four brain bleeds, one of which was very concerning, the one in the brain stem. This was the one that would determine if she would ever get better. She broke her back in five places, shattered her pelvis, broke her nose, had a collapsed lung, and was torn open by a tree as she landed, and it ripped her vagina and anus open (this is why the state police officer asked me if she had been raped). She was in a coma and on life support. She had a central line in her brain to cool it down and to help stop the inevitable swelling of the brain. She had towers of medications being pumped into her body, two tubes in her brain, one to measure her inter cranial pressure, the other to drain fluids so she wouldn't get meningitis. Meningitis? This was the same thing that killed her brother.

They told me she was in grave condition, to hope for the best. I didn't want to ask how much worse it could get. I knew what the next step was, so I accepted what was in front of us and prayed. I prayed for strength to endure every step of her journey. I prayed for God to help her fight. I told her to fight! Not to give up! I told her she was the biggest fighter I know and that she *would* beat this! It was all in her and God's hands.

The first night was very tough. My boyfriend, Jeff, had to go back home because he had a business to run, but Anthony, my son, my rock, was there. With him being there, I didn't feel alone. He knew the situation I was in and was absolutely the person I needed to be there with me. He understood more than anyone what I was feeling. There was no way I was going to leave my baby. Everyone else had left to get a motel room, so I was alone at the end of the night in the hospital with Sierra. I knew I wouldn't be sleeping, so I went in and out of her room all night long.

The doctors told us that her inter-cranial pressure (ICP) could not go above twenty, and if it did, we had to leave her room because it could be detrimental to her. Sometimes as soon as I walked in, I spiked her ICP, so I would have to walk out. She felt me, and it hindered me from being able to stay in her room by her side. So I walked the halls of the hospital and hospital grounds, just thinking and praying. Then I would go into her room to see if she could handle my presence. When she could, I rubbed her; I told her that I would be with her until she got better. I told her she didn't have to do this alone, that I would be by her side every step of the way. I told her how strong she was, how she could beat the odds. Just as she had beaten all the odds all her life to fight for what she wanted. I told her to fight, and when I whispered this to her, I did it in a very stern voice.

"You fight! You will beat this! You don't know failure, so you will overcome any obstacle or hurdle on your path!" Somehow, even with what the doctors said, with all their medical expertise, I knew in my heart that she would recover. I was not being naive. I just had this overwhelming sense of faith, and I just needed to hold on to that. I believed to my core that, eventually, she would wake up from her coma, begin the long journey of recovery, and come back to us. However, the doctors were not as confident as I was.

The next day, more people and more information came rolling in. The news started getting out, and my phone started ringing off the hook. I quickly realized there was no way I could take the multitudes of phone calls I was getting. I answered our families and her very close friend's phone calls and asked them to spread the information that we had at that point. I was too busy between talking to the team of doctors that were trying to keep her alive and sitting with my baby as much as she would allow. When her ICP went up, I would just walk out of the room and watch her from the window. I would talk to her, even though I didn't know if she could hear me. I talked to her about school, about softball, about our family. I talked to her about all the people that came to see her and the people who couldn't see her, so they just sat in the waiting room, hoping for her to live, praying for her to live. At this point, we just prayed for her to make it through this day.

The doctors stressed how serious her condition was. They would not tell me she would be okay. They refused to tell me she was going to live. I begged them to tell me she would be okay, but they wouldn't. They sat her dad and I down and told us what we had to face. That *if* she makes it, she may not walk nor talk nor play softball ever again. But the point they stressed the most was not to get our hopes up. There was a very good chance she wouldn't survive her massive injuries.

At that point, I told them *when* she lives, she will walk and talk and play softball again! I explained to them that they were brilliant doctors, and we needed them, but God was bigger than science. They looked at me as if I was so ignorant, that I had no clue the grave condition she was in. I was very aware of her diagnosis and her prognosis, yet I also told them they had no clue who they were dealing with. She is the biggest fighter I have ever known, and she doesn't fail or give in to the odds that are stacked against her. We have watched her defy the odds her whole life. She loved low odds as much as she loved low, inside pitches. She would just send them out of the ballpark. She would also hit their low odds out of the ballpark, this I was sure of.

Don't get me wrong. I saw what they saw, and it was one of the scariest sights I had ever witnessed, but for some reason, I had complete faith she would make it. Not only would she make it, but she would also soar above the odds against her.

By the third day, more and more information came rolling in. How this happened was our most pressing question at this point. We were told Leslie spilled her drink, swerved off the road, and when she realized, she overcorrected. This is when they started to flip. They rolled uphill seven times, and Sierra and her boyfriend were ejected. Sierra flew out on the last roll. Morke flew out on the third roll. Morke, her boyfriend, was taken to Socorro Hospital with Leslie and Andrea while Sierra was airlifted to Albuquerque's Neurosciences ICU. Then her boyfriend was transported to Albuquerque from Socorro, and I was able to talk to him. My first question was, "Why in the heck was she not wearing her seat belt?"

He explained to me that she was wearing her seat belt, that she had dropped her phone, so she took off her seat belt to pick it up off the floor board. At that precise moment, Leslie lost control of the car, and it started to roll. Since she was bent over when they rolled, she hit the hood with extreme force inside the car. It continued to roll, and she continued to be flopped around like a rag doll inside the car as it was rolling. This why she received such bad head trauma and Morke didn't. He was sitting upright, so he received minor injuries to his head. However, when he flew out, he cracked three vertebrae in his back, which is why he got transported to Albuquerque. We learned that she flew approximately sixty-five feet through the air, downhill, and landed in some trees and shrubbery. It took multiple people to find her, and when they did, she was gurgling on her blood and barely breathing. She was covered in blood and unrecognizable to those that knew her.

By God's grace, a man and his wife were traveling the United States from Germany; I refer to this man as her guardian angel, our hero. He referred to himself as Fabian, Sierra's lifetime friend. He was a paramedic in Germany. He treated Sierra and stabilized her as much as he could until the ambulance came. When they put her in the ambulance, they quickly realized she needed to be airlifted. So the fight to keep her alive was on.

When the helicopter arrived, they loaded her up and airlifted her to Albuquerque where they specialize in head trauma. The prognosis was still grim, even though she was in the best hospital she could be in. If she made it, it would be the hardest fight of her life and ours as well. The doctors also told us to count on being in Albuquerque for at least a year, maybe two. If she made it, she would be in the ICU for months and in their hospital for at least a year, then suggested to us that it was probably a good idea to rent an apartment because this was a marathon, not a sprint. But, again, they stressed, if she made it at all.

Leslie and Andrea were both wearing their seat belts, and there were airbags, so their physical injuries were minor in comparison. Leslie got a gash on her head that required stitches, and she was released within a few hours. Andrea broke her wrist, which required surgery. Her recovery took longer than Morke's broken back. He was back to playing baseball within six weeks. It took her several months between surgery and therapy to get back to softball. Although Leslie received minor physical injuries, her emotional scars proved to be her massive internal injuries. She loved Sierra. They had played high school ball together and brought their high school to the first softball championship their school had ever won. Now her friend and college roommate was lying in the ICU, fighting for her life because she spilled her drink. It was too much for her young mind to handle. She could no longer drive because of the trauma of the accident. She had to seek professional expertise to help her cope with the trauma that was impossible to deal with at the time.

She couldn't go see Sierra. The guilt and the fear kept her from coming to the hospital. Sierra's dad and I also knew this young lady. We were very aware of what a beautiful soul she was. I never blamed her nor made her feel bad about this tragedy, but other people in our family were not as understanding.

My thought was that any one of them could have been driving, and it was just a terrible accident. She loved Sierra and would never, ever want to hurt her. This crushed her spirit, and I did not want that. So I contacted her mom, Georgia, and explained to her our position. I loved her daughter and didn't blame her. "I understand it was just a terrible accident that could have happened to any one of them. I hold no ill will toward her at all. I love her. She has always been such a sweetheart, such a kind and respectful young lady."

Her mom was very grateful for those words and would pass them on to her.

This was also the day that "the vultures" set in. The hospital apparently had a special set of people that attacked the families as soon as they got there. No matter what condition your loved one was in, they wanted to know how they were going to get paid. One group of people came and talked to me about food and lodging. They asked where I was staying, and I informed them that this hospital was my new home. "Until my daughter is discharged, I will stay here with her."

So they reiterated that this was a marathon, not a sprint! Of course, those words fell on deaf ears. I didn't care how long it would take; I would not leave my baby girl. So they informed me that they would get me food vouchers, find a bed for me to sleep in, and a place to shower. I thought this was all so kind of them. I thought they were looking out for my best interests. When they found out that I would not give them our insurance information, they changed their tune. They tried to convince me of how important it was to get our insurance information, how she needed the best care possible so that she could have the best chance of survival. In my mind, they had to treat her; they had to save her life. I was right, they had to save her life, but that's it. They didn't have to continue treatment; they just had to save her life, and then they could release her. I told them they needed to go after the car insurance or the driver, but we weren't paying for this. Needless to say, I didn't get food vouchers or a place to sleep or shower.

After this whole conversation in the hallway, we were brought to a room with about five case managers. They told us that they needed our insurance information so they could get paid, so I told them to go through the car insurance. For some reason, that was not an option. I refused to give them her insurance information and told them to go to hell. I tried to go back into her room, but I was so upset I jacked up her ICP, so I had to leave.

I walked through the hospital; I walked the hospital grounds, wondering how people could be so callous. Our baby was lying in there about an inch away from death, and the only thing they cared about was how they were going to get paid. They came in sheep's clothing, as if they were there to help us get through this terrible tragedy we were brand-new to.

But, in reality, they only cared about the money, and they attacked us at our weakest point. I couldn't wrap my head around all of it. It was way too much for my brain to process. How could they be so heartless? We were told that if we didn't give up her insurance information, she would not get the care that she needed. It was as if they were a pack of wolves and we were the injured prey. We were hit at our very lowest point, and it was inconceivable to us that if we didn't give up our insurance info that they could actually deny proper care. I asked them if this was even legal. They informed me that everyone had to get paid and she was going to be there for a long time, and the medical bills would be astronomical. Yes, we understood that, but why were we responsible for payment when she was a passenger? This happened to her, she did not cause this. So she has to lose everything she has ever worked for, and we have to fund it? It just wasn't right.

At this point, I had not eaten or slept. My mind was clouded with fear, anxiety, lack of sleep, and now another blow. She wouldn't get the care she needed if we didn't give our insurance information. These words were so inconceivable. Where is the humanity? Where is the compassion? They saw Sierra lying there in a coma, tubes sticking out of every inch of her body, and yet their only concern was how they were going to get paid. They asked us if they could file for Medicaid for her because she was a student. I gave them permission to do that and thought maybe that would be enough, at least to keep them at bay so we could just focus on her. This proved to be unsatisfactory for them.

When the first pack of wolves didn't get the information they needed, they sent a whole other set of wolves, only this one included a pastor. He asked if he could pray over our baby. Of course, the answer was yes. We wanted as much prayer flowing her way as possible. He was actually the first one that showed us any sort of compassion. He tried to explain their position, but again, it fell on deaf ears. I thought because she was a passenger that the car insurance should be responsible for all the medical bills. I soon learned how ignorant I was. We quickly learned that health care was no longer health care—it was health care-less.

At this point, I asked her dad to take care of financial vultures so I could keep my focus on our baby. It ended up being a good choice because just entering her room was exhausting, but having to deal with her and the vultures was way too overwhelming.

Up to now, her dad was unable to go into her room; he couldn't see his baby girl in such a grave condition. I kept him informed from a parent's point of view, and the team of doctors kept us both informed from a medical standpoint.

In the midst of all the first day's chaos, my phone would not quit buzzing with texts and ringing with phone calls. The news was spreading. She was very well known in the softball world of Las Cruces, Las Vegas, and Albuquerque. She had been playing softball since she was four years old and earned a full ride to college for her outstanding pitching ability. She was nineteen now, so that was fifteen years of people that she had touched. That was just her softball world. She was also a beautiful human being and touched everyone's lives that she came in contact with. Because of this, there was a plethora of people who wanted information on her.

It was at this point that I realized there was no way I could answer all the phone calls and texts coming in continuously. I decided to start posting on Facebook. I explained that we could not answer all the inquiries. While we appreciated everyone's concern, the only way I could keep everyone informed and be there for Sierra was to open my Facebook page to the public. I wrote to the people that were on my friend list in the beginning. I told them to spread the word to people that weren't on my friend's list that if they wanted information on her to send me a friend request, and I would accept everyone who requested me.

Immediately, I started receiving friend requests. It ended up being a brilliant idea. I was able to keep the hundreds of people that were concerned about her informed, and I was also able to be there for our baby girl. Every day, I got more and more friend requests from the people that wanted to follow her journey.

In the beginning, I posted a couple times a day because her condition changed from minute to minute or hour to hour. It was like a roller-coaster ride that never stopped. Doctors and nurses constantly came into her room with more news and updates on her condition. As we got the information, I would pass it on. I tried very hard to keep our feelings out of the posts and just focus on Sierra and her medical condition. I didn't talk about how hard it was on her dad and me, how we couldn't sleep or eat, how her dad tried to put on a strong face for me, and how I roamed the hospital halls and grounds all night long like a zombie. All the while, I prayed, I cried, I bargained with God to please keep her alive.

At the end of the day, when everyone went to their motel room, I stayed at the hospital and roamed the halls and kept a bedside vigil with her. I talked to her, I combed her hair, I told her all the things we would do when she beat this. I told her not to listen to the doctors because they didn't know her; they only knew her condition. They only gave us their medical advice according to their experience. But I wouldn't let that sway my opinion because I knew something they didn't know. I knew the young woman lying there, fighting for her life. I knew you never let obstacles keep you from reaching your goals.

Almost immediately, her friend and high school catcher, Krystal, jumped in to help in any way she could. She started forming fundraisers and got a hold of the media. Our local news program aired her story—the story of Sierra, the young woman who played softball her whole life, who earned a full ride to college because of her amazing pitching abilities, who was one of the Mayor's Top Teens when she was in high school, of how she helped bring her high school into the first state championship in the history of her school and taught younger children how to play softball. They spoke of how she was fighting for her life because of the horrific accident she had been in.

Krystal, along with the help of many people from her softball community, formed a softball tournament to help raise funds for us, mainly me, to pay my bills as I sat with her in the hospital. It was a great success! So many people came out to support her. One of the city's softball teams donated shirts with her picture of her on them that read "Battle for Sierra" and "Team Bdog" printed on them. They sold the shirts while the girls who played for her, her old team-mates, wore them as they played their hearts out for her. Every girl in the tournament was, at one time or another, playing on the same field as our baby girl. And this was how they showed their support for her. There were probably a hundred people who donated their time between putting everything together to make the tournament happen, people to sell t-shirts, work the concession stand, take tick-ets, make rosters, and everything else in between that made it so successful.

My friend, Rebecca, who I had gone to school with, imme-diately made a GoFundMe page. Within days of the accident, she made a special trip up to Albuquerque to bring me money she had raised to help me until the GoFundMe page had started to produce funds. She brought $300 she had raised in just a few days. I was so grateful for her as well. My niece, Sarena, also started a GoFundMe page from California. She made a tremendous effort to get the news out to as many people as possible. I was so grateful for everyone who thought about us and knew what we needed, even before we would realize how badly we needed it.

A couple I had done many jobs for throughout the years decided they would give me $150 every month until she got out of the hos-pital. Roger and Sharon Odom are Christian people. They love the Lord and truly do his work by helping so many people, and one of those people happened to be me. Before her accident, I knew their love of God and their willingness to help people, but I was lucky enough to be one of the recipients of their generosity. Every month

Sierra was in the hospital, Sharon called my sister to come pick up a check to deposit in my account. They reached out to me, and I felt very blessed to have them in my life as well. They followed her story and prayed for her every day. When I think of true Christians, I think of these two beautiful human beings.

I received care packages from the softball girls' parents; I received gift cards to Walmart and so many people offering anything they could to make this terrible situation as smooth as possible. So our only focus was Sierra. Mostly, I just asked for prayers, which was the one thing that everyone can do, and that was what we needed the most. We were overwhelmed with the outpouring of support. I didn't need much in the beginning. I wasn't eating, I didn't have a change of clothes, I didn't leave the hospital, so I didn't need money for a room, I didn't have my truck. I only needed a toothbrush and coffee to keep me awake, so if anything changed, I would be there for her.

As the days passed, my mind was more and more foggy. Lack of sleep and lack of food takes such a toll on a body. And it really did on mine. I couldn't hold a clear thought. My mind knew what it wanted to say, but it was so hard to put it together so I could get the words out of my mouth. The doctors kept telling me that this is a marathon, not a sprint! They told me I need to sleep and I need to eat. But I couldn't, I was so sick to my stomach at the sight I faced every time I entered her room. And every time I would lay my head down to rest, I saw her lying in a coma, on the brink of death. I thought I couldn't sleep because what if my baby died and I was sleeping? If I fell asleep, I couldn't be there for her.

During one of our many conversations with the doctors, I thought I heard them say her brain should stop swelling within five days. So those five days were full of anxiety, stress, and heartache. Doctors were constantly coming in to talk to us, telling us not to get our hopes up, explaining what a bad shape she was in. They were trying to educate us so we wouldn't get our hopes up.

My niece, Donnie, worked there at the hospital, so she made it a point to come see Sierra every day and talk to me. She told me about how the system worked, why the vultures acted like they did. She told me how to go about getting things done that I felt weren't being addressed. She taught me what questions to ask. She had inside information that helped me a lot. But, mostly, she just sat with Sierra and I. Her presence was soothing.

I thought that if I could get to day five, things would change. Her brain would stop swelling, and maybe I could get some sleep or eat something without it making me sick to my stomach. So my focus was five days. All we needed to do was get her to five days which, ironically, was my birthday. So I, along with several other parents who stayed with their children at the hospital, would brush our teeth, wash our faces, and perform as much hygiene as possible in the bathroom. Then we would all meet downstairs around 7:00 a.m. when we got kicked out of our child's room between 7:00 and 8:00 a.m. This is when the doctors did rounds on all the ICU patients and no one was allowed in their rooms.

This is also where we found strength. We listened to each other's stories about our children and the fears we all faced. We were all in our own little hell, but here we found people that could relate. We were all in such fear of losing our child; we became each other's support system. We saw so much tragedy; the helicopter flew in about five times a day, and each time they landed on the roof, we knew there would be another person fighting for their life. With that came a family that would be in the same situation as all of us. Our stomachs would sink into oblivion at the thought of another parent having to go through what we were going through, another child being airlifted. Every time a helicopter landed on the roof, we would all just look at each other as if to say, "We know the fear! And God bless that family connected to that helicopter." We were all in such a helpless position. The only thing we had was prayer. We had God to carry us, and we all used him every day. We begged him and pleaded with him to spare our child.

When I started posting her story, a man named Christian found her story, and it touched him so deeply that he had to reach out to me. I asked him who he was and how he found her story. He explained to me that he just happened to run across her story while on Facebook. Her story really touched him, and he felt he needed to reach out to me. That really touched my heart. This man, who knew nothing about us, became part of her story and part of my life. From that day on, this man, who was a complete stranger to me and to Sierra, started texting me every day. He texted me every morning and asked me how I was doing, how Sierra was doing. He prayed for both of us, he lit candles for Sierra, and told me how he prayed for us every day. It was a small gesture that meant so much to me. I started to look forward to his texts. They were soothing, and it felt good that a complete stranger could care so much for someone he never even met.

Because of Sierra's tragedy, I started to believe in humanity again. So many people were there to help us, to reach out to us. So many people cared about her and about her welfare. It was so overwhelming. In this world of self-centered people, I had been losing faith in humanity. Unfortunately, it took this tragedy to open my eyes and realize there are truly good people left in this world, people who were willing to do whatever they could to help us through this hell we were living. It made my broken heart feel better knowing that it wasn't just Sierra and our family that were trying to live with this tragedy. It was our family, friends, and even strangers that became part of our family, part of our fight to get her back.

My son was my rock during it all. He and his family drove up to Albuquerque, and he told Sierra and I that he wasn't leaving until she is out of a coma and could tell him that she loves him. Jeff was commuting back and forth from Las Cruces to Albuquerque as much as possible. He drove Anthony, Lee, Zoe, and Sebby back to Las Cruces so he could take his family back home and drive my truck back to the hospital. This made it possible for me to have a vehicle. He could stay as long as he needed to, and my daughter-in-law could go back to work. He took on tasks that were too hard for her dad and I. He talked to the doctors and gave us the information as gently as possible. He was there when she needed to be turned or sucked out, when they had to do knuckle rubs on her chest and anything else that was too hard to watch for her dad and I.

He and I would spend almost every night sitting on the tailgate of my truck watching the sunset. We talked, he comforted me with his words and with his presence. He let me cry and held on to me and talked to me so I would have enough strength to go back in and do what had to be done, and at the end of the day, he could go get some sleep so we could do it all over again the next day. I parked my truck on the east side of the hospital parking lot at night so I could watch the sunrise, and I parked it on the west side in the afternoon so he and I could watch the sunset for our evening talks.

This Is How Sierra's Journey Began

> I'm on my way to Albuquerque. Sierra was in a car accident and is being airlifted to Albuquerque. She is in surgery right now to relieve pressure on her brain. I'm asking all my Facebook friends to pray for my baby girl. #TeamBdog

This is my first of many posts. I didn't know it at the time, but this post would be the beginning of Sierra's journey. My boyfriend was there when I got the call from her coach telling me she had been in a terrible accident and was airlifted to Albuquerque. I was scrambling around the house, looking for my shoes and my driver's license so I could get on the road. I told him I have to go, and he quickly replied, "You *are not* driving! I will drive you!" So we started the longest drive of my life. It actually only took us about two hours because we were doing about a hundred plus miles an hour, but it seemed like a lifetime.

Immediately, my niece, Sarena, in California, and my friend, Rebecca, from Las Cruces, got online and began a GoFundMe page for me because we knew that I would have to quit my jobs and stay with her until she beat this…or she would die, and I would not be able to work for quite a while, if I made it at all, which was doubtful.

My son, Anthony, and his family showed up, and he told me that he would help me through this. That eased my mind because her dad and I were divorced, so I didn't know how much we would be able to lean on each other. Anthony and I shared blood with her, and he was just as scared as I was. Our family has always been very close. We always make time to do the simple things in life together. We have cookouts, movie nights, game nights, and we all enjoy and appreciate our family time.

August 25, 2017

> She made it through surgery. But she is in very
> bad shape. Doctors are doubtful and try to make
> us understand that most people don't make it
> through this much injury. #TeamBdog

This is the day we were gathering so much information on her injuries and her prognosis—and none of it was good. A group of people from the hospital came in to talk to us about how they were going to get paid. I told them to go after the car insurance, and they told us that was not an option. They said they needed her dad's insurance information so that she could get "proper care." Her dad and I refused to give it to them. Our position in all this was that it wasn't her fault, so we shouldn't have to pay them. They explained to us that everyone has to get paid, and I retorted with, "We *are* paying! We are paying the highest price of anyone! And she is right down the hall, fighting for her life!"

This was unacceptable to them, so each time they came to talk to us, they sent a different group of people, trying to get money from us. Besides being there for our daughter, we had to fight off the vultures.

Family was rolling in throughout the day. More and more friends came, my sister, Yvonne, and my nephew, Bubba, her softball teammates from Las Vegas, her dad's family from Las Cruces and

Chamberino, and her grandma and Papa drove in from Utah. They all came for support or to say goodbye. Many of them couldn't even go into her room to see her, yet they sat in the waiting room helpless, crying, and praying. It was all so somber in the waiting room. So many people but eerily quiet. I also received the picture of the car, and my heart sank. We realized being ejected from the car probably saved our daughter and her boyfriend from imminent death. They were in the back seat, and it was crushed.

This is the car after they rolled seven times.

August 26, 2017

> AM Update on Sierra… She hasn't started her day of well today. She is not responding like she should be. There are a lot of details behind that, but too much to go in to. So we pray that her day gets better. I will continue to keep everyone informed throughout the day. Thank you ALL for your continued support. This is going to be a long road to and I appreciate the fact that you're all out there for us. #TeamBdog
>
> Follow-up on AM update… I'm not sure if I made this clear, but she is in a coma, and has been since the accident. She is on life support, has tubes in her brain and throughout her body. But we are trying to stay positive. She is in a very dangerous situation. She has several other issues, such as four brain bleeds, a broken pelvis and she broke her back in five places. We are just trying to stay positive. From some of your posts, I didn't know if I had made that clear. #TeamBdog

She wasn't responding to anything. The doctors tried knuckle rubs, they stroked the bottom of her feet, they pinched her, and nothing, no response at all. After her stimulus checks, the doctors and nurses would look at me as if to say, "She's not going to make it." Every time I have to talk to the doctors, my heart sinks, and it feels like someone punched me in the stomach. Watching them do the stimulus checks was very hard. She started to get a bruise on her chest from the knuckle rubs. There was one of her nurses that I started forming a relationship with. He explained everything they had to do to her in detail and why it was necessary for her. He was very knowledgeable, compassionate, and seemed to be invested in her recovery. So when I asked him about the knuckle rubs, he explained to me why it was so important for them to get some kind of reaction from her. They didn't want her to slip into oblivion and die, so they had to stimulate her as much as possible. Although it was so hard to watch, I realized the necessity of why they had to do it.

> PM Update on Sierra…we're waiting for her to get another CT scan. She's not responding on her stimulus check. She was earlier and now she's not. Her numbers have been fluctuating all day and night. Her Inter Cranial Pressure spiked to 38, this is very, very bad because the doctors told us that they don't want it to go above 20 or it can damage her brain further. We are trying to see the light at the end of the tunnel when we can walk out of here with her. We have to believe that. Morke was transferred here from Socorro because they realized he broke his back so he needs more intense care. #TeamBdog

The tubes in her brain were measuring her Inter-Cranial Pressure (ICP). If the numbers go above twenty, she was in grave danger. This is why too many people couldn't go in her room. Too much stimulation would raise her numbers, which could mean death. We decided at this point, only her immediate family was allowed in her room, and then only if her numbers didn't spike. Sometimes I would go in her room, and immediately, her numbers would shoot up, so I would have to turn around and walk out. I found a pond at the university across the street. It was a nice walk and the most peaceful place I could find in all this chaos.

When the situation got too overwhelming, and someone else was with her, I would walk over there and sit by the waterfall, listen to the rushing water, and just think and pray. I thought about how your life changes in one instant, how my baby was fighting to stay alive. I thought about the vultures and how they didn't even care about people's lives; it was only about money for them. I wondered how I was going to pay my bills or just sell my house and get an apartment here. But mostly, I prayed. I begged and pleaded to God to bring our baby back to us. I cried and cried; the pain engulfed my entire being. I felt so helpless. I knew the only way I could possibly get through each day was God. I prayed continually. I knew it was in God's hands, so I begged and pleaded for him to spare her.

> PM update on Sierra and Morke… Morke was able to get out of bed today. We wheeled him down to see Sierra, which by the way, their doctors and nurses thought was a great idea to help Sierra. It was very hard on him, as it is for all of us. We don't know if she knows, she's just lying in a coma, lifeless. We hope that she feels his love for her. So he is on a good road of recovery. As far as Sierra goes, today is a big day for her, day 3! So far she's okay. She's not better, but much more importantly, she's not worse! #TeamBdog

Morke was her boyfriend who was also ejected from the vehicle, cracked three vertebrae, had cuts and scrapes, and some head contusion, but we knew he would be okay. When we arrived the first day, the doctors told us her brain would continue to swell for at least three to five days. In my mind, they said it *would* quit swelling in three days. So I was under the assumption that if she made it through this day, her brain would quit swelling and she would be on the long road of recovery. That's not what they said, apparently. Now we were waiting for up to five to seven days. That's tough to hear.

One day, with all the information we received on her update, prognosis, and outcome, one day was so exhausting. Now they were asking us to wait up to seven days? After absorbing that information, we did what we had to do to help our baby, whatever it takes, and pray.

> Follow-up on pm update… Also, for all of you trying to call or text for answers, I appreciate all of your concerns, however, I'm not able to answer everyone individually, I apologize for that. I wish I could, but things are a little crazy here. So what

I can do is post updates on her every day. So please follow my page and that way I can keep everyone that loves and cares for her informed. Thank you all for your concern and understanding. #TeamBdog

My phone was continuously going off from people wanting to get information and ask if they could help us with anything. It occurred to me that I had to make my Facebook page open to the public so that I could update everyone, every day at the same time. Then I asked friends and family to pass the word on. The lack of food, sleep, and the emotions that come with it all is catching up on me. I hadn't showered since we'd been here. I had no clothes to change into, and I already felt worn out. This was so bad because the doctors told me that this was a marathon, not a sprint.

I had to start forcing myself to eat. My boyfriend would bring me clothes so I could go shower at her dad's motel room. I was so overwhelmed this morning that I walked to the duck pond and took a nap on the grass by the waterfall. It was the most relaxing place I could find and still be close to the hospital.

August 27, 2017

This morning's update on Sierra… It was a very scary night but she got through it. Now the doctors are saying we need to get her past seven days because the brain can continue to swell that long. It's pretty tight in there and she's got brain bleeds, but this morning, right now her numbers are good. We are asking people not to come up right now. There are so many people here now and we believe it's too much stimulation on her brain for so many people to be here. I realize that everyone loves her so much but she *needs* rest right now. Many of you have asked me what they can do and here it is…what I am asking of all of you is to pray at five o'clock tonight. That's New Mexico time. If we all take thirty seconds to pray at five pm tonight, there will literally be thousands of prayers sent to God at exactly the same time. So please get on board with this and thank you all for your continued support, prayers, concerns, and everything. For our Las Cruces family… there will be people meeting at the high school soccer field at 5pm today for a prayer vigil for her. Everyone in Las Cruces is more than welcome to join. Otherwise, please pray at 5pm MST wherever you are. #TeamBdog

Tonight's update on Sierra…her numbers are good today. For some reason the tube in her brain is showing lower numbers than the one in the hemisphere of her brain. There are opinions about that, but without an MRI, it's just speculation. We kept everyone out of her room today with the exception of her dad and I. Even we only had short visits just to let her know we're here, we love her, and about the prayer vigil…which, by the way, was awesome. Thank you all of you Las Cruces people, we felt the love penetrating our baby girl.

Unfortunately, we are on the verge of another much more dangerous surgery if there is any more pressure because her brain is still swelling and there is almost no more room for it to swell. She is not better yet, the doctors said she's still the same as when she came in, *but she's not worse! Thank you, Lord!* Her brother is taking over for us when she has to be turned and sucked out, or any other tests they have to do on her… thank you Anthony. Her dad and I can't do it. My dad is also here for us. I was finally able to get a quick nap on his shoulder. My mom passed away over twenty years ago, I sure could use her and her wisdom and love right now, but my dad is here with me and that helps tremendously.

It's way too hard on us. Just being here every day to see her is so exhausting. Thank you everyone for all of your prayers and being involved in our 5pm massive prayer. Please continue to keep her in your prayers…they are keeping her alive and will bring her back to us.

Also, Morke has been released. He can't walk, but for some reason, they released him. He is on his way back to his college. He has to go to school because of his student visa. So please keep him in your prayers as well. He had a very, very hard time leaving Sierra, but he has a great plan for their future, and part of that is him going back to school. So we have the utmost respect for him. We will get him here to see her as soon as he is able. For now, he needs prayers as well.

BTW…thank you everyone who takes their time to pray, read updates, and share comments. I really appreciate it. I go through them when I'm not with Sierra; they are very uplifting to me. It's nice to see how many people love our baby girl. She's touched so many hearts. It's unbelievable! To know her, truly is to love her.

The prayer vigil turned out to be a great success. There were about a hundred people that showed up at the high school to pray for our baby. Not only was that a success, but Sierra went to school with kids from Dominican Republic, Panama, Guatemala, Puerto Rico, and several other countries. Because of that, we also had people praying for her from those countries as well. Including people all across our country that were praying for her, all at 5pm MST.

My dad led our prayer at the hospital, and as he prayed, I felt the comfort of the Lord penetrating every inch of my body. Even people we didn't know took off their hats and paused as my dad prayed. People called me and text me to let me know that they prayed, their families prayed, and their countries prayed, all for our baby girl. We absolutely believe that is why she is still with us. #TeamBdog

Prayer vigil at the high school in Las Cruces.

August 28, 2017

Morning update on Sierra...she had a good night. She gets agitated from the stimulation tests now, but I think she is responding to my touch because they jack her numbers up with their tests and then I touch her and talk to her and her numbers decrease. I saw a picture of the car and realized God does work in mysterious ways. It is very likely that they both would have been crushed had they stayed in the backseat. Divine intervention took over because a man from Germany and his wife just happened to be traveling the United States, on the same highway, and he was one of the first on the scene. This man happened to be a paramedic and he treated her and kept her alive until the ambulance showed up. We also learned that medics from Germany are much more trained than the United States paramedics. He is her guardian angel. Many other circumstances we've learned has made us realize God has been there protecting her the whole #TeamBdog

The man's name was Fabian Grub. He and his wife came up on the scene of the accident, and he knew exactly what to do. He assessed everyone else that was in the accident, and they were okay. Then he learned that there was a fourth passenger. He, along with several other people that had stopped for the accident, looked for her.

She wasn't visible, so they started a search. She was finally found in some bushes down by the road. She had flown sixty-five feet downhill and landed in some shrubbery. He immediately went into action to save our baby girl. She was gurgling on her blood and barely alive, and he stabilized her until the ambulance came.

After going to the crash site, we also realized this could have been so much worse. There were large gorges; some were a hundred feet down that they could have flipped into, and then we would have had to attend four funerals. The back seat was smashed in, and Sierra and her boyfriend would have likely been smashed had they stayed in, but at the very second Sierra had dropped her phone on the floor board and took off her seat belt to pick it up, Leslie spilled her drink, lost control of the car, overcorrected, and flipped seven times uphill. If it were seconds earlier or seconds later, they could have fallen into one of the many gorges surrounding the crash site.

I have no doubt at all that God saved her from death and she will come back to us. Everything happened exactly as it had to happen for our baby girl to be alive.

August 29, 2017, 12:46 a.m.

> It's my birthday, thank you for the birthday wishes already. What I want the most, the best present I could ever receive in my entire life, is for this very important day to be good for her. Please pray for that! #TeamBdog

After midnight, people started sending me birthday wishes. They were short and sweet. But what do you say to a mom who's standing by her child's hospital bed, praying she won't die? This is day five. The next day we've been waiting for. The doctors said her brain would continue to swell for five to seven days after it didn't quit swelling on day three. It will be a wonderful birthday present if the doctors come in and tell us that her brain has quit swelling. That will be our first of many hurdles to jump over.

Since we were told that her brain would continue to swell for five to seven days, in our minds, this was day five. So I hoped that today would bring good news. It would be a beautiful birthday present. I thought tonight would be the first night I could sleep. Until this point, I had not slept much at all. I roamed the hospital grounds and went in Sierra's room. I prayed, I posted, I shared stories with the other parents that couldn't sleep because their children were also there, fighting for their lives. That was my support system. The doctors are still trying to get me to eat. They said that she would need me if she made it, and if I don't sleep or eat, I wouldn't be able to do that. Yet that's easier said than done. I was amazed at the fact that I was still standing. I had caught a couple naps since the accident, but I was definitely running on empty. Up to this point, I had a total of about five hours of sleep.

August 29, 2017, 3:05 a.m.

> So I'm sitting outside while she gets her 3am chest x-ray, sitting, thinking, and praying…I've been showing her nurses her picture so they could see the beautiful young woman they are actually treating. Several of you have been sending pictures of you and her over the years. That's great! I love them, I remember them all. Please continue to send them and will continue to show her doctors and nurses, which has become quite a large number. My thought is that if I humanize her to them, it will become their personal battle as well.
>
> Her team of doctors and nurses are great, and very knowledgeable, but I want them to have a personal interest in the person we have come to know and love, instead of what they see. So please, if you have pictures of you and her, or just her, send them to me and I will show them to her doctors and nurses. I don't mean to imply they are not doing everything they can to keep her alive and make it so she comes back to us, because they truly are amazing. She is in the best place she can be right now, but I want/need them to see who they are really treating. I realize most of the pictures will be of her on the ball field, and that's great too, after all, that has been her entire life, the life she chose, the life that brought her to many of you.

I look forward to all the memories to share
with her staff. Also, something has been bothering me deeply...the driver, Leslie is in agony. Her
heart hurts so badly. So if you all could pray for
her I would greatly appreciate it. She is a beautiful
person as well and she *needs* prayers too. Thank
you. Also, when I get the pictures, I will re-post
so you all can share the memories. #TeamBdog

I asked people to send pictures of her so I could make an album
of memories. I thought when I was having conversation with the
nurses I would show it to them. Most of them seem to take a personal
interest in every patient.

We're very impressed with the care she's getting here. Several of
my family members were very upset with the driver of the car. I never
felt that. I only felt the pain of my daughter. I realized it could have
been any one of them driving. I know Leslie; I know what a beautiful person she is. She went to the same college as Sierra for a reason,
and that reason was Sierra. I knew she was in her own hell knowing
she was responsible for the accident. We didn't need to add to her
personal agony. It's very easy to point the blame. But whoever is to
blame doesn't matter; what matters is that we focus all of our energy
on our daughter.

I didn't let anyone speak any negativity around her, so when
the subject came up of Leslie, or when the doctors came in with bad
news, I made them leave her room and give us information where
she couldn't hear, under the assumption that she could hear, even
though she was in a coma. This is a new brain forming, and I refuse
to let anything negative in while she is fighting so hard and making
new connections.

August 29, 2017

AM Update on Sierra... Very rough day today.
She's very sensitive today. Her numbers are spik-
ing continually. There is not very good news to

tell today, so I won't tell it. But tomorrow could
be different. #TeamBdog

From the time the doctors did their rounds at 7:00 a.m., the
bad news started. For morning rounds, the doctors told me she was
in bad shape that her brain is still swelling. We need to prepare ourselves for the fact that she may not make it. They told me that she
would probably need a craniotomy. They explained that they would
have to saw a chunk of her skull open and take it off to let her brain
continue to swell. They also explained to us that her brain was swelling so much that she no longer had room in her skull for it to swell
anymore and this is the next step.

This is also the day that KVIA ran news coverage on Sierra.
They talked about how she is a softball player, how she helped bring
her high school into their first state victory, she was one of the may-
or's top teens, how she showed the little kids how to play softball and
how to pitch. They talked about her wreck and her condition. They
showed pictures of her while telling her story. All the while, I cried.

This is the Sierra we know and love. Fierce passion in every pitch.

We also received copies of the Panama paper talking about the wreck. Her boyfriend was an all-star baseball player in Panama, so they did an article on him and included Sierra because she was his girlfriend. They both received the worst injuries. However, Sierra had received the worst by far. This was not the birthday I had hoped for by any means. From the beginning to the end, we received bad news, discouraging news. The doctors started in the morning, telling us not to get our hopes up, and ended with, "She is probably not going to make it."

My boyfriend had to go back home to close his business, and my dad and stepmom told me that they had to go back home as well. I remember walking outside at night after everyone had left, feeling so downtrodden that it took my breath away. I just needed my mom. I felt so alone, and it was my birthday. By the end of the day, I had received so many birthday wishes. I appreciated them very much, but with every birthday wish I received, there was one missing—my baby girl's. Her intention was to come to town early from her college so she could spend time with me for my birthday. She had a softball game down here, so she wanted to drive down instead of coming on the bus. This way, she could spend time with me for my birthday. Instead, I was praying for my baby girl to make it through another day. But, at the end of the day, she was still alive. And that was enough of a gift for me.

August 30, 2017

> Sierra's morning update… There is good news this am. And please understand with a brain injury as severe as hers, updates are in this minute. And this minute is good. She is completely off sedation and holding her numbers. Spiking sometimes but bringing her numbers down on her own. They brought her down for her CT scan last night because she was stable enough to be moved.
>
> She turned her head when I talked to her, I don't know if she knew I was there, but I'd like to think that was the case. She moved her arm

and tried to stop her nurse from sucking her out. These are tiny steps, but they are in the right direction. Please understand everything is up and down, so these are good signs that can change at any minute. I stress that because people have been forming conclusions from one piece of information. So my posts are accurate *for right now, this minute*! Thank you and please continue to pray. She is still not, not, not, out of the woods, but right now we can all enjoy some good news for a change. #TeamBdog

Tonight's update on Sierra...her good day has turned into a good night. She's getting angry at her nurses for moving her and brushing her teeth. She's pulling her legs up. We think she's responding to her dad and me. No sedation all day and she is bringing her numbers down all by herself. Her gag reflex is working and she's trying to cough. She's also setting off the alarm on the breathing machine because she's trying to breathe over it. This is all good news for today. Goodnight my Facebook friends, until tomorrow. And thank you all, I appreciate every one of you for your prayers for our amazing baby girl. #TeamBdog

PM follow up... So she got a male nurse tonight that just seemed to 'go through the motions,' he came in and started moving her, turning her, doing everything the other nurses have to do, but with no emotion at all. She was just a patient that he didn't care about, and I didn't like it at all! All of the other nurses have been very compassionate and understanding. So after he was done with her, I decided to go for a walk. While on my walk, I was thinking about that nurse and how much it bothered me. I am her voice and I have to speak up for her. When I went back into her room, I pulled up my profile picture of her and showed it to him. And I told him, "*This is Sierra* (as I stuck my phone in his face), *not that*!" as I was pointing to her lying in a coma, unrecognizable to those of us who know her. When he looked at her picture, all he could say was, "Oh!" as his jaw dropped to his chest, like he was surprised to see such a beautiful young lady. And I retorted with "Yeah!" Now he will see 'her' from now on and not just what he sees lying in an ICU bed. It really worked; I saw the transformation in his attitude immediately. #TeamBdog

This!

This is one of my favorite pictures of Sierra. It shows the sparkle in her eyes. When she smiles, she lights up the room. Not only with her smile, but her personality is just as beautiful as her smile.

Not that!

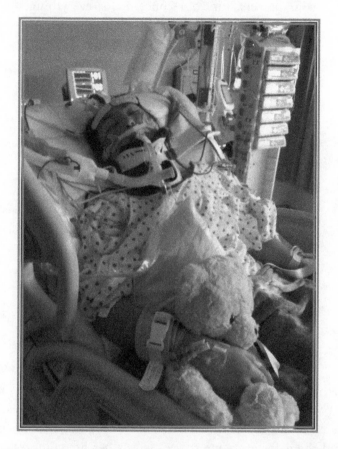

This picture, on the other hand, is one of the scariest pictures I've ever witnessed in my life. It still doesn't show the entirety of her injuries. There are towers of medications and tubes in so many parts of her body, broken bones, and parts of her body that had to be stitched back together that don't show.

August 31, 2017

AM update on Sierra... This is just a small update for now. I was so excited and wanted all of you to share the great news. Her brain is no longer swelling! Thank you, thank you, and thank you *all* for your prayers, for your concern, for everything. I have had such an incredible show of support; it's amazing how many people our baby girl has touched. She is so loved, it melts my heart. Many of you are obviously waiting by your phone for her updates because as soon as I post, people start commenting before I have a chance to put my phone down. My phone is constantly going off every day that we have been here.

You people are amazing. I can't express my gratitude for all of you. There are so many people wanting to help, asking if they can do anything for us. The answer is yes! Keep praying! Because *when* she wakes up I want to show her what our community, our country, and many other countries, have done for her and Morke. Thank you again. I know I've said it over and over again, but you people out there, praying for her, supporting her and our family, *you rock*! #TeamBdog

When I asked people to send me pictures, I had no idea how many I would receive. I received so many pictures of her and her friends and softball teammates. I made an album with them and reposted them for everyone to see. It was her life compressed into one video. Every one of the pictures was a beautiful memory, a story behind the picture, and I remember them all. It made me smile. And then it made me cry. I wondered if this was it. I wondered if we would get anymore pictures and memories of her or if this was it, the end of the selfies, the pictures of her on the pitcher's mound, on the ball field, pictures of her with her family, with her coworkers and friends. All I could do was pray that it wouldn't be the end of any of them. We had too many things to do still. She had too many things to accomplish before leaving this world. She was on a great path to a bright future, and I prayed for her road to continue, for God to give her another chance at making our world a better place with her in it.

PM update on Sierra… Not only is her brain not
swelling anymore, but her whole team met today
and decided that she is doing so well bringing her
numbers down on her own that they decided to
take the tubes out of her brain. Softball tournaments are being put together to help her dad and
I with expenses so if you want any information
on this, please contact Krystal. #TeamBdog

Many people in our hometown have started putting fundraisers
together for her. There will be a softball tournament for her and the
field was donated. My friends from work are having another fund-
raiser at the VFW for her as well. It's beautiful to see people come
together for her. A printing company from El Paso helped us with
these shirts to sell at the softball tournament, and one of the softball
teams from Las Cruces paid for them. That is our baby girl; her smile
and her shine are captured in this picture. This is how we remember
our Sierra, not the person lying in a coma, fighting so hard to come
back to us.

Battle For Sierra

Shirts were also donated for the softball tournament. Many of the girls she has played with in the past built a team and played their hearts out for Sierra. Everyone felt so helpless, and this is something her friends and old teammates could do for her. I was unable to attend, but her dad and Auntie Von traveled back from Albuquerque to represent our family. It was a massive turnout, and every one of the people that attended were there because our baby girl made such a good impression on them through the years that they wanted to help in any way they could. There were literally a hundred people that volunteered their time to put this softball tournament together, all from her past softball world. We were so very grateful for every one of these people; it's hard to put into words how good it felt that so many people would do this for her, for us.

September 1, 2017

> Afternoon update on Sierra… I've been talking to doctors all morning. I've been getting a lot of good news. She is starting to follow commands, which means her brain is starting to make new connections. This is great because she has what they call 'shearing.' This means the two hemispheres of her brain are shifted, and she will have to relearn everything she knew, such as walking, talking, breathing, eating, everything we take for granted every day. I saw the MRI and she literally has no space between her hemispheres. Her brain is so swollen, but it's not swelling anymore. One of her brain bleeds is in her brain stem, which is affecting her left side. They can't get her left side to respond yet, but I know she will get there. The doctors are trying to get her to breathe on her own, she is still getting oxygen, but she is also breathing on her own to some degree. Her Neurologist said we can't say she is 'out of the woods' yet, but she is headed in the right direction. Thank you again for continued support and prayers, please keep them coming. #TeamBdog

When I saw her MRI, my heart sank into my stomach. I couldn't believe she was still alive. I suddenly became more aware of the doctors' positions. This picture of her brain is their information, and it was very clear to me why they looked so grim. It had been nine days, and the bad news had pummeled us every day that we'd been here. I was operating on almost no sleep or food. I couldn't close my eyes because I didn't want to be asleep if my baby died. I didn't want to think like that, but all my defenses were down. The team of doctors told me every day that I had to eat and I had to sleep, but I just couldn't. The neurologist was impressed with how much knowledge

I had gained since her accident. While he was explaining the MRI to me, I interjected with what I had learned since we'd been here.

He was not only impressed with what I have learned but the fact that I was proactive in learning so I could help her on her journey to recovery in any way I can. He showed me all of her brain bleeds and all of the damage to her brain. It was so scary, but it also empowered me to help her in any way I could because, after all, knowledge is power. The most concerning brain bleed was definitely the one in her brain stem. He explained to me, "This is the one that will determine her ability to get better or not."

September 2, 2017, 12:51 a.m.

> Update on Sierra…she is amazing. She has responded several times throughout the day. They have a fifteen point scale for brain function and she jumped up two points today. Yea! Sometimes she is trying to breathe over the ventilator, this is very good news, hopefully she will be off life support soon. If she doesn't get off it soon, that could cause a whole other list of problems. She got her central line out today because her brain quit swelling, and the central line was pushing cool saline through her body to help keep the swelling down in her brain, and now that it's not swelling, it was safe to take it out.
>
> The Neurologist actually told me today that he believes she's going to live. Awesome news! An incredible weight lifted off my chest and my heart. She has a bleed in her brain stem, which affects the entire left side of her body, but our hope is that as the blood dissipates, she will regain the use of her left side. If not, we will deal with it. As long as she lives, we will learn whatever we need to know to take care of her. She's still trying to come out of her coma. It may take some time, but we'll take it,

she's alive, and whatever else we have to face, God will be there to help us through it.

Her Neurologist told me today that this improvement is *her*. They do what they can, but she's the one that has to fight the fight. He also stated that her whole team is very impressed with her already, and she is not even awake yet. Imagine their surprise when she does wake up and they realize the amazing, beautiful person she really is. We still have a very long journey to go, but whatever arises, we will get through it. I love all of you for helping her to get to this point because of your prayers. Please keep them coming so we can get our baby back. Morke is also getting better every day. He leaves voice clips on my phone and I play them for her. We don't know if she can hear them, but I will continue to play them for her under the assumption that she can. #TeamBdog

September 2, 2017

AM update for Sierra… She has fever, but she has been maintaining it. For now it's not increasing. Last night she actually held my hand…that was better than anything I could imagine! She moved her lips when I asked her to, and when the nurses turned her, she tolerated it much better. I had to get out for morning shift change so that's all I have for now. #TeamBdog

Follow-up on morning update… I want to thank my long-time friend Becca for coming up here to offer her support and prayers to our baby, and what was great is that Sierra lifted her hand to her, as if to say bye when she left. What a wonderful gift to leave with. #TeamBdog

Update for tonight... She is still running a fever, and her white blood count is up, which indicates infection. The doctors think she is developing pneumonia. But it may have something to do with them taking her central line out, or it could just be coincidence. Sorry so vague, but that's what I got from her doctors, so that's what you get. However, she was pretty responsive today. She lifted her thumb on command, and wrapped her hand around our fingers. It is only small steps, but good news for tonight. Goodnight all, and thank you for your continued prayers. #TeamBdog

When the doctors told us that she may have pneumonia, part of me thought that this was the beginning of the end. I cried so much at the thought of her getting this far, fighting so hard, just to have her die from pneumonia. What a cruel joke. I went to the waterfall and cried and prayed to God to please help her fight this on top of the tremendous fight she has already shown. When I got back into her room, I stroked her hair, I rubbed her, and I told her that she would fight this and she would overcome this as well. I told her again that she didn't fail, that she would fight and she would beat this. She didn't have a choice. I insisted she get better, and I would not accept anything less.

My friend, Chris, came to hang out with me today. He's always been a joker, and it was nice to get some smiles in and relief from the continual tragedy we had to live. Doctors confirmed that she was getting pneumonia. Becca came and brought me cash and a gift card for Walmart that she had collected from our Las Cruces people.

After she left, I was on the phone, and when I was done, I set my phone (in the case that holds money and bank cards) down. I just sat outside for a minute, just contemplating the situation, and then I went back into her room. As soon as I got there, I realized I left my phone outside. It was just a few minutes, but when I got back downstairs, it was gone. All the money and my credit cards, bank cards,

ID, SS card, everything. It was gone in that amount of time. How can people be so cruel?

My friend made a special trip here so I would have cash, and now I had nothing. I couldn't even buy a bottle of water. But her ICU nurses would not accept this. So they went on a quest to find my wallet and my phone. Well, they succeeded. When they called my phone, one of the fourth floor nurses answered and explained that someone dropped it off at their station. They went up to get it, and all the money was gone. That was very disheartening. Everyone here was in distress, and to steal from someone who was already in agony was just incomprehensible. I prayed for that person that took it right there and then. I prayed that it helped them more than it would have helped me. I didn't have the heart to tell Becca.

September 3, 2017

> Morning post… This is not an update on Sierra. This post is for all of you. I have had so much time to think about everything since I've been here. I think about the outpouring of love and support we have gotten. I have so many stories of kindness. Some want to stay anonymous, so I will not mention names, but you know who you are. I will tell you that people have made trips to Albuquerque to see Sierra for five or ten minutes. Sometimes they can't even see her at all because it was too traumatic on her. Yet, you keep coming, you offer your support, your prayers, care packages, your money, hold prayer vigils for her, and have fundraisers so that I can still pay my bills and live with Sierra. You people are amazing! You have been on this journey with us since day one.
>
> Besides Andrew, this is the hardest, most heartbreaking tragedy that I have ever had to deal with in my entire life. I can say thank you for the rest of my life, and it wouldn't touch how truly

grateful I am to every one of you. People across our country, all of Panama, and many other countries have been supporting us. If it were not for every single one of you, I could not have gotten this far. And my family feels the same. So this post is about all of you and me, saying thank you from the bottom of my heart. I will forever be indebted to all of you. We *all* got her here. And because of all of you, our baby girl's will to fight, prayers, and God, we *will* get our Sierra back! #TeamBdog

Afternoon update… She's very sleepy today. Not much response so far today. The doctors said it's very exhausting for her to try to breathe on her own and she has pneumonia now. This is one of the valleys they explained to us. It's very hard for us to accept the bad with the good, but I am still thankful for the good. We have to believe that she will get through this as well. In the meantime, we continue to pray and believe she will come back to us. #TeamBdog

PM update on Sierra… It's been a very sleepy day for her, and a very restless evening. Her Neurologist said that restless is good, so we'll take it. It's very hard to watch, but if it means improvement, then we'll watch and just know that it's a good sign. Her heart rate went up really high but they gave her happy drugs to calm her down, and it worked almost immediately. Her heart rate went down almost forty points to about normal. So she is resting peacefully now.

She got antibiotics for the pneumonia and tomorrow we'll see how well she's reacting to them. Her teams of doctors were talking about taking her off life support, but with the pneumonia we'll have to put that on hold for now. She's

> still fighting and actually tried to get her hand up
> to the breathing tube. It obviously bothers her
> now, which is really good because she is becom-
> ing aware. Goodnight for now and I will post in
> the morning when I know more. #TeamBdog

In my mind, when her doctor told me she had pneumonia, that was it. She was fighting so hard just to stay alive; I couldn't see how she could fight that too. Besides the fact that I had read enough to know that many people in the hospital that were idle die of pneumonia. I prayed and I tried so hard for these thoughts not to overtake me, but I couldn't get it off my mind. Yesterday, when the doctors told our family that it may be pneumonia, it was very hard on us all. But today, when they verified the fact she had it, everyone's faith was challenged.

Many people contacted me, stating their fears, which only heightened my own fears. The only thing I knew to do was pray. I pleaded with God to heal her; I explained that she'd come too far for him to take her now. I promised him that she would be such an asset to our world if he spared her life. Of course, he knew, but I had to speak it with my mouth. I knew that I had to speak it out loud, not only for God to know but to convince myself as well.

On the other hand, the fact that she was trying to get her hand up to the ventilator and getting restless was a very good sign. It was hard to watch. She appeared to be in agony, but not knowing exactly what she knew almost seemed harder than knowing what was happening to her.

September 4, 2017

> Afternoon update on Sierra… She's off the venti-
> lator! Her doctor took it out just as I was walking
> into her room. It was a very scary sight because
> she was struggling to breathe, but they gave her
> a nebulizer treatment to bring the swelling down
> in her throat and it worked very quickly. She only

has a mask pushing O2 and she's holding her level at 99%. Amazing news! But that's not all, her temperature is going down and she's responding very well to the antibiotics. She is overcoming every obstacle that arises. She's amazing and she's amazing! Thank you everyone for your prayers. We still have quite a long journey but she continues to defy all the odds against her. I'm hoping the next step is when she comes out of the coma and says, "Hi, Mama." #TeamBdog

I had left her room for a little bit to go downstairs, and when I walked back into her room, I saw them taking the incubation tube from her throat. She was gagging and gasping for her first breaths on her own since the accident. My heart sank into my stomach; it was so scary. The doctors explained to me what they were doing and why she reacted like that. It was normal for her to struggle immediately after getting the tube out that had been breathing for her for twelve days.

Only twelve days! Incredible. She was supposed to be in ICU for months according to her medical team, but she had defied the odds once again. I wished they had let me know so I could be there for her, but I am thankful I got there when I did. I was able to talk her down and soothe her while she was gasping and struggling to breathe.

September 5, 2017

AM update on day 12… The neurologist said he believes she will walk out of here on her own two feet. Since she got off the ventilator they put a mask that pushes air into her lungs, then about midnight they took her off that and put her on a mask that just blows oxygen and humidity because she has something called 'strider' which means it sounds like she's struggling to breathe and her breaths crack as they come out. Her team of doctors said it's getting better, yet it's scary to watch and very hard to hear. Another one of her neurologists said that she is doing amazingly well on her progress. We are thankful for that. I am trying to give you the most positive words and updates that I can give you all. But what I see every day is so incredibly hard. Sometimes it takes its toll on me which is why I didn't post last night.

A lot of people text me and called me wondering where her pm update was, so I apologize for not posting last night, I just took some time to decompress and build some strength. Her team said she's still in a comatose state; it's like an altered state of consciousness. We don't know what her neurological abilities will be or how much of our Sierra we will get back. We have to continue to believe that eventually we will get our baby back because the Sierra we all know and love isn't here anymore. #TeamBdog

Tonight's update on Sierra…she was in and out of different states of consciousness. I guess that's the best way to explain it. She's still fighting. Her temperature is going down, and her strength is improving, I actually had to use some muscle to hold her hand down, which is a great sign. Her breathing is getting better, she still needs the mask to push oxygen, but it's getting better. She looked towards her dad and her brother today and it was very nice. It actually looked like she made eye contact. She usually looks like she's just staring off into space because she's still in her altered state of consciousness. Goodnight, all, and thank you for the continued prayers. #TeamBdog

This is the day we learned that even though she was trying to come out of her coma, she wasn't "awake." It's not like you see in the movies where they come out of their coma and remember everyone and everything and start talking to everyone, and when they come out of it, they are in a conscious state of mind. Until this happened to our baby, I believed that.

When the doctors said she was coming out of her coma, we thought she would be coherent and look at us and talk to us. We thought "the light would turn on!" That is so far from reality. Her eyes were glazed over, and she couldn't communicate. Her eyes were open, but she was not here. The only thing that ran through my mind was "the lights are on, but nobody's home." That's the best way I can explain to anyone who hasn't experienced this.

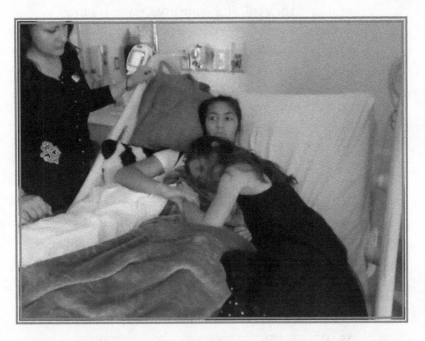

This is what the trance-like state of being actually looks like. Zoe, Sierra's niece, overcoming her fear to be by Auntie's side.

Post from Georgia:

> There are different fundraisers going on this weekend for Sierra and her family! Please come out and support in any way you can by donating, volunteering, etc.

Banner donated for the softball tournament

I called the people I had been working for and let them know that I would be living with her at the hospital until she was ready to come home, which could be a year or more. I remember making those calls. I broke down many times; I could hardly get the words out of my mouth. My daughter was on life support, fighting for her life. We may be in Albuquerque for a year or more, and I would continue to live at the hospital with her. If she made it, her road to recovery would be a very long, excruciating journey. "I will no longer be able to work for you because there are only two outcomes: death or a very long journey until she gets better, and I will not leave her side." They were all very understanding and prayed for the best outcome possible for our baby girl.

September 6, 2017

Update on Sierra, day 13…she is progressing nicely. The doctors said she's taking the right path forward. She's yawning now and sometimes making sounds. This makes us more hopeful she will get her voice back. She reacts to Morke's voice text, that's nice that love crosses all boundaries. The physical therapist came in to work on her joints so she doesn't atrophy. She said her joints are nice and flexible, which is great news as well.

The nurses have to reposition her constantly because she moves around so much. She flops around constantly like she's trying not to drown. She has a look of terror in her eyes. I try to talk her down, but she just continues flopping around all over her bed. We put the rails up on her bed so she doesn't fall on to the ground. They want me to get words out of her now so that's what we will work on until she succeeds. Sorry for the late post, it's been a crazy morning. #TeamBdog

Pm update… We are hours away from two weeks! Unbelievable! She is irritable, and becoming more aware of the situation she is in and that she has tubes throughout her body. Because of this, she tries to take off her leads, tries to pull out her IVs, and pulls on her feeding tube. This is all wonderful news, but it means we have to constantly watch her and make sure she doesn't pull anything out of her body, and we also have to put padded gloves on her so she can't get them out. She definitely doesn't like them, but they are necessary.

Aunt Susan and Uncle Bob came up to see her and I was just holding on to my sanity at the time, so I had to leave and go to the duck pond to take a nap since they are with her. She tried to say Mama today. Then I told her to say it, and she moved her mouth… I'll take the effort. Right now she is resting comfortably, so I'm going to take this opportunity to try to catch some sleep. Goodnight, all…

PS, there are people out there who are concerned about me; all I have to say about that is, don't worry! I will have my moments of weakness, but I got this! Anything I have to do for her, I will, even if that includes taking care of me. Thank you for your concern though. #TeamBdog

At this point, she didn't talk, eat, or respond to commands very often. We were just beginning to work on her, show her how to brush her teeth and wipe her face. We were trying sign language or anything to get her to interact and communicate with us. Aunt Susan and Uncle Bob came up today. I know I was out of sorts. I hadn't slept much, ate much, my heart hurt so bad, I was on the verge of exploding, and they saw that. I could hardly talk to them, so I went for a walk to the university to sit by the water and watch the ducks. They have a pond with a little waterfall; it was peaceful there.

When the situation became too overwhelming or when I couldn't be in her room, I would walk there and just sit by the waterfall and cry, then I would compose myself to get ready to go back in her room and do whatever I had to do to help her through this day. This was my new world, and I was trying to work it out in my head.

September 7, 2017

Update on day 14… So last night, after the nurses were constantly harassing me about getting some sleep, I finally gave in. They set up a chair that folded into a bed in her room, so I decided to give in and lay down about 9:30pm. I was awakened about 11pm to one of her nurses who I had never seen before, telling me, "Lee Anne Wake Up! Wake Up! We're moving Sierra to a step down room. You need to pack your stuff and bring it to your vehicle because they don't have room for your things up there."

So, in my very confused, sleepy mind I asked what the heck is going on. And in her very abrupt and outright rude tone of voice, she told me that she's not critical anymore so they're going to move her to the fifth floor to a big room of brain damaged patients where there is one nurse's station in the middle of the room.

All the while, I'm trying to wake up and another woman was packing her things into a big trash bag. I told her that no one told me about this move and she informed me that she knew for three days. I informed her that I only knew for about five minutes and that she needed to quit being so rude and callous. I then asked her if I could take some things down to my truck and come up for the rest. We both had accumulated a lot of stuff during her stay. I had a suitcase that I lived out of, and Sierra had so many things that people had brought and sent her.

We brought her photo album that my friend and I made for her graduation present, the one that I put on the table in her room so that the nurses and doctors could see the person they were treating. There was no way I could get it all in one trip. She informed me, in a very rude manner that I wouldn't be allowed back in her room, that I have to take it all at once. Then she proceeded to inform me that they would leave the things I couldn't take in the first load out in the waiting room and I can come back and get the rest of our things from there.

I wondered why no one had even given me a heads up about this transition. The fact that she wasn't critical anymore, and that she was doing well enough to be moved was a fantastic step forward. However, where they moved her was horrific and proved to affect her adversely. When I finally got up to this 'step down' room, I almost puked, I was scared and Sierra was scared. She started flopping all over the bed. She couldn't speak, but she didn't have to. I hate it, and she hated it! It was terrifying for both of us. They put a chair next to her bed and told me this is my space. I sat with her for a while and I had to break down so I went for a walk and cried and cried. I felt so helpless, and my heart hurt so badly. I cried so hard that it made my stomach hurt, my muscles tightened up so much, my head was pounding, I felt like I was going to explode. I squeezed myself so hard, trying to catch my breath; I rocked back and forth, trying to soothe myself. I finally composed myself enough to go back into her room, which was more like a mosh pit.

There was a man that screamed and cussed all night long. He screamed, "I want my mom! I want my f——g brother! F——k you!" For hours, this is what we heard. Sierra is freaking out; she's flopping all over the place. I laid my head on her bed and rubbed her until she calmed down. Apparently I fell asleep for a few minutes and awakened to a man across from her just staring with a creepy smile. This man could eat and drink and walk and talk. I didn't understand why he was in this room. He was really scary looking though. I hadn't noticed, but when they moved her from ICU, they had taken off her underwear and I woke up to this man staring at her vagina with a very creepy look on his face. I flipped out and covered her up and spent the rest of the night awake, watching over my baby to make sure she was covered up. This is not what I was expecting when they told us that she would get 'the best care' if we gave up our insurance information. #TeamBdog

Imagine my surprise first of all to get waken up so abruptly, then for her to get moved to this giant room with brain-damaged people. Different degrees of brain damage, but all of them more advanced in their healing than our baby girl. It created so much anxiety I thought I was going to have a heart attack, and my heart ached having my baby girl in this room. The nurse saw it as soon as I arrived, and she was trying to explain why Sierra was there and what to expect. Then she looked at me and asked me, "Are you okay?"

I was so far from okay. I couldn't even see it from that position. She knew I was far from being okay. She tried to explain to me how this was a better room for her to be in and how it meant that she was good enough to be moved from ICU. But, as I looked around the room, I realized this was not going to work for me or for my child. Every time the man across from her started screaming profanities, she reacted adversely.

She was just coming out of a coma; she had no way of communicating with us, so she flailed her hands continuously with a terrified look on her face. I tried so hard to shield her from where she was, but the screaming and yelling from the patients upset her terribly.

This night was extremely terrifying and heartbreaking; it seemed that daylight would never come. When I woke up to see the man across from her, staring at her vagina, I flipped out and broke down and cried. When her dad came back to the hospital the next morning, I explained to him, with tears flowing down my face, what had happened throughout the night. He wanted to see what I was talking about, so we went back up to the mosh pit so he could see for himself. When he saw where they had transported her, he was very upset and agreed with me that she had to be moved immediately.

We went straight to the administrator and told him what the night consisted of. I cried so much that her dad had to tell the administrator what happened because I couldn't get the words out of my mouth. He explained that we wanted her moved now. He said he would work on that right now and for us to go back to her room and get her ready to be moved. Within the hour, she was moved to the fifth floor where she shared a room with another girl.

> PM update...obviously by my rant earlier, you all know she's been moved to a step down room. She is getting moved again right now to a semi-private room. It's by the nurses' station because she still needs 24-hour care but she is no longer considered critical. Great news of course, and I'm trying to see that side of it now. She is moving like crazy, flopping her arms around, she seems very distressed. She has moments of clarity, and we are truly thankful for that. Overall, she is coming back to us a little at a time. #TeamBdog

Her dad got back to hospital about 7:00 a.m. As soon as he got there, I unloaded on him. I explained to him what happened last night and how terrible it was. We both went back up to her room, and as soon as he saw her and the environment she was in, he flipped out as well. We both headed straight to the administrator's office. Art explained the night we had with all the detail I had given him, and I cried. I couldn't say a word. I just sat there and cried. I'm good in the face of adversity, but when it's done, I break down. Now that her dad was there, he could be my strength, and I could cry enough to carry on and get ready for next hurdle we had to jump.

The fifth floor was a much better setting for her. She was right across from the nurses' station so she could be monitored 24-7. Hopefully, she would do better here than she did in the mosh pit. It's amazing that you can find comfort even in the most horrible situations. ICU was so hard on all of us, but somehow, we found some security in her being there. Now that she had been moved, the insecurities and fears had taken over again.

September 8, 2017

> AM update on day 15…she is advancing a tiny bit every day. She gets very agitated, or soothed by her environment. After taking her out of the big room we call the mosh pit, she was much calmer. She got a feeding tube in her stomach today so that she could be fed through that instead of the NG tube down her nose. It was obviously bothering her, we had to strap her hands down so she wouldn't pull it out of her nose, so we're hopeful this will be a better solution to feeding her.
>
> Radiology took her to a CT scan to make sure it was in the correct place, and thankfully it was. During one of our many one sided conversations, I told her to look at me. She actually turned her head and looked at me, actually seemed as though she looked through me, but it was in my direction. It was great! I'm still working on her saying Mama…soon, though. Thank you all again for everything you have sent our way. Money, food, lodging, cards and flowers sent to Sierra, and prayers, Prayers are so powerful, I see how they are working every day in our Sierra. #TeamBdog

Follow up on AM post… I have decided to call this *Sierra's Journey*. #TeamBdog

PM update on day 15 of Sierra's Journey… she had a big day today, and it really wore her out. She's already asleep, resting peacefully to Beethoven's Moonlight Sonata. She started her day with the surgery to put the feeding tube in her stomach, and, of course, she rocked that. The nurses have a machine that vibrates and they have to use it on her lungs so they can keep the congestion moving and she doesn't start to get pneumonia again. It looks like it hurts her but she can't tell us. She can't speak, and she doesn't have emotion, so it's very hard for us to tell. I make the assumption that because her back is broken in five places that it has to hurt to some degree.

These nurses on the fifth floor don't have near the compassion and care the nurses from ICU had. It's a very hard transition and I feel like I can't even leave her alone for a couple of minutes because they seem to ignore her because she can't speak up for herself. Her Physical Therapist came into her room and told her that they were going to work with her and Sierra proceeded to lift her foot over the bed rail and kick her, twice. That was cool. Afterwards she rested for a bit, but it didn't last long because she started flopping all over the bed again.

This evening when we were just hanging out, she snapped her fingers, or at least did the motion to snap, without the sound. But it was an effort so we'll take it. I saved the best for last…Anthony had to go home today, and he was so distraught because when he first got here after the accident, he told her that he is not leaving until he knows she's going to be okay, and she tells him, "I love you." He and his family have been here since day one, but it was getting financially tough. So he regretfully told me that they had to go home for a few days and he would come back after they got paid. When he was explaining to his little sister that he had to go home but he would be back in a few days. Then he said, "I Love You Kid," as he had done all her life, and Sierra signed "I love you" back to him. After that he was actually ready to go home. Her gift made the ride back to Las Cruces much easier on all of them. Thank you, *all*. We are getting her back because the power of your prayers. #TeamBdog

Anthony was so distraught that they had to go back home for a few days. He was in tears, telling her that he had to go home for a few days. So when he was telling her goodbye, he told her, "I love you, kid!"

And the most amazing thing happened; she signed, "I love you." At that moment, we both broke down and cried. This is the first interaction we got from her. It felt so good; the only reaction we had was to cry. She was so restless tonight. I felt as though she wanted me to know or she wanted to tell me something, but she can't communicate. She could only get restless and move around, flailing her arms. I have played Beethoven for her since she was a baby, so I thought that her brain might still relate to it. I played "Moonlight Sonata," rubbed her head, and talked very gently to her, and it worked. She fell asleep and slept like a baby.

After being spoiled by the doctors and nurses in ICU, this was 180 degrees in the opposite direction. Seeing as how she couldn't talk or communicate at all, they ignored her. They didn't turn her when she was supposed to get turned; they didn't brush her teeth, change her leg brace from one leg to another, nor change her diaper when necessary. I had pretty much taken over. I asked for a toothbrush, a washcloth, and diapers so I could give her the care she needed.

Anthony has been my rock. He loves both of us. He's has been my voice of reason since day one. He has a lot of medical knowledge, and what he doesn't know, he learns. So having him here was helpful in so many ways, but now he's gone, and I feel alone again.

September 9, 2017

AM update on day 16 of Sierra's journey… She has made tremendous strides since yesterday. Almost every time we ask her, she tries to interact and respond to our questions. I asked, "Do you know you're in the hospital?" She gave me a thumbs up. She also gave me a thumbs up when I asked her if she's in pain. It's so hard to tell because she doesn't have emotion, so I feel like she's living in her own hell and she can't even tell us. She just has to wait for us to ask the correct question. She is in pain so she got her happy drugs to help her relax. Her dad found a song by Rachel Platten called "The Fight Song." We play it for her all the time and she appears to relate to it. When it comes on, she gets very still and contemplative. Now I can ask her if she wants to hear it and she can give a thumbs up to let us know that she wants it. If she doesn't do anything, we know she doesn't want it. At this point she can only give a thumbs up, not thumbs down. Next we will teach her blink once for yes and twice for no, that way, as long as we ask her yes or no questions, we can give her what she wants. The trick is to ask the right questions. She wanted to watch TV this morning, so I surfed through the channels to find a show with no negativity. This is a new brain and we will not let anything negative in it. We settled on Sponge Bob Square Pants. Her attention span is very short, so if she wants TV now, in two minutes, she could want music. So after watching Sponge Bob for about a minute, she turned her head to the Kindle, which means she wants music.

It's like learning a whole new language. We learn how to communicate with her by trial and error. The best part of the day is the fact that she has signed "I love you" three times already. Oh my gosh! It's such a gift! Thank you everyone for the prayers. We are really seeing the miracles they bring to our Sierra. The softball tournament started today and they had a great turnout. #TeamBdog

Art and my sister went back to Las Cruces for the softball tournament they were holding for her. All my family had gone back home. They went back to represent our family, so Sierra and I were on our own. Up to this point, I had her dad to take care of the paperwork, the vultures, and all the red tape. I also had my son and Jeff to help me emotionally, my sister, my dad, and stepmom for support as well, but now they were all back in Las Cruces, and my dad and stepmom went back to Utah. We decided very early on that her dad would take care of all of the paperwork and the vultures and I would take care of Sierra. They are so heartless. I just couldn't do both, so he took that part of it so all my energy went to Sierra.

Now it was all on me, and I was scared. I had forced myself to eat, to drink, and to sleep as much as possible. I had put my needs on the back burner since the accident, but I could no longer go on doing what I had to do every day without energy from sleeping and eating. I couldn't leave her because she did not get the care she needed. The girl she shared a room with was on suicide watch, so she had doctors and nurses coming in to check on her many times a day. They had to walk past Sierra to get to her roommate, yet they still managed to ignore her. I had to throw a fit and stand by the nurses' station just to get them to give her the medication she needed, particularly her pain medications.

So far, they had made her wait in pain for at least two hours past the scheduled time, so Sierra was in so much pain it made her face red and her eyes show terror in them. She flopped around and looked at me like she was scared to death. We didn't know how much she understood, but I got very upset with the nurses when they made her wait for her medications.

Since she had been moved to the fifth floor, she had not gotten the care that was necessary for her to progress, and I was so mad. I waited by the nurses' station and continually told them she was in pain, and they just abruptly told me they'd get there when they could. This floor sickened me, and I prayed that she was not aware enough to know what was happening. I cried every day and I prayed to God that he intervene so she could get the care she needed, which were actually just her medications. I did everything else for her, but I couldn't give her the medications she so desperately needed.

> PM update on day 16 of Sierra's journey... Okay, I have to say she is probably one of the most amazing determined little fighting machines I have ever had the pleasure of knowing. I just happen to be the one who is blessed enough to be her mama. She had a sleepy day, but when she was awake, she tried to kick the Social worker who was talking to me about her next placement. Apparently there are no acute care rehabs for traumatic brain injury (TBI) in New Mexico. There is one in El Paso, Denver, and Austin.
>
> Anthony and Lee will go check out the one in El Paso to get a feel for it and see if it is a good fit for her. Also, if any of you out there have any information on the one in El Paso, I would appreciate your feedback. The good news is that she's almost there. She's at the point that they're thinking about sending her to the next step. She's

progressed much faster than the doctors expected with the severity of her injuries, mainly her brain of course.

   She hugged me today, she put her arm up and put it around me, and then she pulled me down to her chest, patted my back and played with my hair. This has got to be one of the best days of my life. I'll be back in the am, hopefully with more good news. #TeamBdog

Apparently, she understood that the people dressed in street clothes bring bad news. She was very limited as to what she can do, but somehow, she could get her leg over the rail of the hospital bed to kick anyone that came in with a notebook and street clothes, and she always used the leg with the brace. It was a nice break from the constant stress. I watched her when they came in, and now I knew her intentions. She kicked them, not hard, but enough for them to know she didn't want them there. The discharge caseworker came in with pamphlets full of information on several different facilities. There was a Rancho Scale that they measured her progress from. She was in between a one and two at this point. She would still need twenty-four-hour care for quite a while.

   I was hoping we would find a facility close to home, but it was more important that we find a place that was best for her. Since I opened my Facebook to the public, I figured I would ask everyone out there because I wanted word-of-mouth suggestions. Everyone's pamphlets looked and sounded great, but we had learned wolves came in sheep's clothing. And Sierra was noncommunicative. I didn't want her to be a horror story you read about, the one's about people that should be getting good care. Instead, if they can't communicate, too many times, they don't get the care they need or are completely ignored. We were living that fact right now. Thank God she was doing so well because the care she was getting now was less than average. I wanted her to get out of here as quickly as possible, and her surpassing their expectations was exactly what we needed for her to do that.

September 10, 2017

AM update on Day 17 of Sierra's journey…
Sorry for the late update today. She's had a pretty
lazy day. She is more aware of things that bother
her now. We take off her gloves, and she tries
to scratch the stitches on her head, scratch her
neck because the brace bothers her, she tries to
pull off her leads, etc. Anthony, Lee, and grand
babies just left and that seemed to upset her,
but she signed I love you with both hands when
her brother said, "I love you, kid." It was nice
to send him off with that. She must be thirsty
because she wants me to rub her lips with the
spongy toothbrush and she's starting to suck on
it. She even swallows the water that builds up in
her mouth when I'm rubbing her lips. We know
that they are only baby steps, but all in the right
direction. #TeamBdog

PM update… She had a sluggish day, it
seems as though she's getting more and more
frustrated and irritable. That is actually a good
sign. It means she's trying to come back to us. I
finally got her calmed down tonight when I put
my head on her chest and talked to her very gently. Now she's sleeping peacefully. She loves her
Beethoven's Moonlight Sonata. #TeamBdog

She had to wear padded gloves now that she was trying to come
out of her coma-like state. She was somewhat awake but didn't understand the importance of everything in her body. The stitches on her
head were healing, so they itched. She tried to scratch them, but it
did no good with padded gloves, so I scratched around the stitches
to try to give her some relief. The neck brace was definitely irritating
her skin because there were marks all over her neck from the plastic
and Velcro. When she was lying down at thirty degrees, sometimes I

loosened it just enough to bring her some relief. Although we didn't know if she understood, I explained to her why everything in her body and on her body was necessary.

September 11, 2017

Day 18 of Sierra's journey... She is definitely becoming more aware of her surroundings. She was frustrated this morning, probably because she felt my frustration with the lack of care she is getting up here on the fifth floor. She pulled my hair and scratched me to show me how upset she was. I'm starting to learn more sign language and will try to teach her so she can communicate more. Maybe she won't feel so trapped. Any time a social worker, or someone who doesn't belong in her room, comes in, she tries to kick them. Now when she gets upset, she shakes her right foot. I just don't know what her frustrations are yet.

It looks like we're going to Denver. With the information we have been given, it seems to be the best choice for her, and her injuries. We asked how long she would be there and we were told that it depends on her advancement. So today I had to deal with the bureaucracy and she *does not* like it at all! Her discharge caseworker came to talk to me today about her next placement. We went out to the hallway so Sierra wouldn't get agitated. She was pushing me to send her to Austin. I continually told her that Austin was not an option. I told her that we're from Las Cruces and El Paso was our other choice. The more she talked to me, the more upset I became. She was also all about the insurance. She needed it so wherever they place her, she can get it to them.

I asked what if I don't give it to you. She very abruptly informed me that they would release her because their only job is to save her life. I jumped out of my chair because I wanted to punch her in the face. Thankfully my friend Chris was there and knew exactly what was happening, and he jumped out of his chair too. I'm sure it was to stop me from punching her. That snapped me back into place. I asked her if that was even legal? She retorted with, "Our only job is to save her life." I asked her how heartless she has to be to do this to people every day. She explained to me that it's just her job. I had several more things to say to her, none of which was nice. Then, again, she started trying to get me to go to Austin. I asked her why she's trying so hard to send us to a place that is suffering from the hurricanes. Surely the hospitals were overflowing with patients from the area. She told me several times that it was fine. I was so angry at this point. All I could say is, "Watch the news!" It was all over the news, and she outright lied and told me everything was fine in Austin. She was just a liar, and nothing will set me off more quickly than people lying to me. So I have decided to no longer give this woman any of my precious time. I have to focus all my energy on Sierra, and I will not let this woman take any more of my energy, or time that I'd rather give to our baby girl. Thank you for all your input about her next placement. #TeamBdog

P.S. The #18 is and always has been her number her whole softball career, so maybe today will be her day! Also, we love the flowers, stuffed animals, and other things people bring. However, there is nowhere to put them. Cards are great. I am saving them for her but I can't store anything else. You're more than welcome to get them for her and when we get back, we can have a big cookout and you may give them to her then, but she is sharing a room with someone else and there is no room to store anything. Thank you for understanding. You may want to hold off on sending them snail mail because we don't know exactly when we're leaving. I will post information on how to send cards, drawings, pictures, and mementos when we get to Denver. We Love you people! #TeamBdog

PM update on day 18 of sierra's Journey… Quite a big day today. First of all I'd like to start with change of plans…we are not going to Denver. Through all research and phone calls Anthony, Lee, and Art made on getting information about her next step, Anthony and Lee learned that there is actually an Acute Neurological Rehab for TBI in Las Cruces! We are coming home! Well, not quite home, but to our hometown. Anthony and Lee found this out when they went to visit the El Paso facility. They said that unfortunately she wasn't ready to be in their hospital, but she does qualify for the one in Las Cruces. Her dad went to check it out and get a feel for it. He said that it had everything she needed and we wanted for Sierra. We were also informed that being around people she loves and who love her will enhance her recovery tremendously. She is ready for the next step neurologically, but not medically.

As far as her progress, she has brushed her own teeth about six times today, she wiped her own chin when the water ran down it, put on her own ChapStick, mostly on her lips, and rubbed her lips together to spread out the ChapStick. She gave me a thumbs up that she wanted to hug me. So I leaned down on her chest and she hugged me and stroked my hair ever so gently. And, because I like to save the best for last…we have a thing that every time we leave each other, we say, "I Love you forever!" So today she signed "I love you," and I said, "Forever," and she held up four fingers! Oh my gosh. It was amazing! Thank you, all! Our prayers are being answered every day. #TeamBdog

She was still not getting the care she needed, so I couldn't leave her for very long. She had already gotten infections in her catheter, so it was very important to change her immediately after she used the restroom. When I went back into her room, I realized she must have had a bowel movement as soon as I left the room because she had a puddle of diarrhea between her legs, and it had already begun to dry around the edges. She had to have several suppositories everyday so that she didn't strain to use the restroom because she could have a seizure if she did. So when she had to have a bowel movement, it was always very runny, and it puddled up between her legs. I had taken the responsibility of changing her since she got moved to the fifth floor, and this is exactly why. They didn't change her, turn her, switch her leg brace, brush her teeth, or any of the care that she needed.

The only time we saw a nurse was when they came in to give her medications. Even then, I had to track them down and throw a fit so that she could get her necessary medications. Even still, she had to wait an hour or so before they finally came in. They had yet to come in on time to give her the pain medications she needed, so I had to go to the nurses' station and find the charge nurse to tell her that Sierra was in pain because she was an hour past due for her medications. It was so hard to see our baby in so much pain and know that they just didn't care.

Thank goodness for my very long-time friend, Chris, who came to sit with me and let me unload on him quite often. Today was fate that he was sitting there when the discharge nurse was talking to me about going to Austin. When he saw me jump out of my chair, so did he, and that was enough to snap me back into reality, and reality is that if I punched her in the face, I would not be able to be here for our baby girl.

September 12, 2017

> AM update on day 19 of Sierra's journey... She is doing great! I asked her if she's happy that she's going home and she gave me a thumbs up. It's hard to tell because she has no emotion, at least we can't see it, and she can't communicate it. She says she is very excited to see her family and friends. A lot of the time she will respond with a thumbs up or "I love you" sign. We just have to ask the right questions. She gives her nurse the thumbs up sign when she's in pain, and she can even localize the pain when they ask her where it hurts. It's good to know that she can respond to yes or no questions. She's just amazing!
>
> I'm waiting for the discharge caseworker to tell us when we are going home. I don't think she wants to face me because of our heated conversation yesterday. Also, Anthony and Lee told me about the TBI rehab in Las Cruces, so I asked the nurse about it. She apparently told the discharge woman because I had left Sierra's room for a little bit to deal with more red tape, and when I returned, there were pamphlets and information on the rehab at home. I was furious! All along, while she was trying to push us to go to Austin, she knew about the rehab in Las Cruces. She deliberately withheld this information from me. So now we have to wonder what kind of kick back she was going to get, and what kind of person would send us to a place where there are hurricanes and logic dictates that the hospitals would

obviously be overflowing as well. I just keep asking myself, "What kind of person is capable of this?"

I've made quite a name up here. I am her voice, and I will do whatever it takes to get her what she needs. So sometimes I have to unleash "the witch" on their superiors to make sure they're doing what they should be doing to give Sierra the proper care they assured us she would get if we gave them her insurance information; such as them giving her pain medications when she needs them, instead of making her wait in pain for an hour before they get to her, or change her diaper when I'm not in the room, and to stop leaving her unattended. I haven't punched anyone in the face yet, and I'm pretty proud of that. I have to bite my tongue, or at least make the words coming out of my mouth much nicer than the ones in my head. I have to keep my cool so Sierra doesn't pay for it. There is already a lack of care for her now, and I have to be out of her room a lot more now that her dad isn't here so I can deal with the bureaucracy. Because of that, I'm not always there to change her as soon as she needs it, and they rarely check on her. She has already had to have her catheter changed out because they let her set in her feces when I was downstairs trying to figure out insurance issues, and she got infection. I have to stay with her, but I have to make sure she continues to get the care she needs, so I also have to take care of the red tape side of it and I can't do it in her room. But several times I have come in and she is setting in her own feces and around the outside, it was dry. She must have gone as soon as I left, sometimes I'm talking on the phone for an hour with very necessary phone calls, and when I come back in, she's got a dirty diaper. I'm looking forward to the best care they promised she would get when we gave them her insurance information. We are excited to be coming back to our hometown where, hopefully, she will get the care she needs. Love you all! #TeamBdog

Today I found out how very low her discharge planner could go. After I talked to Anthony and Lee and they told me about the rehab hospital in Las Cruces, I almost blew a lid. I looked for the discharge planner, and it was probably very good that fate stepped in and Sierra needed me because I had a lot to say to her, none of which would be nice or kind. I was actually livid. When I finally tracked down one of Sierra's nurses, I told her that my family learned that there was a rehab in Las Cruces that specialized in TBI, and she obviously didn't care. However, she apparently passed the information to the discharge planner. After I told the nurse about my newly found information, I had to go downstairs to make some very necessary phone calls, and when I went back into Sierra's room, there were pamphlets on the rehab in Las Cruces. She obviously had the information all along, and yet she tried to get us to go to Austin. At that point, I wanted nothing more than to meet that woman on the street and teach her a lesson she would never forget. I was so angry and was all alone with Sierra. She was sleeping, so I took a much-needed break to calm myself down. I walked the halls and made some more phone calls to my family, and they helped me calm down enough so I could go back into Sierra's room and tend to her.

Even though she was out of her coma, she was still in an altered state of consciousness. When I looked at her, she didn't look back; she just stared off into space. The nurse told us at some point "the lights would turn on." But we were obviously not there yet, so now, "the lights are on, but nobody's home" is the best way I could explain her current situation.

PM update on day 19 of Sierra's journey… We ran into some snags, we were told that we were good to go, but another advocate of the for the facility in Las Cruces said that they need to review her records to be sure they can accommodate her Rancho level of TBI. I know this will all work out, it's just one more bridge that we have to cross. We should know in the morning, so when I know, you will know.

She is making a little progress every day. She blinks now, one for yes and two for no. She's using her pointer finger up and down for yes and side to side for no, signing "Thank you" and "I love you" have become almost commonplace. She gets her Oxycodone and sleeping medications so she sleeps most of the night, which makes me feel better when she's resting peacefully and healing her brain. Besides the fact that if she is sleeping, she doesn't need as much care from the nurses, so their lack of care doesn't affect her as much. Please Pray that Las Cruces comes through. It sure would be nice to be home. Thank you, and goodnight, all. #TeamBdog

At this point in her recovery, I was maxed out. Her dad and I, together, had dealt with everything else that came with getting Sierra the proper care and placement she desperately needed to heal. Just taking care of Sierra on a daily basis was so emotionally draining. On top of that, we had to deal with doctors' and nurses' opinions about how very bad her situation was and how she may never completely come back to us, she may never walk or talk or eat, let alone play softball again.

On the other side of the spectrum, we had to deal with insurance who we had to fight to pay for the necessary treatment she needed to progress. The caseworkers whose only job was to make sure they got paid, and there was a long list of them. The discharge planners whose job was to find her next placement and try to convince us of their opinion of where they think she should go for her next step of recovery, or in this case, where they would get a kickback from—every one of them obviously had a personal interest, and it was not Sierra.

Now it was all on me, and I didn't know if I had what it took to continue this on my own for much longer. It was unimaginable to me that they could look at Sierra and still be so heartless, and to know that their only driving force was money. In the meantime, Sierra was getting a serious lack of care since she was moved to the fifth floor. Going from the care she received in the Neurosciences ICU to the lack of care she received on the fifth floor was wearing on my spirit, I felt as though I was going to completely lose my mind from anger, heartache, and helplessness. We needed to get her out of here as quickly as possible.

September 13, 2017

> AM Update on day 20 of Sierra's journey… I've been waiting for the call from Las Cruces, but haven't heard anything yet. We are still praying that Las Cruces comes through. Her neurosurgeon came in this morning and said, "This is miraculous! She is definitely a miracle!" She has come so far in just three short weeks, and he is extremely impressed. He went on to tell us that people who come in that are in her condition, if they make it, they are in the Intensive Care Unit for months. She was only in ICU for two weeks, and she's already signing and communicating. Of course, we were very jazzed about that. He just couldn't believe what he was witnessing.
>
> I told her whole team from the beginning that they didn't know who they were dealing with, and now they're beginning to understand. She's ready for her next step, scary, yet exciting.

Even though this is a very scary place, scary situation, I have some comfort in being here, I have learned that the broken step coming in from the parking garage is my cue that is the floor I need to go into to get to the hospital, and I didn't like the revolving door because I saw it stop one day with people in it, and where to get the best coffee. I learned the schedules of the doctors so I could talk to them. I learned the nurses I could talk to, and the ones that were truly invested in her progress. I have the pond I can go when it all gets too much.

All of it was strangely comfortable. It's very hard to explain. I have come to know this place, the people, the nurses and doctors. So it's scary to go into the unknown. I wonder if she'll really get the care she needs. Will they be kind and understanding? Will they care? Will they invest themselves in her recovery? After researching more, we feel more comfortable with her going to her next step, as long as they are what they say they are. Progress is progress, and it's good, no matter how bad she is right now, she's progressed enough to go to the next step. So, next step, here we come. I know this will work out and we'll be homeward bound soon. We are thankful to all of you. #TeamBdog

Strangely comfortable—it sounds like a contradiction in terms, but it is the best way I can explain it. There is chaos, heartache, and fear just looking at our baby girl. Apparently, the staff was used to seeing this sort of trauma because they had obviously become complacent. They didn't look at our child as a human being who was loved by so many people; they saw her as just another dollar sign. I was appalled at what our health care system had become and even more appalled at the people who chose the jobs that used the victims as prey. They had hit us at our lowest point and told us she would not get the care she needed if we didn't play their game, playing on our emotions, knowing that we would give in to them and their requests in the hopes of getting the care she needs. The staff in the ICU was amazing beyond comprehension, but the staff on the fifth floor was less than average. I was so ready to get out of here no matter where we went. It had to be better than where she was now.

September 14, 2017

> Day 21 of Sierra's journey… I apologize that I didn't post last night, without going into too much detail, I feel like I need to stay at the hospital until I drop. I want to make sure she's asleep for the night before I leave her. So the only thing I could think about last night after I left her was bed and sleep. I don't like to do that because I know a lot of you are following her posts closely and when I don't post, I get calls and texts asking what the heck? So, it was a big day yesterday.
>
> A woman from Craig in Denver came to evaluate Sierra. When she was talking to me I got the feeling she had no idea of Sierra's capabilities. It sounded like she thought Sierra was in a vegetative state. I asked her how she got her information and she informed me that she read her records and they state that she doesn't respond at all. So I retorted with, "They are way off! They completely neglect her so they have no idea where she is in her recovery." I told her that she helps brush her teeth, wipes her chin, and she is starting to communicate with basic sign. She wanted to witness for herself. Sierra had just had her Oxycodone about half hour before so she was pretty sleepy. Even so, she followed some commands from her and me. I told her there's more

but she informed me that she had seen enough to know the records are not updated with her progress. So, on the Rancho Scale, instead of the Level 1 they had her at, she put her at a possible Level 3. I have to say, the Neurosciences ICU here is extraordinary, but the fifth floor is far from competent.

She is now signing "I love you," "Thank you," and "Peace out." She brushes her teeth or at least helps me brush her teeth several times a day, and her new thing is pushing the nurse's button. I showed her that if she needs anything, to push that button and keep on pushing it until they come. Sometimes she pushes it and I ask her if she needs the nurse. And she signs 'no,' so I ask her if she's being ornery. And she pushes the button again. I think she's playing around, but it's hard to tell because she still doesn't have emotion.

Yesterday, her neurosurgeon came to check on her again, and I threw a huge fit to him about the lack of care she's getting up here. I told him everything and I was crying uncontrollably, it was so emotional for me. He was very angered at what I was telling him. He couldn't believe it. He told me that he would talk to them and that would change. After he left, they waited on her hand and foot. They were in there every hour checking on her, turning her, switching her leg brace, and checking her diaper. Finally, she's getting proper care.

After that shift changed, it was right back to neglecting her. I asked them if I could get a nurse in there for five minutes. I want them to just knock her out for the night so we can get through one more day. It seems that every nurse that is assigned to her, has an emergency with another patient, or checking on another patient, but they don't seem to make it to Sierra's room unless I go to the nurse's station and tell them she needs something, and then stand there and wait until someone comes.

We need to get out her of here where she's treated like a human being instead of a patient with no voice. So I'm known as a real witch around here, but I'm okay with that. I am her only voice, and I will continue to be until she can speak for herself. We're still waiting on word from Las Cruces. #TeamBdog

PM update on day 21 of Sierra's journey... We got the word today that Las Cruces Rehab accepted her. They were apprehensive because of her medical records from here. As I said before, the information they had on her was incorrect. I explained to them that she is starting to follow commands and she is more aware than what they have written in her charts. Again, if they spent any time with her at all, they would have realized this.

The social worker informed me that if I had not fought against their medical records, she would not have been considered advanced enough to accept her. Now we have to wait for authorization from the insurance company and they said it could be as long as the 18th, but we'll take it. At least there's light at the end of the tunnel. Today the physical therapist came in and sat her up for the first time since the accident. She also had her follow basic commands and Sierra rocked it. When she decided that she had enough, she started trying to kick her therapist. That always makes me laugh, because sometimes

I would like to do the same thing, but without a brain injury, it's not near as acceptable.

She is eating ice chips now and I let her play candy crush on the notebook. She can only get a few lines right now, but it still helps her on so many different levels. It's great to see her brain starting to reconnect. I have continued to show her the nurse's button. I have to show her every day, multiple times a day because she forgets. So when I had to step out of her room again, I showed her the nurse's button and told her to ring it if she needs anything, and keep ringing it until someone comes in. They turn it off at the nurses' station, many times without even coming in to check on her, so I tell her to keep ringing it and ringing it. So now she can have some control over her care. It was quite funny today. She would push the button and it would get turned off at the nurses' station, so she would push it again. They would turn it off and she would push it again.

She was in pain and was way overdue for her pain medications, and again, they didn't give them to her on schedule, they tried to ignore her. But now that she has the nurses button, I tell her don't quit pushing it until they come. All the while, I go hunt down a nurse and tell them she needs her pain medications, actually she's way overdue. That's my baby; she will beat them at their own game, even with brain damage. I'm so very unhappy about the lack of care they give her here.

I'm looking forward to getting her out of here and being in our hometown. I've heard many good things about the rehab in Las Cruces since we started doing research, and now I feel very good about her next placement. Besides that, we will be home where her friends and family are. All of those ingredients make for good progress. See you all very soon. Love you all. #TeamBdog

When her neurosurgeon came in to check on her progress and he started asking questions about how she was doing, I literally broke down. I had watched doctors, nurses, and techs come in to check on the girl she shared a room with and walk right past Sierra like it was an empty bed they were walking by. All the while, Sierra was being neglected on a daily basis. I told him that they didn't change her diaper, they let her sit in her own feces until it was dry on her skin, they didn't brush her teeth, they didn't switch her leg brace or move her from side to side—they actually didn't do anything for her except give her medications. Even then, she had yet to get her medication on time; they made her wait for at least an hour in so much pain that Sierra had a look of terror in her eyes, and her whole face turned red because she hurt so badly.

I had taken over her complete care. The only thing I couldn't do was administer medications, so she never got them when she needed them. When he heard about the lack of care she was receiving, he was terribly upset and couldn't believe what I was saying. Immediately, he consoled me and assured me that would change today. He was right. It did change tremendously. The nurses came in and switched her brace every hour, brushed her teeth, gave her medications to her on time, and turned her from side to side. I still changed her diaper because I didn't know if she knew what was happening to her, and I knew her old brain wouldn't want anyone else changing her. That was short-lived. As soon as that shift was over, they went right back to ignoring her; it was extremely disheartening.

September 15, 2017

AM update on day 22 of Sierra's journey… We're still waiting for word on when we're getting out of here. I am working on her dexterity, so I downloaded candy crush and let her play it. At first she just sat and watched the screen, then moved the candy three times in the correct direction. It was so exciting. She's pulling on her tubes less and less now because I explain to her everyday why she has them, the purpose they serve, and the damage that it will cause if she pulls them out. I think she's starting to understand. She still just looks through me, but she appears to understand. She's getting there, slowly but surely.

This morning, Coach came to see her and ratted her out. When they were on the road for a game, she snuck out of the hotel room and went to the movies. As he was telling me, she actually smiled. Actually, it was a half-smile, but the attempt was great. She obviously knew what he was saying. This is the first expression of emotion that I've seen. It was beautiful. He also talked about how she was his singing partner, even though she isn't the best singer. She smiled again. That smile is her web, the reason everyone loves her. It's so captivating; it just draws people into her. I've missed that smile so much, and now it's coming back, and it's very warm in my heart.

When I know more about when we're leaving, you will as well. It's just a waiting game. But we are more than ready to get out of this place and hopefully start working on her recovery, as opposed to me constantly harassing the staff here to give her some attention. I have been responsible for changing her, brushing her teeth, dressing her wounds, turning her, and everything else that she needs because they continue to neglect her since she's been moved to the fifth floor. She still has stitches where they sewed up her vagina and anus as well, so changing her promptly is a necessity, yet they still don't care. We believe the next placement will be much better for her, and her recovery. Thank you all for the continued prayers. #TeamBdog

PM Update on day 22 of Sierra's journey... We are coming home! The word right now is that we should be leaving Albuquerque at 5:30am and she will be transported in an ambulance. Yet another thing I had to pitch a fit about. The case worker wanted to send her home in a medical transport van with no medical staff. I raised hell about that and explained to her that I am *not* okay with that. She said it was standard procedure but I was not willing to accept that. If something happens to her on the ride home, there would be no one with any medical knowledge to help her, and I will not allow that to happen after how far she's come.

Her dad came to see her today and I showed him how much she's learned in the past week, and he was so very proud of her, as I am. She will need familiar faces to enhance her rehabilitation. So we look forward to seeing family and friends very soon. Please contact us before coming to see her. The staff said they absolutely encourage people to come see her, but she can't handle too much stimulation at one time, so we can't allow too many people to see her at once.

The doctors estimate that she will be in Las Cruces for about six months. After what she has shown us, we highly doubt it will take her that long to progress to the next step. She has blown away their expectations to this point, and we believe she will continue to surpass every obstacle on her path to recovery. However, if that's what it is, then she will conquer it as well. After Las

Cruces, she will go to El Paso for her last stage of rehabilitation so we can get her back to being independent and 100%. Thank you, thank you, and thank you to everyone out there. Most of you are lucky enough to know her, some not. Some just found her story on Facebook, and began to pray for her. It's just warms my heart. True humanity! I love all of you for what you have done for us. Her story is not over; she still has a lot of healing to do. Her new life and new beginning is approaching. Thank you Lord! Please pray for our safe return. And I will let you all know when we get on the road. #TeamBdog

Follow up on PM update... Okay, I did not realize my phone would blow up with texts and phone calls after I posted. So, for all of you that want to welcome her back to our hometown, I will post when we leave Albuquerque, and it should take about three and a half hours from our departure time. I'm sure she would love to see her family and friends welcome her back to Las Cruces. She is being transported to the rehab hospital in Las Cruces. It is up by the hospital on Lohman. I'm too excited!

We look forward to seeing you all there to greet her when she gets home. No pictures please. We will save that for when she can tell us that it's okay to show them, until then I ask that you respect her privacy. Thank you. #TeamBdog

Getting to this point had been extremely tumultuous. I was jazzed to be getting out of here and going back to our hometown. We could only hope and pray that she wouldn't remember this part of her journey. I would never forget it. I would never forget how amazing the ICU was, and I would never forget the treatment—or lack of it actually—that she received up on the fifth floor. I cried more for her on the fifth floor than I did when she was in the ICU. At least when she was in ICU, we truly believed she was getting the best care possible.

She had been Coach's favorite since she started college and played softball for him. They had a special bond that exists to this day. Every chance he got, he came to visit her and tell stories of their time together. He talked to her about her past shenanigans but also their future together when she got better and he was able to coach her again—a goal we all hoped for her to ascertain.

September 16, 2017

> AM update on day 23 of Sierra's journey... Getting ready to get on the road. We are coming back to our hometown finally. I am so looking forward to being in our hometown. We should be arriving about 9:30 or 10am. #TeamBdog

Before we left, I met the ambulance staff at the hospital. When I saw her being wheeled out, my heart sank. I was so afraid of her being on the highway. There were three paramedics transporting her, one driver, and two of them kept watch over her while they drove the long stretch back home. I gave her photo album to one of the paramedics, the one that shows her softball life and high school years. I told him if she gets agitated to show her the pictures in the album. She related to them, and I hoped it would help her. I didn't even know if she knew what was happening, but I didn't want her to freak out if she knew she was on the same highway that they got in the accident on.

> PM Update on day 23 of Sierra's journey... We made it home safely. She's a little agitated but settling in. I will update more this evening after we get her situated. #TeamBdog

The photo album turned out to be a good idea. The paramedics said that she was looking around and getting agitated. They thought that she knew she was on the road. She tried to grab his notebook out of his pocket, so he gave it to her and gave her a pen, and she tried to write, "Be careful!" It was barely legible, but it reinforced the fact that she knew she was on the road. She wrote other things as well, but we couldn't make them out. When we arrived at the rehab, there were multiple people out there to greet her. She was very agitated when she got there, so they took her immediately to her room to let her settle down a bit. I went to her room and began telling her where she was, that she was okay, and this was her next step on her path to recovery. She just stared into space, so I hoped that she understood.

Follow-up on PM update... She's settled in and seems to be quite pleased with her surroundings so far, I know I sure am. What a difference from what we just left. Today she wrote her brother's name, and it was actually quite legible. On the way back from Albuquerque, she grabbed the paramedics' pen so he gave her a notepad and she actually tried to write something. Most of it wasn't legible, but the fact that she tried is amazing. We had no idea that she was able to write so we will get her a notebook to help her communicate with us. She smiled when she saw Krystal and tried to throw her the stress ball. I asked her if she knows that Krystal is her catcher and she smiled and dropped the ball in her hand. After that, she tossed the ball with her brother.

Jeff was teasing her because I said she is only allowed to watch positive shows on TV. So he asked her if she wanted to watch the Trump debate, and she smiled at him and gave him the finger. It was pretty funny. We know all too well how she feels about Trump, and there's no positive vibes coming from that name. She has also

started writing to communicate with us. It's very
hard to read, but we are learning to make most of
it out. As time goes by, everything, including her
writing will get better. Goodnight for now, and
thank you for the prayers of a safe homecoming.
#TeamBdog

As soon as we got home, my sister was there to greet her, and I
just broke down in her arms. I don't know what happened. I just saw
her, and she hugged me and told me how proud she was of me. Then
the floodgates opened. I cried so hard, and she just held on to me
until I stopped. I needed that so badly. I had been on my own with
Sierra for the last week, and it was so hard on me, so when I saw my
sister, I just lost it. I had to unburden my heart so I could continue
the fight to get our baby girl back.

It was very nice to see her react to her long-time friend and
catcher, Krystal. They worked great on the field together, and she
remembered that connection, and it was great to see. We didn't know
if she would recognize anyone from her past. So when she recognized
Krystal as her catcher, it made us smile so big not only to see the two
of them but to realize that she has memory of people that were in her
life before the accident.

Since we realized that she can write or at least attempt to write,
I went and got her a notebook immediately. Most of what she wrote
was not legible, but the effort was there, and it was our first hope of
her communicating with us so we could learn how much she really
knew. The lack of emotion and lack of communication had been so
hard for us; we couldn't imagine how hard it was on her.

September 17, 2017

AM update on day 24 of Sierra's journey… She
had a very restless night. She is becoming more
and more aware of the tubes in her body, and
they are making her very uncomfortable. She is
trying to communicate more with her writing,

but it's very hard for us to make out what she is writing most of the time. We are trying different forms of communication, such as pictures, flash cards, and number scales to show her level of pain, and we made a list of things we think she might need or want so she can just point to it. So far we have words like water, food, family, and pain. We're still trying to figure out what works best for her.

She had more ice chips today and handled them very well. Choked a couple of times, but she is still learning to swallow. She really wants to sit up, and she wants the neck brace off, but her neck is not strong enough to hold her head up yet so we have to keep her at 30 degrees so her head doesn't droop. Also, we were informed that she has to wear the brace because her head can detach from her spine if we don't keep it on and her head stable. She lit up when I asked her if she wants to talk to Morke. He is walking much better, climbing stairs a bit, and he will finally be starting therapy next week. He is very excited about that. Now we will work on a way to get him back down here so that he can see her. Signing off for now. Thank you all for your support. #TeamBdog

PM update on day 24 of Sierra's journey... She had quite a big day today. They already scheduled her for physical, occupational, and speech therapy. They have to work her in slowly, so we waited until the gym was empty and when her therapist wheeled her down, she took her straight to the east window where she could see the Organ Mountains. Sierra handled it very well seeing as how she has had no contact with the outside world since the accident, and we have kept her stimulation level to a minimum. We made her flash cards today to help her communicate with us, and oh my gosh! Now we know that she feels pain all the time, and it is always a ten on a scale from one to ten. That breaks my heart. Since she has very little emotion or expression, we had no clue the agony she has endured. She is just barely starting to show emotion and expression, so when she gets one of her terrible headaches, there's a look of terror on her face, and her face turns as red as a tomato. We feel so helpless, we want to just take it all away, but we can't. We can only request medications to help ease her pain. I rub her and talk gently to her trying to get her to sleep. That seems to be the only peace she has.

She took a shower today for the first time, with help from her occupational therapist and I of course. She stood up out of her wheelchair for the first time as well. We transferred her from her wheelchair to the shower chair, she was wobbly but held her own weight for just a couple seconds, yet it's still progress. She's very unstable now, but it will get better as time goes by. Tomorrow she starts a full load of therapy, so please pray for her strength. Goodnight all and thank you for your prayers. #TeamBdog

I feel like so many things have happened in one day. She got here, and immediately, the staff had a vested interest in getting her started on her road to recovery. We realized she attempted to write what she was thinking, that she was in massive pain, and she was aware enough to know she was on the highway, and it scared her. When her occupational therapist came in and told me that she was going to take her to the gym, my heart sank. I didn't know what to expect. I didn't even know she could be put in a wheelchair. I remember when she wheeled her down to the gym, it was empty and very bright. We put sunglasses on Sierra because she reacted adversely to light. As she wheeled her down, I took video of it, and all the while, my heart was pounding out of my chest. I was so afraid for her because I didn't know her capabilities.

Until today, she just lay in bed, and now they had her in a wheelchair in the gym. When she got to the window, she stared outside in her trance-like state. We didn't know how much she could see or how much she knew of what was happening to her. She just stared out into oblivion, no reaction, no emotion, just a blank stare. The staff explained to us that they were going to start her on therapies immediately because the longer they took to start, the longer it would take her body to recover. They were the experts, and we had to believe they knew what they were doing. Easier said than done. She was our baby girl, and we are completely ignorant as far as brain injuries were concerned, but we were learning.

September 18, 2017

> AM update on day 25 of Sierra's journey… She had quite a big day today. She had physical, occupational, and speech therapy. We made her flash cards to help her communicate, and oh my gosh! Now we know that she feels pain all the time. On a scale from 1–10, she always picks ten. She's getting expressions now, and the look on her face is so hard to bear. We're very happy she can communicate with us more now, but there is nothing I can do to take the pain away from my baby. So we anxiously await medication time. She gets high doses of pain medication, and that is the only thing that takes off the edge enough to let her relax and sleep. Sleep is the best thing for her brain; it's the only time her brain doesn't have to do anything but heal.

She took a shower today, with the help of her occupational therapist and me. She seemed confused and a little scared, but I talked her through it so we were able to wash some of the blood out of her hair. It will probably take a few more showers before we get it all out because it is so clumped up and has been in her hair for twenty-four days now. I told her to close her eyes so the soap doesn't get in her eyes, but the truth is that I didn't want her to see the red water that filled the shower floor. Her OT and I just looked at each other with sadness in our eyes, as she sat in her shower chair oblivious to what was actually happening.

Besides the shower, she got into the wheelchair today as well. She actually put weight on her feet for the first time since the accident. We haven't been able to sit her upright because of the damage to her tendons and ligaments in her neck. Up to this point, we had to keep her at a thirty degree level because she couldn't hold own head up without the help of the neck brace. It is still very wobbly, but it's getting stronger and stronger as the days go by.

Because she did so well today, she will now have scheduled therapy on a daily basis. They will only push as far as she will accept it, but they will push. I explained to them that she is an athlete, so she is used to having a coach push her. I asked them to act like a coach because they will get the best response possible. Goodnight All, and thank you for your continued prayers. #TeamBdog

PM update on day 25 of Sierra's journey... Today, in speech therapy, she ate ice chips, sipped water, and brushed her teeth. Her speech therapist said she does have her voice, but she just has to find it, which she will in her own time. The occupational therapist came in today and massaged her left arm trying to stimulate the nerves so she can regain movement. She also worked on her hair, trying to get the knots out so we can get the rest of the blood out. It's in such a big knot from lying in bed for so long. Her physical therapist got her in the wheelchair again, and she rocked that. She's holding the weight of her head much better, which means the tendons and ligaments are getting stronger the more she is forced to use them. She is so awesome. Every one of the medical staff that encounters her is very impressed with how much she has progressed in such a short amount of time. I tried to tell all the medical staff since the beginning of this journey, they don't know Sierra, the drive and determination of this young woman. Now they are beginning to understand what I meant as well, and maybe I'm not as naive as they thought I was.

A few of her friends came to visit her today and she hugged them and signed "I love you" to them. She apparently loves pregnant women because Cole and Lexi came in, and she rubbed their bellies and signed "I love you" to the babies, it was adorable.

We love it here at the rehab, the staff is amazing, and Sierra is reacting in a very positive manner. They all appear to have a vested interest in her healing process. All the doctors, nurses, techs, and therapists treat her with kindness and compassion; it's so wonderful to feel like this is where she belongs, where we will get her back.

Because her days are so busy, full of therapy and healing, I don't know if I will be able to post twice a day because I want to be with her every

step of the way. I hope that I can, but if not, I
will definitely let you all know at least once a day
how she is progressing. Goodnight All. Thank
you for your prayers...they are definitely working because she is soaring much faster than any of
the experts thought she would. We're getting her
back, slowly but surely. #TeamBdog

We are both settling in here. It is so much different than
Albuquerque's fifth floor. They gave me a fold-out bed so I could
sleep next to her. She had her own room, and the nurses continually
checked on her. Since I had already been changing her diaper, I told
the staff I would continue to do so. At first they were apprehensive
about it, but I explained the lack of care she had been receiving and
how I had to take over her care, so they agreed to let me take over
that part of it. I showed them I was very thorough and cleaned her
stitches very well so she wouldn't get an infection, and they agreed to
let me continue to change her. We didn't know how aware she was
or if she had modesty, so I felt better that I could take on that part of
her care. We made sure she was never alone. If I was not in her room
with her, she was with her dad, her brother and his family, or other
family members.

So far, I am the only one who had spent the night with her,
and it was what she was used to. It was not only for her but for me
as well. She didn't like it when I was not with her at night. She got
very agitated and restless until I came back into her room and rubbed
her head and talked very gently to her. I told her every night how
amazing she was and how proud we all were of her. I told her she was
the biggest fighter and how much God and her family loved her. She
wanted me in her bed every night, but I had to sleep in the chair next
to her because I didn't want to accidentally pull out her IV or any of
the other tubes she had in her body. So I got in her bed with her and
rubbed her and talked to her until she went to sleep so I could get in
the bed next to her and get as much sleep as possible. Her day started
at 7:00 a.m., so I tried to get her to sleep as early as possible so she
was ready to fight when she woke up.

For insurance purposes, I had to prove myself to her medical staff. I had to show them that I knew how to change her and dress her stitches. She had about ten stitches that sewed her anus and vagina together. It hurt her when I had to clean them, but I explained exactly what I was doing and why it was very necessary. Again, we didn't know how aware she was, so we assumed she knew what was happening, so we tried to ease her mind. It was very sad to see this injury and imagine how it happened. We believed she hit a mesquite bush on the way down, and it ripped her open.

The doctors' assumption was either that or when she landed after flying through the air, the impact blew her open. They explained that more than likely, it was a tree because she also had a gash that needed stitches on her butt. The brain injury was definitely the scariest injury, but the stitches in her groin area were the saddest. Even the staff had a sad face when they were dressing those wounds.

My friend, Veronica, gave me a homemade cream for her so I could rub it on her head when she got headaches. It obviously helped because when she got a bad headache, she would swipe her finger across her forehead, and that meant for me to rub the cream on her head. Then I would hold her close to me, and I would talk to her very gently. I told her how beautiful she was, how she was going to beat this, how proud we all were of her. I told her about her family, how we were all here to help her in every way we could until she was 100%. All the while, she just lay there.

I think she understood because she went limp in my arms when we did this. It felt so good that I was her security. Whatever stage she was in, she needed me to help her get through it. She held on to me, and when I tried to get up, she pulled me back to her chest so she could rub my head. In those moments, my heart was so full of love and gratitude that it felt as though it would overflow.

September 19, 2017

> PM update on day 26 of Sierra's journey… She had an amazing day today. She started with a shower, and held most of her weight on her own.

She found her voice today! It's only a whisper for now, but we know it will get better as her vocal cords heal. Today she ate for the first time, it was only applesauce, but she has to be taught to swallow again, so her speech therapist is introducing soft foods to begin with. The more she tolerates soft foods without choking, the more she will be introduced to thicker foods. Then she's on her way to getting the feeding tube out of her stomach. It bothers her very much, she's tried to pull it out many times and it gets infected and bleeds.

She had a video chat with Morke today; I believe it was good for both of them. He told her how proud he is of her, and she smiled her little half smile. I took a video of her, saying, "Hi, Morke" and "I love you." It's very touching, to say the least. I have to hold the phone, so I'm right up in their conversation, but it makes my heart smile and hers as well obviously.

The catheter finally came out today. It took some convincing on my part, the doctors weren't quite as convinced as I was about whether or not it was time. Her wounds were a major part of the decision, of course, but I was able to convince them that I would take care of her needs and it wasn't necessary anymore. I explained how much it bothered her. She has tried to pull it out so many times, and when she does it makes her bleed so her bag is full of red urine. I can see the pain in her eyes because it hurts her so badly. The risk of infection increases tremendously if she is not changed in a timely manner, but I'm always with her, so I can do it all now that she can help a little bit. I won this battle, and that feels good because I can see the relief in her eyes. When her doctor took it out, I could see how much it hurt her, but once it was out, the pain started to subside and she felt better. Auntie Von was in the room, and it upset her because it hurt Sierra so badly. When the staff walked out, Auntie said something derogatory, and Sierra flipped them off and smiled. Oh my gosh! My sister and I laughed so hard, it even made Sierra laugh, which she wasn't capable of until today. Then she flipped me off, and we all laughed. So I told her not to flip me off, and she proceeded to do it three more times. After that, I asked her why she was flipping me off with her little half smile, and she just shook her head no. I asked her if she flipped me off and she shook her head no again, smiling all the while.

I don't really know what she knows, or what she is aware of, but it was fun, a wonderful moment of interaction, and that's great. It just makes me feel euphoric to see our baby coming back to us. She is apparently in the stage where she's trying to regain her filter, so we have been informed to expect things out of her mouth, and actions she may have, but not to take them personally, she's healing and doesn't know any better right now. I think I'm going to like this stage. That may not sound quite right, but this journey so far has brought so many tears, so if we can get any laughs out of it, we'll take them. Today was a good day and we are so thankful for that. Thank you, all, and goodnight for now. #TeamBdog

This was the stage that her doctors warned us about. They said that she had no filter, which meant that whatever was on her mind was what she said or did. We all have a filter, the one that tells us that we can't tell our boss off because we may lose our job. Or the many things we all face every day when we really want to punch someone or want to tell them how stupid they are, etc. She didn't have the ability to stop herself from saying or doing things that were on her mind. Hence, the flipping people off. It's what she felt, so that's what she did.

Her physical therapist, Lisa, told me she just wanted her to talk, so even if she cussed her out, it was okay. So we were ready for this completely inappropriate stage. I was actually somewhat excited to see her go through this now that she could smile and laugh. I thought we would all get a few laughs. I realize that may sound wrong in some ways, but we had cried so many tears since day one. We could all use a few laughs. If it was at the expense of being humiliated or embarrassed by some of the things she said or did, it was just fine with us.

Getting the catheter out was such a relief for her. She had pulled on it to the extreme that she had blood in her urine bag so many times because it constantly bothered her and rubbed on the stitches, so she tried to scratch continuously. Even though she found her voice, she didn't talk very often at all. She mainly used her notebook to communicate. So when I asked her if it felt so much better for her, she nodded her hear yes vigorously.

September 20, 2017

> PM update on day 27 of Sierra's journey… I truly believe I am witnessing the most incredible acts of strength and perseverance I have ever seen. She is getting better, so much better every day. Her staff is amazed by her. All of them! They have certain goals the want her to achieve, and she surpasses every one of them. She was scheduled to go to the gym on Monday, but she was doing so well, they took her down there today. We went later in the day when there were very few people in there because she still has a very hard time with stimulation, but she handled it very well. Her therapist told her to just focus on the mountains, so she just stared out the window for a long time.

Her eyes don't work so well, so I had to wonder what she was looking at, what she was thinking; could she see the mountains from here? I wondered where she was at in her head. Does she know where she is? Does she understand that she was in the accident and how bad it was? Does she know she has to be re-taught everything? She was just frozen in front of that window, and it was eerily quiet. She has only seen hospital rooms for the last month, and this was a big change. She rocked it though. She walked the parallel bars, with a lot of help, but she didn't give up. She knew she was in pain, but wanted to push through it, some things haven't changed. I'm in awe of what I'm watching on a daily basis. Because of your generosity, I have been able to stay with her every day since the tragedy, and I can't even begin to tell you how much that means to all of us.

This has proved to be very time consuming, not only for Sierra, but for me because I want to be involved in every step of her progress, so she's very busy getting better, and I'm right next to her. Tonight we were lying in bed and she fell asleep. I was whispering softly in her ear how much I love her and I looked down and she was signing I Love you to me in her sleep. It felt so good and so warm in my heart; our baby is coming back to us. I accidentally woke her when I was getting in my bed so I asked her if I needed to put her glove on her right hand so she wouldn't pull on any of her tubes, and she shook her head yes and put her hand up in the air so I could put the glove on. What a moment! Tomorrow's another day, full of surprises I'm sure. We're getting her back and we are so thankful to God, to Sierra for fighting so hard, and to all of you for your kindness, support, and prayers. Goodnight All. #TeamBdog

This was also a very confusing stage for us because she did interact a lot of the time, but she still looked like she was in a trance. When she looked at you, it looked like she was looking through you. She just stared off into space all the time. We didn't have any inkling as to what she was thinking because she couldn't process her thoughts enough to tell us. We asked her to write what she was thinking and, for the most part, she couldn't. Sometimes she just wrote things that didn't make sense to us, but maybe they did to her. I wanted to get in her head so I could help her.

Even though she didn't seem like she was "here," she still tried to participate in her therapies. She followed commands, for the most part. Sometimes she just looked at us as if she didn't even know us. Yet she worked hard to gain her strength back and wrote Morke's name in her notebook daily. When I asked her if she wanted to talk to him, she always said yes. Other times, I asked her questions, and she just stared off into space.

Having to wear the glove to keep her from pulling out the tubes in her body had become something she accepted. She knew enough to know that she needed to put them on at night, but she didn't know enough not to pull on her IV, her catheter, and her feeding tube. If we were not watching her, she would pull on her feeding tube continuously. I had to clean it every night because she wouldn't leave it alone, and it got infected. She had puss oozing out of it, and I'd show her and tell her that's what happened when she pulled on it. Hopefully, now that she was starting to eat solid food, it would come out very soon.

The problem with that is that it had to heal inside before they could take it out, but it couldn't heal if she was always pulling on it. But she wouldn't quit pulling on it because it hurt her. It was a vicious circle. She gave me a very sad face when she was pulling on it and wrote in her notebook that it hurt and she wanted it out.

PM update on day 28 of Sierra's journey... She had a really rough night last night, which turned into a rough day for her as well. They switched her feedings, and it really upset her stomach. Before they could push it all in through her feeding tube, she was throwing it up. Her therapists decided to take it easy on her today because they could tell it really took a toll on her. She has been pushing so hard, so they figured she earned an easy day today.

We had a family meeting in her room to talk about her progress because she couldn't handle the stimulation outside of her room today. I asked Sierra if she was okay to have the staff in her room to talk about her progress. She agreed so her physical therapist, occupational therapist, the social worker, and a couple other staff members were present. They all stated how proud they were of her. Then she let her physical therapist talk, she spoke very highly of her determination and how far she's come, after that, the occupational therapist reiterated what the physical therapist said. All the while, Sierra is listening very intently. When it came time for the social worker to speak, Sierra immediately motioned for all of them to get out. They tried to convince her to listen, and she just pointed to the door, shaking her finger towards the door, so I informed them she was done with the conversation and they needed to leave her room, so they all reluctantly left. As they were walking out, she gave them the peace sign and flipped them off. It was like she was "the Godfather" and she had complete control. It was beautiful...and funny. She associates street clothes and notebooks as something bad, that's why she always tried to kick them when we were in Albuquerque. I'm sure if they were close enough this time, she would have done the same thing.

Apparently her new brain flips people off, because this has become a common occurrence with her. If she doesn't like something, she flips it off. If someone irritates her, she flips them off. Sometimes she just looks at me, but it looks like she's looking through me, and she decides to flip me off, I find it quite amusing.

She asks to talk to Morke on her own now, so they video chat. The smile on her face and the look in her eyes is priceless. We love him. Thank you all for your prayers. Goodnight for now. #TeamBdog

When this journey started, all the medical staff agreed on one detail: there would be peaks and valleys. We had no conceptual idea how true that was. Even though we heard their words, we couldn't conceive of what they meant. By now, we had a much better understanding of what they were talking about. There were such high peaks and very low valleys. Her good days actually found us smiling sometimes. For example, when she started to brush her teeth on her own and then realized water was running down her chin and she was actually able to recognize it so she wiped it off. It seemed so small to us, but for her, it was a giant hurdle that she triumphed. When we realized she could write, when she recognized us, when she ate for the first time, when we realized that her stuffed bee brought her comfort, and the first time she smiled, oh my gosh! That was a day where so much pent up anger and sadness melted away. And when she started to realize what she wanted and what she didn't want, like the staff with notebooks and how she would flip them off and swirl her finger and point to the door when she had enough of their gibberish—all these things brought smiles to our faces and warmth in our hearts.

On the other hand, there were so many tears we couldn't begin to count. When we saw her being wheeled out from the operating room the first day, watching her lie in a coma on the brink of death for two weeks, praying for another day; when she finally came out of her coma but the lights didn't come on, so to speak; how she stared into space, even when she looked directly at us; how she flopped around uncontrollably; how she had a look of terror every time she got a headache. She held me so tight as if her life depended on it.

When she learned to write, which meant she could communicate with us, we began to learn the hell she was living in. It was so heartbreaking, and that came with a tremendous sense of helplessness. We wanted so badly to help her, but there was absolutely nothing we could do for her. She had to do this on her own. She had to fight the biggest fight of her life, and we could only watch and be by her side.

September 22, 2017

> PM update on day 29 of Sierra's journey... She started her day off with occupational therapy, which includes a shower, working on getting the tangles and blood out of her hair. She helped wash her body, rinsed her body off, and actually used her left hand to push herself up, pull up her pants, and dry herself off. These are great accomplishments. She sat in a chair for fifty minutes today. When she started to lean, I would prompt her to straighten up, and she did all by herself. Seeing as how her head is still wobbly, I have to remind her to pick it up. It just seems like it's too heavy for her to keep upright, and she doesn't know to pick it up until I tell her. The muscles in her neck are getting stronger all the time, as are the muscles in her body.
>
> Now when I tell her, "Honey, your left hand." She knows to lay it flat. Because of her

brain injury, and the fact that the blood in the brain stem affects her left side, her left hand automatically curls up so we have to remind her to straighten it out. Sometimes I still have to uncurl it and help her lay it flat, she's starting to do it herself when I tell her, but sometimes I still have to help her. Her understanding of everything is constantly progressing. Now, before she goes to bed, I explain why she needs the tubes in her body, and the purpose they serve. I explain to her that we have to put the padded gloves on her when we sleep because she tries to pull them out when I'm not watching. But if she quits pulling on them, she won't have to wear them anymore. It really seemed to intrigue her because she hates the gloves. After our talk, I asked her if she wanted to try sleeping without them and she shook her head vigorously yes, so we're trying a night without gloves. I really hope she understands because lately when I go to sleep, I have found myself sleeping so hard that I wake up to her upside down on the bed or part of her body hanging off the bed, and then the guilt sets in. I wonder how I could be asleep when she needs me to keep an eye on her, but I'm so drained, I find it very hard to stay awake even in daylight hours.

Today Aunt Sue Sue went with her to physical therapy. So she got to see Sierra actually using her left hand. There is still a major deficit on her left side compared to her right side, but they're working very hard on trying to get it to work. She picked up cones with her left hand today. Sometimes she dropped them, but she was able to grasp some of them and we are very thankful for that, it all shows improvement and gives us hope that she will regain movement and control over her left side eventually.

She flipped off pretty much everyone she saw today, including me. The smile that comes with it is priceless. So she is definitely in the inappropriate stage. Her filter is not working, so when something bothers her, the only response she knows is to flip it off. She flips off people and inanimate objects. If it irritates her, it gets 'the finger.' She also has inappropriate responses and actions that she cannot control, some are funny, and some are hard to understand. The staff here is absolutely amazing, they keep us informed as to what to expect on her road to recovery. This is just another stage that we believe she will surpass.

Krystal and her family came today to visit. Sierra signed that she wanted ice. So I asked her if she wanted Krystal to feed her ice. She shook her head no and pointed to Esther. Apparently they used to eat ice together, and she wanted Esther to give it to her instead of Krystal. So this means she is making connections, which is totally awesome of course.

We are trying to get her to use her voice more often. We know it's there, but it's very weak, so we work on it every day to help her get to the day she can have a conversation. She wants to write out her needs, but we push her to use her voice and ask for what she wants. It really frustrates her sometimes, but she does it anyways. In her writings, she said she wanted her sissy to come see her. So her dad called her and she came down to hang out. They got sister time today and it was very sweet, and much needed for both of them I'm sure.

> Every day and every night we are watching
> this beautiful miracle before our eyes and it is
> so fantastic. Goodnight, all… Until tomorrow.
> Thank you for continued prayers. We see them
> working constantly. #TeamBdog

She was obviously in the inappropriate stage. She flipped me off regularly and anyone in her wake that had irritated her in the least. It was also a sexually inappropriate stage. She asked if she was pregnant multiple times a day. She also asked if she was pregnant and lost the baby in the accident. When we tell her no to both, she told us she wanted to get pregnant. She made inappropriate comments and gestures. Her staff was very understanding because they understand brain injuries, and this was all a part of it.

We were very thankful that she remembered people in her life. That was a big fear of mine, so when she made the connection to Esther and the ice, and Krystal catching the ball, they were big moments in her recovery. She remembered how much she loved Aunt Sue Sue. She wrote in her book that she wanted her to go to therapy with her. When they came back, they were both smiling. Sierra was smiling because she was happy that Aunt Sue Sue went with her, and Aunt Sue Sue because Sierra was alive and fighting.

Her notebook has become her best friend. She preferred writing everything to us as opposed to talking to us. I tried to push her to talk, but she just banged on the notebook to state her points.

She and her sister had good quality time today, and it was very nice to see the interaction she had with people. She was so genuine and didn't know how to be anything else.

September 23, 2017

> Day 30 of Sierra's journey… So I'm sitting out-
> side, thinking, as I have come to do a lot lately.
> I know I did this in the beginning of Sierra's
> journey, but a lot of people have joined us since
> then. Some of you have been with us since day

one; you have lived this nightmare right along with me, and our family. Some two weeks in, and some are new to her journey. So this is to each and every one of you… Thank you for everything you have done for our baby girl. Our family is facing the hardest struggle we could ever know. We have witnessed tragedy after tragedy while living in hospitals, all the while, living our own personal tragedy. We have also witnessed people at their finest; the kindness we have received is overwhelming sometimes. Because of every one of you that have prayed and offered your time, your gifts, volunteering for fundraisers, sending care packages, and money. You are all a true blessing to our family, and mostly to Sierra, it really helps put our faith back in people and humanity.

There are people we don't even know that have been touched by her story, so they are following her journey as well. Like Christian, he started texting me one day. I didn't know him so I asked him how he found her story. He informed me that he was surfing Facebook and found her story. It touched him so much that he felt he had to text me. From that day on, this stranger became a friend I had never met. He text me every day, asking me how I was holding up, how Sierra is doing, he informed me that he prayed for both of us every day. He lit a candle for her and sent me a picture of his list to show me that she is at the top.

I have quit my jobs, and because of all your monetary donations, I have been able to stay with her all day, every day without the burden of how I will pay my bills. So "Thank You" doesn't even touch the surface of how grateful I am, her dad is, our family is. And by family, I mean our whole family, not just blood relatives. I read your comments every night after she goes to sleep; they have become my strength when I don't feel so strong. I needed to say thank you all for helping me specifically, but also my family who also struggles through this with us. We have a long way to go but with continued support and prayers we will all get through this, and we will get our baby girl back. I truly love and appreciate all of you. #TeamBdog

PM update on day 30 of Sierra's journey... She woke up a little stubborn today, being lazy with her commands. After a while and some encouragement, she snapped out of it. We have a list of words that help her to communicate with us. So I was asking her questions about them, and she got nine out of ten of them. That was so cool. She got a break from therapy today so we worked on her brain together. She played candy crush on the notebook, and she did much better than she did just five days ago.

After that, she wanted to hear her "Fight Song," and as she listened, she sang two verses of it. Then she looked at me and said, "I still got a lot of fight left in me!" I just can't express the joy in my heart. I told her how very proud of her I am; she smiled and decided to play it again. As she was listening to it, she swiped the side of the screen, pulled up messenger, and found Morke's name and decided to video chat with him. I didn't even know how to do this myself, so I was pretty amazed when she did it on her own. She smiles so big when she talks to him, it just warms my heart. He tells her how proud of her he is and for her to keep fighting. He tells her she's "the fighter," and she uses her voice to say, "I love you." Oh my gosh! It's a beautiful sight.

Her dad and I were talking outside when we saw the light go on in her room and our hearts sunk. We ran into her room and she was sitting up on the edge of her bed ready to pull herself up with her IV pole. We both lost about five years on that one. I decided to come home tonight and leave her in the very capable hands of her brother so I can get a good night's sleep...hopefully. Goodnight, all, until tomorrow. #TeamBdog

Because of the outpouring of love and kindness we have experienced, I feel it very necessary to write my gratitude to our readers. Every day is such an emotional roller coaster with her recovery and so inspirational with her fight to get better and the people following her story. The comments people leave are so uplifting. Sometimes they are the only thing to give me enough strength to go back in her room and fight for another day.

She continued to amaze everyone she came in contact with and even those she didn't. Many people who read her story every day didn't even know her. Yet they were inspired by her and her continuous fight to get her life back. The "Fight Song" had become her inspiration. We played it about fifty times a day, and now she was starting to sing the verses. I showed her how to play games on the tablet, trying to help her dexterity, and she had improved tremendously in just one week. Now that she knew how to video chat with Morke, it was hard for her to focus on much else. She asked me if she could chat with him all day. So we had made it her reward. If she did well and worked hard in her therapies, she got to chat with him afterward. We would let her anyway, but it was good incentive for her to work hard, even when she didn't feel like it.

I agreed for her brother to stay with her tonight because I had been with her every night since the accident, so he told me to go home and get some rest. Besides her dad, I don't think there is anyone else I would trust to stay with her overnight. I didn't get as much rest as I had hoped because I kept thinking of who was going to change her diaper if she used the restroom. I didn't want a male tech changing her because we didn't know how or what she thought about modesty, and I didn't want it to be something she remembered because it scared her. I explained that to her brother, and he just said, "Yes, Mom, I know, I know!"

September 24, 2017

> AM update on day 31 of Sierra's journey… Today caught up on me. I was so busy taking care of her, and so exhausted in my mind and my body, I just didn't have the strength to write a post today. My mind was so cluttered with fear, anger, and the unknown. I want to believe so badly that my baby will get better, but these stages she goes through are so incredibly hard that sometimes I can't bring myself to write anything positive, so I didn't, I just couldn't. #TeamBdog

That post says it all. All the stages, the tears, the fear, and the heartaches got so unbearable at times that I had nothing to give. I tried to make her posts, even the terrible day's posts, as positive as I possibly could. I told about the terrible days and ended with "Tomorrow would be better" or "We pray for better days." Today was different; I was on the verge of giving up on her posts and giving up on trying to be strong. But with help of my family and friends, I made it through this day to write again.

> PM update on day 31 of Sierra's journey… Today she started with a nice visit from Britt. They lay in bed together, they were so happy to see each other. They are lifetime friends, and Sierra is making these connections. She just lit up when Britt walked in the room. When she took a shower, Auntie Lissa helped her. Sierra knows that she is

a nurse, so she was okay with Auntie helping her. There are very few people on the list that were able to help change her or shower her, so Auntie Lissa was very happy that she trusted her enough to help her shower. While she was showering, she was able to cross her mid line. This is a great feat because of her brain injury; she couldn't cross one side of her body to the other. So if she is washing the right side of her body, she can't cross over her mid line to the left side, but today she did. She used her left arm a lot today as well. Auntie Lissa went to the gym today for her therapy where she separated pegs by color and put them in specified holes. It was very intricate, and she studied them very hard before making the choice as to which peg to choose and which hole to put them in. She and Lizette played with the balloon today, and she did very well. She was able to track it through the air to be able to hit it.

She and Morke video chat everyday now, she lights up when she talks to him. Even though her smile is only a half a smile, but it is so beautiful nonetheless. He tells her how beautiful she is and how proud he is of her. He tells her how he's working on their future. He's doing therapy so he can recover enough to come see her. His therapist said that he could be playing again in about six to eight weeks, which is amazing. He is a male version of Sierra. He is driven, focused, passionate, and he works hard for everything he's got. And they both achieve great things because of it. He is fighting for her as well, it's very touching.

Her sister and her family came to visit her today. The kids had to stay out in the lobby with their dad because she couldn't handle the stimulation, so they had to take turns coming into her room. Because its flu season, young children aren't allowed into the rooms, so we had to take her to the waiting room in the front so she could see the baby. He was a little weary around her. It was obvious he didn't understand the wheelchair or how his auntie looked. How can you explain that to a two-year-old?

Today was a very big day for her. It really took a toll on her having so many visitors, so she is sleeping like a baby right now. I love when she sleeps because she doesn't have to fight, she can just sleep and let her brain heal.

Although we have taken everyone's advice on how to get the huge tangle out of her hair, we have tried everything you all have suggested, to no avail. It is so tangled and has so much blood in it still; she has decided to cut it all off. She is adamant that she wants it off. Because it is just a clump of hair, it bothers her when she sleeps or tries to sit up in her bed, so after asking her for the past week, she has decided to cut it off. She does the sign for scissors and shakes her head. I have repeatedly asked her and she answers yes that she wants it cut off. So tomorrow she will be sporting a new hairdo. Thank you for all of your suggestions. It's only hair, it will grow back. Goodnight, all. #TeamBdog

I was happy that her dad's side of the family all decided to come see her today. I also felt some measure of relief that my best friend, Melissa, and her daughter, Brittany, came from Phoenix to come help me and see Sierra for the first time since the accident. Melissa and I have been best friends for about forty years, and Sierra and Brittany have grown up together since birth. It was nice to see that Sierra remembered them because they have lived in Phoenix for several years, and I didn't know if she would remember them. Melissa helped me with everyday tasks and hygiene that I had to perform on her on a regular basis, and I was happy to have her there with me.

After heeding everyone's advice on how to get the huge tangle out of her hair, we had realized the only thing to do was shave it off. I'd been preparing her for this for a couple weeks, so I hoped that when she got it shaved, she would be okay with this decision. I told her if it made her feel better, I would shave my head as well. I could see the wheels turning, but she decided against it. I had asked her repeatedly if she was okay with shaving her head, and she continually told me yes, I think because it bothered her so much she was okay with it.

September 25, 2017

> PM update on day 32 of Sierra's journey... She got a shower first thing this morning. Then she got her hair cut off. It was bittersweet to see all that beautiful hair go away, but good to know it will no longer get in the way of sleeping or sitting up straight without a huge knot getting in the way. Yvette has cut her hair for years, so it was only fitting to have her cut if off as well. We are grateful to her that she came up to the hospital to cut it off. Thank you for the suggestions on how to get the tangles out, we tried all of your suggestions, but sadly, none of them worked. She looks great! It's only about a quarter inch long, but she sports it very well.

Sierra sporting her new do

This is Yvette and Sierra after she cut her hair off. She is the only one that Sierra would let cut it off. She made a special trip to the hospital just to cut her hair at no charge to us. She felt honored that Sierra trusted her enough to cut it all off.

While in occupational therapy today, she did really well standing and holding herself up with some help from the parallel bars. She played a memory game trying to match tiles, but was unable to achieve this game as of yet. It was just a little too much for her at this point in her healing process. She'll get there, we're sure of it, just not today.

One more obstacle holding her back was taken out today. The IV that is a continual hindrance for her has been removed. Yeah! This is one less obstacle on her road to recovery. The doctor took blood today to check all her numbers and they all looked great. There was no infection, and everything else is within range. She was cleared to eat soft foods today, so yet another hurdle conquered. She had fish, rice, and broccoli. She ate like she hasn't eaten for weeks, maybe because she hasn't. #TeamBdog

She didn't even like fish, but she devoured it as if she had never eaten. I had to tell her to slow down multiple times, but she just stuffed her mouth with food and continued stuffing it before she could even swallow what was in her mouth. She was working on fine motor skills and she was doing such a great job for about five minutes, which was about as long as her attention span was. The IV was no longer a hindrance to her in everything she did. She was so happy to get it out, and she smiled and told me, "One more thing, Mommy!" Yes, it was one more thing she had overcome and was now a nightmare from the past.

September 26, 2017

PM update on day 33 of Sierra's journey... She started her day at 7am, she went to breakfast and we ran into her Nina, who is also here for rehab on her knee. They have made a pact to fight together. Then she had speech therapy, and decided she wasn't going to talk today. She stayed true to her word; she didn't talk, all day, not a word. She looks very angry, and stares at everything like she is mad at it, including people. I thought if she talked to Morke she would break her silence. It didn't work; I called him and explained to him what she said so he tried to get her to talk, to no avail. Not a word to him either.

She still isn't capable of showing emotion, she doesn't cry, not on the outside anyways. We think she cries on the inside, because her face gets really red like she straining, and she gets a look of terror in her eyes, it's so gut wrenching and painful to see our baby like this. This is just another stage that she has to go through on her way to 100%. So far each stage has lasted anywhere from three to ten days, so on the bright side, we know that each terrible, frightening stage will pass as her brain heals.

I wanted to do something I thought she would enjoy, so I made her some chocolate covered blueberries and we decided to lie in bed and watch TV while enjoying them. I could tell she was upset, so I asked her, "Honey, are you okay? Are you upset? Are you sad? Frustrated?" She shook her head yes! She then pointed to the door and did her swooping action with it. I asked her if she wanted me to leave. She wrote Yes, and pointed to the door again. So I left her writing in her notebook, I hope she is able to express herself in it. We don't know exactly what she's thinking, what she knows, if she knows why she's here. Her writing is so scattered and sometimes not very legible so we have to decipher what she is trying to make us understand.

Good news is that she reached a Rancho Level 5! This is fantastic news, of course, but the medical staff informed us that this is the stage where she will most likely be inappropriate. That her words and actions may be very offensive, she may hurt our feelings but not to take it personally. A healthy brain has a filter; it keeps us from saying whatever is on our mind. She doesn't have that yet, so she is actually very genuine, she expresses exactly how she feels, hence me sitting outside writing her post after she kicked me out of her room.

We're also ecstatic to say that she is eating enough to no longer need the feeding tube, which she calls f——g tube. As long as she continues to eat and gains weight, she will be able to get it out. Thank God for that! This tube has given her so much trouble. It hurts her and she still tries to pull it out, and she rubs it and scratches it, which gets it infected, then it hurts her more so she pulls on it more and round and round it goes. One very good outcome from this obstacle is that we will be able to lay her flat in her bed. No more 30 degree angles, which will help take the strain off her back and pelvis.

Her staff has to reconvene earlier than they had anticipated so they can make new goals for her because she keeps exceeding the ones they set for her. Her doctor just can't believe the fight and drive she possesses, and her therapists are thrilled that she doesn't quit pushing herself. No matter how tired she is, or how much pain she is in, she just keeps fighting. Goodnight, all, until tomorrow. Thank you. #TeamBdog

Although she was in the inappropriate stage, it actually had its moments of laughter. When she flipped us off or pointed to the door for us to leave, it brought a smile to our faces. She was finally able to show us what she was feeling, even if it was anger. It was a step in the right direction. Although, at times, some of her actions were completely inappropriate, we took them in stride, mostly because the staff sat us down and explained exactly what to expect during this stage. They explained that even though she appeared to be angry, it was okay. She was just learning to express herself, and it was all progress, so we should not be offended by her words or actions.

Her biggest obstacle that she was aware of was f——g tube. Now that her brain has healed enough to be more aware of what was happening to her, she had control over whether she got it out or not. She was aware of the pain and irritation it caused. She seemed to understand that she had to eat most of every meal to be able to get it out. Although she rarely talked, she had made it very clear how much it bothered her. She pointed to it with a sad face, pulled on it, scratched it, and gave me a look on her face that she had come to use to let us know when something was wrong while she pulled on it. We talked about it all the time. I'd tell her that she had to eat all of her meals and prove to the doctors that she would continue to eat before they'd take it out. If she got it out and then decided not to eat, then they would have to put it back in, and it would hurt more than it did now. She seemed to understand, and when I asked her if she did understand, she nodded her head yes, so I had to assume that she did. It was all a guessing game, really.

On the bright side, her team of therapists and her doctors talked to me about her progress. They were in awe of how quickly she was recovering. They set goals for her to achieve within a certain amount of time, say, two weeks. Within that time, she had to accomplish certain tasks for her to move up the Rancho Scale for brain injuries. Below is the scale that shows the stages in which brain injuries are measured.

Rancho Scale for Brain Injuries

Level One: No Response

- In this stage, there was no response to any stimuli at all.
- She was in a coma and on life support.

Level Two: Generalized Response: Needs Total Assistance

- Starts to respond to painful stimuli—so when they gave her knuckle rubs, she finally started to react.
- When we walked into her room, her ICP numbers started to fluctuate. Too much stimuli jacked her numbers up, and when I rubbed her head and talked gently to her, it brought her numbers down.
- Although she reacted to stimuli, sometimes it took her brain a minute to realize what was happening before she reacted. So when they gave her knuckle rubs, after about a minute, she tried to lift herself.
- Still in a coma.

Level Three: Localized Response—Needs Total Assistance

- Tries to retreat from painful stimuli, pushing the doctors' hands away when they give her knuckle rubs, when they suck her out, and when they turn her.
- Turns toward familiar auditory sounds, such as her family's voices.
- Starting to react to light.
- Beginning to recognize when people walk up to her or walk away from her.
- Starting to pull on tubes and IVs in her body.
- Appears that she is starting to understand simple commands occasionally, gives thumbs up, or blinks to answer simple questions.

- Responds to family and friends, but not so much to strangers after coming out of her coma and off life support.
- Still in a trance-like state.

Level Four: Confused and Agitated—Needs Maximal Assistance

- She is more alert and moves more frequently.
- Tries to pull the tubes out of her body and gloves off her hands.
- Tries to sit up and get out of bed.
- Attempting to pull on the tubes invading her body.
- One minute, she seems to be okay, and the next minute, she appears to be angry.
- She flops her arms and kicks her legs, appears to be involuntary.
- Doesn't speak or eat, incontinent.
- Appears to be afraid of everything.

Level Five: Confused and Inappropriate—Needs Maximum Assistance

- Getting more alert yet still has trance-like stare.
- Environment affects her moods, can't have too much stimuli.
- No conception of time.
- Brief periods of attention span.
- Beginning to understand that she can't pull the tubes out of her body.
- Doesn't remember the accident and confused about the present tense.
- Brushes her teeth with minimal help, may brush her hair with the toothbrush.

- Can't remember simple tasks from one day to the next, but when asked to do them, she can with prompting.
- Can attempt to write so she can communicate, shows the desire to talk.

Level Six: Confused and Appropriate—Needs Moderate Assistance

- Starting to remember her therapies and people that come to visit.
- Beginning to focus for up to thirty minutes.
- Old memories are more vivid than new ones.
- She recognizes her staff.
- Starting to tell us when she is hungry or needs medications.
- Is familiar with old tasks and can relearn them with ease. Cannot learn new tasks with such ease.
- Believes she can accomplish more than she is able to.
- Is more consistently following simple commands.
- Beginning to use her voice.

Level Seven: Automatic and Appropriate— Minimal Assistance

- Goes into the gym and handles stimulation better occasionally.
- Needs very little supervision to complete simple tasks.
- Beginning to remember when learning new tasks.
- Pays attention to accuracy of tasks.

- Beginning to wash clothes and clean up.
- Knows to look at her schedule for the day.
- Beginning to understand safety issues.
- Wants to drive and go back to school, unrealistic goals.
- Combative and argumentative.
- Filter is not intact, often inappropriate responses, yells at people.
- Confabulates and exhibits perseverance.

Level Eight: Purposeful and Appropriate—Very Little Assistance Needed

- Understands place and time more frequently.
- Can focus up to an hour.
- Recall memory is beginning to arise.
- Uses her schedule book to start her day.
- Takes initiative to complete tasks.
- Overestimates her abilities, tries to walk independently and get out of bed with no assistance.
- Getting depressed and angry about her current situation.
- Low frustration level, easily angered.

Level Nine: Purposeful and Appropriate—Asks for Assistance When Needed

- Able to shift between tasks and maintain focus.
- Plans her days by her weekly schedule.
- Becoming more aware of impairments and disabilities.
- Questions consequences to actions.
- Depressed and irritable because of condition.

- Easily frustrated.
- Performs and maintains hygiene with minimal assistance.
- Maintains social interaction for longer periods of time.

Level Ten: Purposeful and Appropriate—Gaining More Independence

- Handles more stimuli and knows when she needs a break.
- Offers ideas to help her memory.
- Beginning to understand limitations.
- Adjusts environment to fit her needs.
- Gets sleepy when she has too much stimulation.
- Still depressed and angry.
- More appropriate social interaction.

September 27, 2017

PM update on day 34 of Sierra's journey… She's been somewhat sleepy today, yet she still pushes through everything. I tell her she's my hero all the time because it is so very true. My heart is so full of pride and joy for our baby girl. She is dealing with some depression issues now, so the rehab has people that come in and talk to her to help her. Auntie Von came and had breakfast with her so I could go home and shower. We still don't leave her alone. I'm with her twenty-four hours a day unless someone comes and gives me a shower break, and today, it was my sister. Thank you, sister.

Her daddy was pushing her around and she saw me and said, "That's my Mama." Oh my gosh! It put such a big smile on my face, and in my heart. Any time she does talk, it's only a whisper for now, but it's a beautiful whisper. Krystal came to see her today; she spent most of the day with her. She got to see how she's kickin' butt in the gym, and working so hard in therapy. She tried to walk with her walker today, she's a little unsteady, but she's fighting every step of the way.

For some reason, she doesn't talk much, and she gets stubborn with her speech therapist. Because of the breathing tube, her vocals cords were somewhat damaged, so her speech is very low and you have to get right up to her so you can hear her. This may be why she gets stubborn, because she doesn't want people getting in her face, but that's only speculation on our part. We don't really know what's going on in her brain yet because she is not at the point where she can tell us. She mainly writes in her notebook to communicate with us, but her writing is still barely legible most of the time. We can only assume that's part of her frustration.

She uses her picture cards that her speech therapist made for her and the list of words we created specifically for the things we think she might need or want. It makes it much easier for her to communicate. She just points to pictures or words to let us know what she wants or needs; when she's in pain, if she wants company, or if she just wants to be alone. And if she is in pain, we show her the number scale we made so she can let us know how much pain she has. Sometimes it's a twenty on a scale from one to ten, but it's always at least a ten. I can see the terror in her eyes when she has that much pain. She still can't cry, so her face turns so red, and her eyes show a look of terror, it's so heartbreaking.

It's Jeni's birthday today, so I went and bought her a card and Sierra actually wrote her name in it and it was pretty legible. Jeni felt it was one of the best gifts ever. We played games last night, and she beat Margie at 'Go Fish,' which is nothing new, we have all got beaten by her at so many games since she was about five, but the fact that she can still beat us is pretty amazing.

Anthony is staying with her tonight at her request. She wrote something in her notebook that leads us to believe she's trying to look after me, to make sure that I'm okay, and that she's worried about me. She wrote that it's okay for me to go away sometimes. It amazes me that she can think of me, and my well-being with the condition she's in. So she is the very good hands of her brother tonight, so maybe I'll be able to get some sleep without bells, alarms, and people coming in all night long. Goodnight all, until tomorrow. Thank you for your continued prayers; we see them working every day. #TeamBdog

So many things happen in the course of one day. She can have the highest highs and lowest lows in the course of an hour. It's a roller-coaster ride that never quits. We don't know what to expect from one minute to the next. We have the Rancho Level Scale to help us understand the stages she is in, but her specific actions are unknown until they hit us in the face. We have learned to accept what is in the moment, but it brings an incredible amount of anxiety thinking about the next stage she has to go through. Watching her go through so much pain is the hardest part. We want to help her so badly, but the only thing that does help is a very high dose of painkillers and sleep.

Jeni almost cried when she saw that Sierra wrote in her birthday card. She didn't know how aware she was of anything, so when she saw that she wrote her name all by herself, it was overwhelming to her.

Anthony has been a major part of her healing since day one. He is the only one, besides her dad, that I feel comfortable enough to leave her with at this point. She needed constant attention right now, and it was not an easy job to keep her safe. He spent a lot of time with her and taught her things we didn't think of. He helped her to communicate. He helped her to understand where she was and what was happening to her in a way that she understood. He was amazing, and I was very lucky to have him. He and my daughter-in-law, Lee, had been so helpful to me since she got in the accident. They came to the hospital almost every day and brought my grandbabies so that I could smile each day. My grandbabies, Zo and Sebby, lay with her in bed and pushed her around in her wheelchair. They rode with her in her wheelchair while the other one pushed it. Sometimes Sebby crashed her into the wall, but he couldn't push her very fast, so she didn't get hurt. But to watch this three-year-old boy push his Auntie around was priceless.

Her nickname had always been Bee. I gave it to her when she was a tiny baby because she was our honeybee. As she grew up, everyone got her bee memorabilia. She has several bee pillows that she sleeps with, she takes on trips everywhere we go, and is very protective over her bee. She never had a security blanket as she grew up, only a bee, and it has been her security since she was a baby.

I brought her bee pillow to the hospital. She curled up with him when she went to sleep, and when she was having a hard time, we gave it to her to soothe her. So far, it was working. When she tried to pull out her tubes, I gave her bee and put his antennae in her hands so it distracted her from pulling them out. When she was restless, I gave her bee to calm her down, and it worked. It's nice to know that we found something that worked to distract her when she got restless or defiant about pulling on her tubes.

September 28, 2017

AM update on day 35 of Sierra's journey... So I'm sitting outside the rehab while she eats breakfast because she apparently wasn't looking out for me at all, she's just doesn't want me around her all the time because I bug her. Hard to handle for sure, but I have to remember it's just the stage she's going through. I've been with her since day one, 24 hours a day, and she obviously gets tired of me. You hurt the ones you love the most I suppose. I believe that Rancho level 5 will bring a lot of tears and heartache, but it's also progress for her, and that's all that really matters. #TeamBdog

PM update on day 35 of Sierra's journey… She started her day with no pain medications. She hasn't had them since 8pm last night. This is great because she is always so drugged up while she's doing her therapy. She said it was very hard waking up and she looks very dazed. She wrote to her physical therapist that she is frustrated about her walking and wanted to work on that. She's tired of being in a wheelchair. So they worked on that and she did really well today. There are several gadgets they use to help her, and the belt around her waist gives her more freedom to try walking with very little help. Her doctor ordered that an alarm be installed on her wheelchair because she is constantly trying to get out of it on her own. There is also an alarm on her bed, so if she tries to get out of bed on her own, it goes off. Today she set it off because she decided to try to get to the bathroom on her own, but didn't make it. She fell on the ground, so when her tech came in, she found her lying on the floor. In her mind, she thinks she can do a lot more than she is capable of at this point in her recovery. She is not continent yet, and she doesn't walk, but her brain doesn't know her inabilities, so safety is definitely an issue at this point in time.

Today she got the rest of her stitches out, and oh my gosh, she definitely has a voice! She let out a scream that almost reached the decibels of her regular voice. They are in a very sensitive area, and it was so painful for her. She had that look of terror in her eyes again, but there was nothing I could do but hold her, talk to her, and explain what they were doing and why. This is the part of her injuries that are more vague because it is so personal to her, and it's not my decision to make. When she is healed and makes the decision to tell people that part of her healing, she can. But, in the meantime, I will continue to be vague on that specific injury. We are just very happy that she finally got those stitches out because they cause her a lot of discomfort. One more obstacle conquered!

We played Mancala and Connect Four tonight. Connect Four is the game that she has beaten all of us continually since she was five. I remember her brother's friends lining up because they knew they would be the one to beat her, to no avail. She beat all of us; it was a little embarrassing actually. So now, she's has a very injured brain, and yet, she still beats us most of the time. Sometimes we get lucky, but it's only because she has an injured brain I'm sure. So tonight, she won eight out of ten games, pretty dang good considering her current situation. Goodnight, all, and thank you for everything. #TeamBdog

Lee and Bee on game night

Although it hurt my heart to realize that she didn't want me to be around her, I tried my best to understand. I had been with her twenty-four hours a day since her accident. I pushed her. I made her fight. I forced her to eat, and I didn't let her give up. I was constantly underfoot, so it was understandable how she got tired of me. It was so important for me to put my feelings in check and understand her need to recover.

She had always been a kind, compassionate human being, so in my heart, I knew that this wasn't her, and she couldn't help it. All in all, if she was getting better, I would take whatever mood, words, or action that arises. As I watched her brain making new connections, I wondered what kind of person she would become. Would she be the old Sierra? Or would she be someone completely different? She had frontal lobe injury, so it was a toss-up. We taught her the same values that we did the first time around and hoped and prayed that they would be part of her core values that were instilled in her soul. When she came out of her coma, there were things that she remembered; she remembered how to read, she remembered her family and friends, and how to write, so we prayed that she got back her kindness and compassion back as well.

When the doctor told me she was going to take her stitches out, my heart sank. This is the injury that turned my stomach every time

I looked at it. Her vagina and anus were completely ripped open by a tree as she landed after she was ejected from the car. I had to look at it every day because I had to keep it clean, and I had to change her diaper, so I saw it multiple times a day. Yet it still makes my heart sad when I see it. I think she understood because when I changed her, she spread her legs wide so I could clean it. So many things were just speculation because her communication skills were still lacking. When the doctor pulled out the stitches, she squeezed my hand so hard and let out a scream with each one that came out. Besides the one in her private area, she had several more on her butt cheek where she had a gash as well. That was the one that lead the doctors to the belief that it was a tree that ripped her open when she landed.

The other assumption was that it blew open because of the impact to her body when she landed. So between the two assumptions, the fact that she probably hit a tree on her way down was more likely.

Her eagerness to walk was taking over her ability to understand safety issues. In her mind, she saw herself walking, she remembered herself walking, so she thought that she could. She didn't understand she had a brain injury and had to relearn everything she once knew how to do with ease, and walking was one of them. She was extremely unsteady when she walked, so her therapist put a belt around her stomach and held it from the back so that Sierra could walk. So far, she only went a few steps, but she had the determination, so we felt certain it wouldn't be long before she was walking independently.

September 29, 2017

> PM update on day 36 of Sierra's journey… She is getting better physically and she wants to walk so badly, so she is working so hard on that. It's so inspiring to see her drive, her passion, her willingness work through the pain and fight to get herself back. It was another big day for her. She graduated to solid food today, she has worked hard on her swallowing so that she can actually

have a meal, and get f——g tube out of her stomach. She's very happy that she can have a salad
now, and she has a list of things that she wants to
eat. She's so tired of pudding and Jell-O, I don't
know that she will ever eat them again.

Her ability to handle stimulus is increasing
as well. This is great progress because she can go
to the gym while other people are there, and she
can have more visitors in her room at once. We've
had to limit the amount of people in her room at
one time because she couldn't handle it, but those
numbers are steadily increasing. Sometimes she
has to tell people "Shhh" or she just tells them
to leave, it's quite funny actually. She is so genuine, like a child. She doesn't have the ability to
lie, and her filter has not redeveloped yet, so she
says exactly what she thinks. Sometimes we're all
talking and she tells us to get out, that we bug
her. I just smile and politely ask everyone to
leave. After people are gone, she decides if she
wants me to stay or if she wants me to leave as
well. Needless to say, sometimes I get kicked out
too.

She told her therapist that she wants her
glove, so her dad went to get it so they could play
catch together. She is only tossing the ball and
misses it most of the time, but she's trying, and
refusing to give up. It's really incredible watching
her progress. She shouldn't be this far in her recovery, but like I told her doctors in Albuquerque,
she's amazing, she doesn't give up, and she's the
biggest fighter I know! A week ago, two weeks
ago, we could have never imagined how far she
would come. She has surpassed every goal that
has been set for her since the day she came out of
her coma. It's better than our best dream that we

could have dreamed for her and for us. God and Sierra are amazing.

Anthony, Lee, Zo, and Sebby came up tonight, and Sebby lay in her bed with her. She was rubbing his head so gently, with so much love emanating from her, it melted our hearts. We went to the game room and she decided she wanted to play Mancala. And, again, she beat all of us. She has no expression so she sits there with a blank look on her face, and just beats the heck out of us, and then awaits her next victim.

Since she's been having a problem with her sleep pattern, I tried to keep her awake as long as I could because she's getting her days and nights mixed up. I've been waking up at night and she's just looking at me, or she's upside down in her bed. We don't really know what she's thinking or feeling, so we don't know why she's doing this. I just try to talk her through it, or get in her bed and rub her head while listening to Beethoven's Moonlight Sonata with the sound of the ocean in the background. That seems to be the only thing that will soothe her enough to go back to sleep. Goodnight, until tomorrow. #TeamBog

Her recovery is day by day, so most every day brings something new. Today, she went to the gym when it was full of patients because she wants to walk. Up to now, she has had to go to her therapy after hours because the stimulation was just too much on her. She was tired of being pushed around in a wheelchair and even more tired of the alarm her staff had to put on her wheelchair because she tried to get out of it and walk on her own. When I pulled her wheelchair out to get ready for the day, she pushed it away and told me she wanted to walk. It was very inspiring; however, she didn't realize that her abilities didn't meet her expectations. Her mind said she could walk, but her body said not yet. Lisa, her physical therapist, was very impressed with her determination, so she let her walk in therapy. She had to put the support belt around her and guide her, but Sierra showed the will to fight every time they went to the gym.

Today her speech therapist came in and told us she could eat solid foods. We were so thrilled because this was the first step to getting f———g tube out. This would also be the first tube that she had the power and understanding to be removed; it was all up to her. When she ate her first meal, she scarfed it down like a little piggy. You could tell she hadn't eaten for a couple months. We had to slow her down because she was shoveling the food in her mouth. We explained to her that she had to eat 90% of every meal for a week before her doctor would even consider taking out her feeding tube, and at this point, that was her only focus because it bothered her so much. She was constantly pulling on it, which in turn got it infected. Then it bothered her more, and she pulled on it more, and the vicious cycle began. I tried to make her understand if she pulled it out, she would have to have another surgery to put it back in, but she couldn't quite reason that out yet.

Also, because of the feeding tube, she had to lie at a thirty-degree angle. So, last night, she woke me up because she was very restless. When I woke up, she was upside down in her bed, and my heart sank. The doctors stressed how important it was for her to be at a thirty-degree angle so she didn't choke. I asked her what she was doing, but she couldn't answer me. She just looked at me and smiled her little half smile. She was all tangled up in her tubes, but thank goodness none of them came out. I gently explained to her again how important it was for her to lie in her bed correctly, but I don't think she understood. I already slept with one eye open, but sometimes I fell asleep so hard and woke up to her pulling on her tubes or trying to get out of bed, but tonight, when I woke up to her upside down in her bed, my heart sank into my stomach.

We talked about the dangers of doing these things, so I taught her to bang on the bed rails if she needed anything. Then we talked about it and asked her if she understood. She said she did, and I asked her, "What do you do if you want something?" Then she banged on the bed rail and smiled, so I believe she got it. Time would tell.

It was bittersweet watching her play games. She obviously knew how to play but just sat there while she played with no expression on her face. When she won, when she lost, it was all the same—just a blank stare, same as when her niece and nephew crawled up in bed with her. She hugged them and rubbed them very gently but had that blank stare into oblivion. The gentleness was there, but the emotion was not.

We were told from the beginning that sleep was so important for her. It's when the brain doesn't have to do anything but heal. So we encouraged her to sleep as much as possible. However, lately, she had been getting her days and nights mixed up, and it was very hard to put her to sleep. Then, when she went to therapy, she was very tired, and it was hard for her to concentrate on anything. So, after much deliberation with her team, we decided to put her on a sleep schedule. Her naps were limited to an hour a day, and her bedtime was set for nine o'clock. Hopefully, this would help her brain adjust to night and day, and her therapies would be more productive.

September 30, 2017

> PM update on day 37 of Sierra's journey… She has a very hard time starting her day off. For anyone that knows her knows she is not a morning person. Now, with her brain injury, it has only amplified that situation tenfold. It seems the best time of the day that she is the most coherent is in the evenings. She is more focused and willing to interact.
>
> Her medical staff has listed her as nonverbal. She told her speech therapist that she can talk, but she doesn't want to. When I say, "She said" or "She told us," what I mean is that we ask her yes or no questions and she nods her head yes or no. If she has a point she wants to make, or she wants to tell us something, she writes it in her notebook and bangs on it. We don't know

why she won't talk to us, we don't even know if she knows why, but we do know that when she's ready, she will talk to us. We are just so thrilled to have our baby back that it doesn't even matter right now.

She loves to spend time outside. We push her around the hospital grounds, show her the mountains, point out landmarks, and just soak up the sun. Being around the street is hard on her because of the cars driving by. That scares her so we don't take her out in the front much. When we do go outside, she takes her ball and glove with her; it seems to be her security blanket, along with her bee. Sometimes we even throw the ball for a bit. Again, when I say we throw the ball around, she actually just tosses it, and she still has no control in her left hand, or her left side for that matter, but she's making an effort, and that's huge. Leslie came to see her this morning and brought her a stuffed animal that made her smile so big. It's big and comfy and soft, so she hugs it and rests her head on it. They lay in her bed together and took pictures. She rubbed Sierra's head and you could see the love they share. No anger, no blame, just love, it was very touching. I think it was good for both of them.

She hung out with her dad, Izzy, Charlene, and the boys most of the day today. When she was done with them, she pointed to the door and shooed them away. It was funny, it made all of us laugh. She's so genuine and we have all come to understand that. Her filter doesn't tell her what is appropriate, she just acts on whatever she feels.

We can't turn our backs on her because she tries to get out of the bed, or wheelchair, whatever she's in. For this reason, I am with her 24/7, unless family is here, or her dad has the day off work, then I get shower time, or just downtime.

We finished the night eating watermelon and grapes, I couldn't think of a better way to end a day with my baby girl. Several people have asked me to let them know when she is able to have visitors. I'm happy to say that day has come. She can now have visitors, not many at once, but she is able to handle more people as time goes by. Please call her dad or I so that we can schedule you all so that it's not too overwhelming for her, but visitors are finally welcome. She has a lot of therapy, and if you are here during her therapy times, you may join her and help encourage her if you'd like. Most times her therapists don't mind as long as it doesn't hinder her progress. So please feel free to come visit her and show her your support. Thank you for your patience. Goodnight, all, and thank you. #TeamBdog

Although she was listed as "nonverbal," it did not mean she couldn't communicate. It just meant she couldn't speak yet or at least she chose not to speak yet. Although once in a while, she did whisper. She had speech therapy today and informed her speech therapist that she could speak. She just didn't want to. We don't know if that's true because someone was with her twenty-four hours a day, and she had made no effort to speak. This may be one of the things that she believed she could do but wasn't quite ready yet. Or maybe she knew she could but chose not to. Whatever the case, she was not vocal, so we communicated with picture charts, number charts, some sign language, her notebook, and by asking her yes or no questions. I have informed everyone that she now bangs on the bed rails to get our attention when she wants something as well.

Because her sleep pattern was off, her mornings were sluggish. She had a schedule, and we had to make sure she stuck with it as much as possible. There was a huge TV by the nurses' station which listed all the patients' schedules, so every day, I rolled her down there and showed her what her staff had planned for her day. She didn't get it yet, but with repetition, I'm sure that she would come to understand it. It started her mornings off with breakfast at 7:00 a.m.; from there, she went to occupational therapy first so she could get a shower. After OT, she went to speech therapy where they worked on her swallowing, speech, and cognitive therapy. She was allowed a one-hour nap after speech and then lunch.

Now that she was eating, she got to pick out what she wanted to eat, and then we had the task of encouraging her to eat all of her food so she could get f——g tube out. After that was her favorite time of the day when we got to go outside and toss the ball to each other. Her attention span was very short, so everything we did was for a short amount of time. After tossing the ball around, we took a stroll around the hospital grounds; it was so beautiful this time of the year, so we got as much outside time as possible before winter comes.

In the afternoon, she went to physical therapy. This was where I took most of my pictures so I could show her the progress she made when she got better. I had taken pictures since day one so that when she was ready, she could see her entire journey. Although I had all the pictures, and I posted every day about her progress, I did not post any pictures yet. When the day came that she told me it was okay to post them, I would do so. Until then, I just stored them on her tablet.

I had talked to her several times about Leslie, the driver, coming to see her. This was a touchy subject because we didn't know how she felt about the whole situation. We didn't know if Sierra would be mad at her or hold a grudge against her. It is human nature to place blame. She loved Sierra, and she was very distraught because of the damage she caused our baby girl. We had learned that she was in therapy because it turned her world upside down as well. She was a beautiful, kind young woman and carried an incredibly heavy load, knowing she caused this to happen to Sierra.

When I talked to Sierra about Leslie coming to see her or about the accident, not one time did she ever express any anger toward her. That made my heart so happy because I was one of a few that felt that way. I was very angry this happened to our daughter, but I had no anger toward the driver specifically. She was living in her own hell, and we didn't need to exacerbate that. So when Sierra agreed to let her come see her, I was very relieved. They shared a bond that I believed would last the rest of their lives, and to see them together brought tears to my eyes.

When her brother, Izzy, came with his family, they learned how much she had progressed and were ecstatically happy to see her doing so well. And then she got tired of them and pointed to the door, which we had come to learn meant, "Get Out!" It was nothing against them; we all got the finger and her pointing to the door to tell us to get out. We just laughed and granted her wishes. While they were there, her Nino, Ramon, and her dad were also there. They all had their Cowboys attire on, and she recognized that. She pointed at me and gave me the finger because she knew I was a lifetime 49er fan, so I got booted out so all the Cowboys fans could hang out together. I tried to convince her that maybe her new brain was a 49er fan, but she wasn't having any of that. She just shook her head no, gave me the finger, and shooed me out of her room.

October 1, 2017

> PM update of day 38 of Sierra's journey… She didn't have therapy today, so she got a nice break and got to enjoy all of her visitors that came to see her. Darryl and Frances came to visit and she barely responded to them. Vanessa, her sister, came up with her family but she wasn't very interested in them. She only responded to the kids for the most part. She did go outside and throw the ball with her sister, but wasn't real interested in that either. She refused to talk to me most of the day. When I talked to her, she just looked up in the air or at her surroundings as if to say, "Is someone talking?" A couple of the softball girls came up and she still wouldn't talk.

I tried to explain to her that people take time out of their day to come see her so maybe she can make an effort to talk to them, and I felt like I was talking to a wall. I would have gotten just as much response. Then her brother Anthony came to visit tonight and she talked to him. There's just something between them that she knows she can't get away with her defiance when it comes to him.

She had a very hard night tonight pertaining to her pain level. She told me she had a level 20 on her 1–10 scale again. Even after her medication, it stayed at a 20. It's so sad that I can't help her ease the pain. I rub her and talk gently to her, but the pain just overtakes her. The feeding tube is infected because she keeps pulling on it. It can't be removed for six weeks after insertion, and it has to heal before the doctor can take it out. Besides the fact that she is not eating enough to sustain her yet, so we have to get her eating well for at least a week before the choice to take it out is even taken into consideration. Tomorrow the doctor is going to talk to us about options. Hopefully it will be sooner rather than later.

She wanted to watch the Cowboys game today. She actually asked me what time they were playing. We looked it up and decided to watch it together. I'm not a big fan, but if it makes her happy, I'm willing to bite the bullet and watch it with her. She didn't really appreciate my humor about the fact that they were losing. She was not happy in the least that they ended up losing. However, when she realizes that the players took a knee to the National Anthem, she will change her tune about watching them I'm sure. After all, her patriotism is just as strong in her new brain as it was in her old brain. Goodnight, all, and hopefully I will have good news about the feeding tube tomorrow. #TeamBdog

After my post about visitors being able to come see her now, they started coming in droves. She had people coming in and out all day. Her stubbornness was abounding. Sometimes, no matter how hard we tried, she refused to talk. When her sister came up with the kids, she hardly paid any attention to her and her husband, David. She did interact with the kids some but still refused to talk to them. She may just be rundown because of all the therapy and stimulation her brain had been getting lately, but without her communicating to us at all, we just didn't know. Even when her sister took her out to throw the ball around, we thought that would bring her out of her funk, but it didn't. She showed no interest in throwing or catching the ball, and then she got tired of them being here, so she kicked them out.

She had a blank stare she gave us. No expression at all. We wondered what she was thinking or what was going on in her mind, but she wouldn't give it up, so we just dealt with the situation at hand. When her softball friends came to see her, they talked to her and told stories of their time in college, and still no response. I was constantly explaining to people that came to see her that they couldn't take it personally; it was just her brain healing. We had to accept whatever stage she was in and help her through it as much as we could. Her friends didn't know how to react; they looked at me for guidance. I explained to them as best as I could. After all, I was not really sure how to do this either. We were all learning as time went by. Some got offended by her actions or lack of interaction, so they didn't come back to visit because it was uncomfortable for them. I wanted to abruptly tell them, "You think it's uncomfortable for you? Imagine what it's like for her!" Now that she was out of her coma but not "acting normal," her friends were fading away.

It's very upsetting how people are so self-absorbed that they can't put past what they feel and try to understand her position. She couldn't help the way she talked or her actions. It was just her brain healing. It was very sad that she had so many friends, and now that she was not what they viewed as normal, they no longer had time for her.

On the other hand, her brother, Anthony, came almost every day and worked with her. Her staff actually requested for him to be here because she listened to him better than anyone else, including me. He was so patient and loving to his baby sister, and he could get her to talk, eat, walk, and do her therapy when no one else could. They had always had a very close relationship, and it showed when he was working with her.

Up to now, we hadn't let her watch any football games because of the stimulation to her brain. So, today, when she actually asked to watch the Cowboys play, I couldn't tell her no. We all had a very hard time telling her no since the accident. We were so thrilled she was alive we wanted to give her anything and everything she wanted. Obviously, we would have to stop that at some point, but not today.

October 2, 2017

> PM update on day 39 of Sierra's journey… She was very stubborn today. While she was in occupational therapy, defying her therapist, she asked me if Sierra has always been stubborn. Of course anyone that knows her knows this is definitely the case. So her therapist proceeds to inform me that whatever her traits were with her old brain, the ones she keeps with her new brain will be heightened. Watching her today, we realized she will be keeping that trait. She is outright stubborn today, and has the "If I don't want to do it, I just won't!" attitude. She did the same thing to me when I asked her to do something. She just looked at me, tapped her fingers on the table, and just looked around as if to say, "I don't hear you." Her Occupational Therapist was trying to be even more stubborn than her. She told Sierra to

try dressing herself today, and she just sat on her bed looking around as if she weren't even there, it was quite funny. Needless to say, her therapist ended up helping her get dressed. Her staff has a schedule to keep, and Sierra does not, so she just holds out and they eventually give in to her. Thankfully she doesn't have many of these days, or she wouldn't be progressing as well as she has.

All of her high school coaches came to see her today and brought her a t-shirt quilt. She liked it very much. Anthony and Lee came to visit with her, which we love because they really work on her, make her think, and don't give in to her stubbornness. He's so dang smart and he has done so much research on how to help her, so he works on her, asks her all the right questions, and makes her listen. He has learned how to communicate with her so she can make us understand what she is thinking and feeling. Today he walked into her defiant occupational therapy session and, all of a sudden, she starts doing what she's supposed to do.

She gets to see her Nina every day because she is in the rehab after her knee surgery. They decided they're going to fight together so they can get better every day. Her daddy came up with her godfather, but the same little Gonzalez came out. She wouldn't talk, or even respond to anyone when they talked to her. She hasn't even talked to Morke for a few days because she refuses to talk at all. Morke is doing much better; he said he hardly has pain, just discomfort. He started jogging and throwing the baseball, so great progress for him. Thank you Lord! He's checking out flights so he can come see her. I hope that he can because she lights up when we talk about him.

We ended our night with the nurse waking us up to give her nighttime medications. I told her to show me that she had swallowed them so I opened my mouth and she thought that was hilarious. We wouldn't quit laughing and the pills were spilling out of her mouth, so the nurse had to ask me to leave the room so that she could take them. She finally got them down and we continued to laugh about it for about a half an hour. It was a great way to end our day. Goodnight and thank you to everyone for your continued prayers. #TeamBdog

Although days like this hindered her progress, it was very hard not to laugh about it. Her therapists tried in vain to get her to do her exercises. They tried throwing the ball to her, and she would just let it hit her, then she would laugh. She tried to lie down several times on the mats while doing her occupational therapy, and her therapist would lift her back up and coax her to get motivated to no avail. This is exactly why her medical team wanted her brother to be a part of her therapy because as her brain healed, she realized she had choices. Sometimes her choices were to be defiant in therapy. However, when she saw her brother, she knew she wouldn't get away with it when he was around. All he had to do was say, "Come on, kid," and she got her fight face on and rocked her therapy.

Her coaches were so happy to see her because several of them hadn't seen her since Albuquerque when she was still in a coma and on life support. It was obvious they were thrilled to see how far she had come yet very sad that she had so much damage to her brain and she was not the person they once knew. She did light up a little when she saw the quilt they brought her, but that didn't last long because she refused to talk or interact with them much at all. I had to explain to them that she had days when she was very coherent and interactive, but today wasn't one of them.

I found myself constantly apologizing for her behavior, and then I'd get upset with myself because I shouldn't have had to apologize. We are ecstatically happy for where she was in her recovery, but people didn't understand how hard she had to fight to get where she was. They just think how uncomfortable it is for them. If you have not been here, there is no explanation that can make anyone understand, so I just apologized.

October 3, 2017

> PM update on day 40 of Sierra's journey... Forty days, wow! I can't believe it's been that long. She has surpassed so many obstacles in such a short amount of time, it's amazing! She's amazing! She rocked her physical and occupational therapy today. She walked around the entire gym on their special walker, twice. It's very hard to describe the exhilaration we get when we see her fighting to get her life back. She worked on her core muscles, and already, it's helping her to stand upright without wobbling and being so unsteady. She got on her knees and threw the ball. She actually put her glove on and moved it in the direction of the ball trying to catch it a few times. We throw the ball after every meal because she has to stay upright for at least thirty minutes after eating. This helps redirect her mind because the only thing she wants to do after she eats, is sleep.
>
> Her staff has decided to put her on a strict schedule so she knows when she has to work hard, and when she is allowed to sleep or have free time where she can play games or just chill if that's what she chooses to do. It's a double edge sword really because her brain heals much more when she's sleeping, but if she doesn't work hard to get herself back, she can't progress. She is still refusing to talk for her speech therapist, we don't know why she doesn't want to talk, and we

don't even know if she knows why. Sierra told her speech therapist that she's annoying, so when they came back from speech therapy, she told me that Sierra fired her. She did do some of the work she was given, and then refused to finish it. She talks more to her brother Anthony than she does to anyone else, so her team asked if we could bring him in to persuade her to do her exercises with her voice instead of answering everything in her notebook.

Her projected discharge date from here is October 18. They said their goal for her is to walk out on her own two feet, possibly with her walker, but on her own nonetheless. Her feeding tube is doing much better, they covered it so she can't pick at it and we put antibiotic ointment on it to help the outside infection in the hopes that it won't get infected on the inside. If that happens she'll definitely have a lot more pain and that can cause a whole slew of other problems. She got through the whole day with no pain, at least not enough pain to need her pain medications and we really like that. Tonight she finally got the opportunity to talk to Morke, but she was really sleepy so he did most of the talking. We have made lists of words, people, and pictures so that she can communicate better with us. Every day she chooses Morke from her list. Love obviously didn't get lost through all of this. She's resting peacefully now and I am going to take this opportunity to do the same. Goodnight until tomorrow. #TeamBdog

When we started each day, I'd wake up and wonder what this day would bring. Because yesterday she had no motivation or wouldn't talk didn't mean that we could expect the same thing today.

Sometimes it was hour by hour. She could be doing great and then she would not. By that, I mean she could decide not to eat, not to do her exercises, not to talk, or not to take her medications. In one day's time, she could have twenty different moods—it was exhausting. I went to most every therapy she had. I was not allowed in speech because she needed to focus as much as possible, but I went to her occupational and physical therapy. I recorded her progress every day. I, along with her dad and anyone that went to therapy with her, encouraged her, helped push her, told her how she was a warrior, and that we were so proud of her. Sometimes she reacted positively, sometimes she reacted with anger, and sometimes she didn't react at all.

It was such a relief to cover up her feeding tube because it bothered her constantly. She was always trying to pull on it and scratch it, which got it infected, then she pulled on it more because it hurt her. Her brain was not advanced enough to know that if she left it alone, it wouldn't bother her as much. We tried multiple ways to explain to her why she couldn't pull on it, but she'd forget. I was going to talk to her doctors to see when she could get it out. It was the last tube she had left in her body, and now that she was more aware, it constantly bothered her. It was almost at six weeks after insertion, so now we would just have to get her to eat all of her food and start putting on some weight before the doctor would remove it.

The good news for taking it out was that they didn't have to surgically remove it. They just pulled it out, and her stomach would close up right after it was removed. It makes me queasy to think about it, but that's what the doctor said happened when they removed feeding tubes. I guess we would have to trust their medical expertise, but I still had to ask multiple people before I was comfortable with that fact.

Her notebook had been an essential way for her to communicate with us since she had been here at the rehab here in Las Cruces. When we found out that she was making the effort to write about the ambulance ride here from Albuquerque, we immediately got her a spiral notebook. In the beginning, her writing was rarely legible. As time had gone by, we are able make out more and more of what she was trying to communicate to us. Besides the notebook, we also counted heavily on her flash cards. We wanted her to talk so badly, but she wasn't ready. I was experimenting with holding things back from her until she used her voice, but she was pretty stubborn. She would rather point to a picture on her flash cards than use her voice. Anthony, on the other hand, could get her to ask for what she wanted most of the time.

October 4, 2017

> PM update on day 41 of Sierra's journey... She started her day laughing so hard she shook the bed. Her tech came in to get her up for breakfast, but, of course, Sierra was not willing to jump out of bed and start her day, especially at six thirty in the morning. So she told Sierra, "I'm going to pull your covers down." And Sierra just smiled and lay in her bed. So the tech pulled her covers off of her, and when she did we realized Sierra had taken her shirt off during the night. It surprised us to see her bareness, but Sierra thought it was so funny and we all laughed about it so hard we had tears coming down our cheeks. What a great way to start her day.
>
> She rocked her physical and occupational therapy today. She's starting to dress herself and when she takes a shower, she's able to wash most of her body. Her left hand still doesn't work very well. She's still using it, trying to strengthen it and make it more functional, but that will take time and perseverance. After her shower, she went to the gym and proceeded to do crunches trying to strengthen her core, she walked around the whole gym with a regular walker and very little guidance. She stood up and threw the softball. She threw overhand, underhand, and even pitched a few balls. They're only going a few feet

right now, but she's just getting started. It will get better as time goes by because she's amazing!

She's been having a problem with depression because she is becoming more aware of what happened to her and her many deficits, so we had a psychologist come in to talk to her. She did most of the talking and just asked Sierra yes or no questions. It wasn't very interactive, but we hope that it will get better as time passes and Sierra is more able to communicate what she thinks and feels. She cried on the inside when the psychologist left. She obviously struck a chord, but we don't know which one or why yet because the lack of communication.

She talked to Morke today and cried on the inside because she misses him. When I say that "she says," what I mean is that we ask the questions, and she verifies with a yes or no nod. And when I say she cried on the inside, I can tell because she has a very faint whine and puts her head down. Because of many people's responses to her posts, I feel that I have not made that very clear. She may be about 50% of what the average person is, so please take that into consideration when I don't make it clear with each post. She is at this rehabilitation hospital to learn to walk, talk, swallow, eat, brush her teeth, shower herself, become continent, and work on her cognitive abilities. Just the basics that we take for granted every day. Her next step rehabilitation hospital will teach her to be independent again, that's the goal anyways. We still have no clue as to how much of her we will get back, but we are shooting for 100%. I hope this makes her situation more clear. Thank you Becca for coming up here to help my son get the Go Fund Me account set up so I can pay some bills and get necessary supplies for Sierra, and for visiting our family, you have become a beautiful piece of our puzzle that will bring our daughter back to us. Goodnight All, and thank you to the moon and back. #TeamBdog

Depending on her schedule, sometimes the techs woke her up to shower her before breakfast. This completely threw her off her schedule. She didn't know to look at the clock, but her internal clock told her that it was not time to get up. So when they came in early to wake her up, she was very resistant. Today, when the tech came in and pulled her covers off and we saw she had undressed herself sometime during the night, it surprised us all. We laughed so hard about it, but then I thought, *Oh my gosh, she woke up during the night to undress herself, and I didn't even hear her.* That struck fear in my heart because I knew that I must have slept too hard, and that could be dangerous to her. The alarm didn't go off on her bed; somehow it got turned off. I don't know if I didn't set it or if she learned to turn it off herself. We'd tried being very careful not to let her see how we turned it on for that very reason.

When she got in the shower, she took the washcloth from me and started to wash herself. It was beautiful because this was the first time she had shown initiative to do anything. She could not cross her midline, so she had to switch hands to wash both sides of her body. Her left side was still quite weak, but she made the effort to use it to wash the left side of her body. I still had to wash her again after she was done, but she was taking tiny steps to get where she could do it all by herself. After her shower, I let her pick out her clothes, and she made the effort put them on. I had to help her a little bit, but it was less and less every day. We were starting to let her make choices—if she wanted to watch TV or listen to the radio; what she wanted to wear; what she wanted to eat; if she wanted to go outside, etc. It seemed to give her some satisfaction and a bit of independence.

Today, she wanted to throw the ball around some, so we went outside, and everyone at the hospital was watching her and amazed with her progress. They told her how proud they were of her, and it really boosted her confidence. She threw overhand, underhand; she pitched a few balls and even tried to throw a changeup. She knew people were watching her, and they all encouraged her, so I believe she did it to show off somewhat. She smiled every time someone told her how well she was doing and then tried different ways to throw it. That was great; she had interaction with people besides her family, which hadn't happened since she's been here. Everyone here knew who she was. She was the youngest patient here, and word of what happened to her spread quickly. They were all saddened by her story, so they really made an effort to tell her how proud they were of her and encouraged her when she was throwing the ball or trying to pitch again. It was like she had a whole other family here.

My high school friend, Becca Reyes, had been so helpful since she was in the accident. She made special trips to Albuquerque to bring me money she had collected and sat with me during the first days when I was so distraught at the fact that our baby girl might die. She checked on me and Sierra's progress daily, and when Sierra was transported to Las Cruces, she had been an inspiration to my family and I.

She started a GoFundMe page to help ease the burden of me staying with Sierra every day. When she read what happened to Sierra from day one, it touched her so deeply that she has made it her mission to make this tragedy as easy as possible for our family. I find it hard to express the gratefulness I feel for her.

October 5, 2017

> PM update on day 42 of Sierra's journey… In her notebook every day, I write the date, and today she saw that it was the 5th, so she wrote "Andrew," and under it, she wrote "dead." This is the anniversary of her brother's death and she remembered that all by herself. It was obviously on her mind all day because she wrote it multiple times in her notebook today. She wrote over and

over, Andrew, dead, heaven. We talked about it
and I asked her if she knew it was Andrew's anniversary? She kept writing his name and banging
on the paper with the pen. She wrote "Heaven!"
I told her, yes, he is in heaven, but it seemed like
she was trying to tell me something else. When
she tries to make a point, she writes it in her
notebook and bangs on it. She continued to do
this all day today. When we tried to have conversations with her, she just wrote Andrew, dead,
heaven. I would confirm and she would bang on
the notebook. There's obviously something she
is trying to tell me, but I'm not getting it. She is
amazing; I know I have overused that word since
she began this journey, but if you all could see
what I see on a daily basis, you would understand
the use of that very word. Today she learned how
to use the TV remote, which also has the nurses'
button on it. So she started pushing the nurses'
button constantly. The nurse would come in and
ask what she needed, and nothing would be the
answer. She has apparently learned to be ornery
because she continued pushing the nurse's button and making the nurse come in. I didn't even
realize she would push it until they would come
in and Sierra would just smile when they came in
to turn it off. I asked her if she was pushing the
nurses' button and she pulled me close and said,
"I didn't do it!" All the while she was smiling.
I finally caught her and asked her why she was
doing that, and she just shook her head no with
her half smile on her face.

She lifted weights today and worked more
on her walking. Cierra, her softball buddy and
longtime friend, went with her to occupational
therapy today, so she could see how hard she is

fighting. We were all very impressed with her drive today. Tonight when her brother came to visit they arm wrestled. She actually made her brother work a little bit to win on the right side. Her muscle mass is finally getting built up. They also tried it lefty; Anthony just gave her some resistance so she can work on her left side. She is definitely starting to use her left side more often, and I don't have to remind her as often to open her left hand. It still curls up automatically because of the brain injury, but it's getting better. She showed her daddy how she's throwing a change up now, at least the motion of a change up. It's very cute to see her advancing and working to get her abilities back. The ball only goes about five or six feet now, but that's further than she did a week ago. It's only baby steps, but they're in the right direction, so we'll take it. She's constantly getting stronger and it's so beautiful to watch.

As I have in the past, I left the best for last... she wrote in her notebook "I'm awake!" I told her, "I know love, I see you're awake." And again she wrote "I'm awake!" As before, she would write it and then bang on the notebook. She continued to write it, and I would read it, and she would shake her head yes vigorously. I realized at that point that she must be thinking deeper, so I asked her if it was her brain. She shook her head yes with a big smile on her face. I asked if her brain woke up, and she answered yes again. She wrote "not cloudy." The look in her eyes when she smiled was magical.

The medical staff in Albuquerque told us after she came out of her coma completely that "the lights will come on." Because we thought when she came out of her coma, she would be coherent, have conversations, and understand everything like you see in the movies. It's not like that at all! When she came out of her coma, she was still in an altered state of consciousness; she would stare off into space like she's just not connected, like she's in a trance. That's the best way I can describe it. Today, the lights came on and it was very exciting for all of us. We don't believe in coincidences, and we don't believe that it was coincidence that her brain woke up on her brother's anniversary. The smile on her face, and the emotion in our hearts was priceless! Goodnight, all, until tomorrow. #TeamBdog

To date, this was the most exciting day since her accident. I woke up dreading this day as I have many times in the past since my son went to live with Jesus. The thought of having to feel the loss of my son on this day and my baby girl trying to come back to us seemed so overwhelming to me. I wasn't sure how I would get through this day. In the past, I had been able to go off alone somewhere and deal with my pain, but today was like no other anniversary. Today, my baby girl was fighting to get her life back. While I was sad, I felt immense gratitude for the situation I was in. I was able to look my baby girl in the eyes and thank God for sparing her life. I knew we had a long road of recovery for her to come back to us, but I was grateful for the opportunity.

When I saw that she had written her brother's name in her notebook and acknowledged that it was his anniversary, I knew she was making connections, and it was thrilling. She knew that he had died and was in heaven. That is a core memory, something that she had grown up her whole life knowing. Now, even with a brain injury as extensive as hers, she remembered her brother.

When she wrote in her notebook, "I'm awake!" I didn't think anything of it at first. I just thought she was letting me know she is awake and ready for her day to start. I never thought that this would be the day that "the lights would come on." It truly was as her medical staff explained it. I could see it in her eyes. The trance-like state she had been living in had lifted. She continued to write, "I'm awake!"

I continued to tell her, "I know, honey, I see that."

Then she would bang on her notebook, which meant she was trying to make a strong point. I didn't get it at first, but after several times of her doing this, she wrote, "Not cloudy!" I finally got it. Then I realized this was much deeper than she woke up to fight another day. And when I asked her if her brain woke up, she smiled so big and nodded her head yes so vigorously my heart filled with so much gratitude. I felt as though I had been given the best gift of my life. Our baby girl may be okay after all.

I realized it had only been forty-two days, but that was forty-two days of round-the-clock care for her. This also meant lack of care for me. I had refused to leave her side against medical advice. The lack of sleep, the lack of food, and the lack of anything to take care of myself had caught up with me. I felt beaten down almost to the point of breaking, but I couldn't. I was a mom first and foremost. I had to be with my baby girl every minute of every day because she needed me constantly. She was afraid if I was not with her. Everyone else may come and go, and she just wrote, "Be careful."

But if I had to go somewhere and leave her in the care of other family members, first, I had to prepare her for it. I had to explain that I was going to the store or going home to take a shower, etc. She actually had to give me permission to leave and accept who was going to be there with her. As of yet, the only people she allowed to take over was her dad, her brother, and my sister for short periods of time. It was not only her that feared me leaving, but it was me as well. As soon as I walked out of her room, I'd get an extreme amount of anxiety. I prayed to God to let her be okay. Not that they couldn't take very good care of her. I just feared the worst all the time.

October 6, 2017

PM update on day 43 of Sierra's journey... Well, she has become quite the joker. Since she had to have an alarm installed on her wheelchair because she tries to get out of it on her own, she has decided to make music with the alarm. She opens it just enough for it to go off. She pulls on it and makes it go off in sequence of one, two, or three. Then she seems to be trying to make music with it. All the while, she had a big smile on her face. Her smile has found its way to her face quite often lately. She smiles, she laughs, a lot of the time it's inappropriate, but we don't care, it's beautiful nonetheless. Cierra, Lee, and I were sitting around laughing tonight and Lee got it on video, it was a beautiful interaction that we can all cherish.

Today in her occupational therapy, she was on all fours throwing bean bags into a crate, and all of a sudden, she decided to lie down. Her occupational therapist was coaxing her to get up and continue, but she refused with a smile. They just looked at each other, Sierra smiled and her therapist tried in vain not to smile. It was so cute. Needless to say, we all started laughing and that put a serious damper on her accomplishing her therapy. We played catch today, and she is making a serious effort to use her left hand to squeeze the glove. I accidentally hit her with the light softball and she just burst out laughing, she couldn't compose herself to continue. This is so rewarding, I am so thankful for her ability to overcome her deficiencies. She learned to call Morke all by herself tonight. I didn't even know she knew how to do that. She blew him so many kisses, which she can do now because her brother taught her how to pucker her lips. I had to run to Wal-Mart tonight and when I got back, she was at dinner and her whole table was full of visitors. Aunt Susan, Uncle Bob, Krystal, Esther, Daddy, Wellies, and Elvis were all with her, and of course, she was cuttin' it up so everyone had a smile on their faces. What a beautiful sight to see. Now that "the light came on," she is much more interactive. Thank God we are getting her back more and more every day. Goodnight all, and thank you for everything you do to help our baby girl come back to us. #TeamBdog

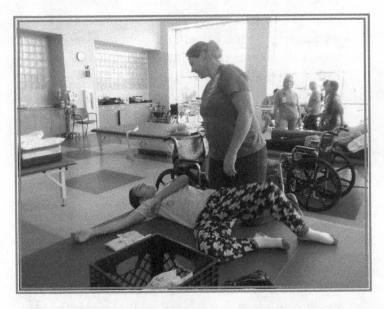

This picture shows her defiant side. She said she didn't feel like doing therapy, so she lay down. The smile on her face is her response to her occupational therapist, Shannon, trying to coax her to get motivated.

Because she thought her abilities were further advanced than they actually were, she tried to get out of her wheelchair. The staff decided that it would be best for her safety to put an alarm on it. Every time she lifted the buckle, the alarm went off. Well, she decided that it was fun, so she was continually lifting it and putting down to make it chirp. Then she started doing sequences like she was playing music with a big smile on her face. There was also an alarm on her bed because she thought she could walk on her own, so she just decided to get up and tried to get out of bed on her own. This caused serious safety issues because she didn't understand she could hurt herself very badly. When we tried to explain to her, she just smiled because she had inappropriate reactions to many situations.

Today was such a beautiful day. There were so many laughs and so many smiles; it felt so good to have such a great day. So many of her days were filled with fear, pain, and tears, so when we got smiles, it was a great day, and we were thankful. I truly believe that God was also watching over me because when I felt like I couldn't continue going through the pain and agony we faced every day, he gives us a good day. It was just enough to recharge and get ready for the next stage she had to go through.

I never liked the cliché that "God doesn't give us more than we can handle." But in our present situation, I believe it to be true because every time I talked to God and tell him, "I'm maxed out" and I started to doubt myself, she had a better day. There had been so much fear, heartache, uncertainty, and tears since her accident; we craved good days like this.

October 7, 2017

> Lack of sleep, lack of any fuel for me caught up
> on me. I got sick and fell asleep, so I will post in
> am. #TeamBdog

Because I talked about a good day or a good night didn't mean that as soon as I was done typing, she continued the same behavior. Everything she did could last ten minutes, an hour, half a day, or days on end. So we woke up every day and had no clue what this day would bring. We took it as it came and dealt with whatever she was going through presently.

At the end of every day, I think about what I am going to write for the day. I don't actually post everything she does because we expected she was going to get better, and I wanted to honor her privacy to some degree. Sometimes at the end of the day, I just didn't have anything else to give. Tonight was one of those nights. Every time she told me she was going to die or she cried or wouldn't eat or drink or she was scared, it all affected me so deeply and drained every ounce of energy I had mustered up for each day. Today was so overwhelming that while I was putting her to sleep, I drifted off myself.

October 8, 2017

AM update on day 44 of Sierra's journey… She has definitely reached the inappropriate stage. We were informed that it would come as her brain heals, and here it is. I've been giving her my tablet to play games and to call Morke. Tonight when she was using it, somehow she erased everything in it. All the pictures, all the videos, everything I have recorded since her journey began. First she changed the password so I gave it back to her to see if she remembered it so we could get back into it. Well, that didn't work. Whatever she did, it wiped everything out. There are no pictures, no videos, everything I have kept track of since the accident is gone, and she made it go back to factory settings. Of course that was funny to her, but so disheartening to me. She laughed while she watched all of us trying to fix it…to no avail.

Everything seems to be a battle for her; Walking, talking, work outs, taking walks, waking up to start a new day, everything. She's pushing through it, but it just seems to knock her down sometimes. Her staff had to put her on a behavior modification plan trying to curb her defiance, so we'll see how it works out. Most of it is funny, but there are some things she does that can be very dangerous to her so we have to watch her every move because she is so fast and impulsive. An example is that she tries to pull out f——g tube, and if we don't catch her before she does it, it can be very dangerous to her and she may have to have another surgery to reinsert it. We definitely don't want that. Because this is the inappropriate stage, she does things to her body that are definitely inappropriate, which we don't care to share. All the while, smiling and laughing at it all. #TeamBdog

PM update on day 45 of Sierra's journey... She has decided not to eat anything so she is back to tube feedings, which makes her sick to her stomach so she can't sleep. Partly because she is sick to her stomach, partly because she is hungry and the anti-nausea medications they give her only last so long. Besides her refusal to eat, she is in a very angry state. Her dad took her to eat because I thought she was just angry with me. Apparently she is just angry. Her dad took her to the cafeteria to eat today and she threw her food at him and threw her drink off the table. She's been hitting everyone, pulling their hair, their clothes, anything she can get a hold of. She has to go sit in front of the nurse's station because of her behavior. Tomorrow she will get a babysitter and they want me to spend less time with her in the hopes it will curb her aggressiveness. This is all a part of her healing, and it will pass just as the other stages have passed. We will get through this one just as we have gotten through the other ones. It's very exhausting. We thought if she got to talk to Morke, it would help her curb her anger. But it only seemed to make her more confused about the situation. She is praying a lot, and we pray together as well, for God to help her through this very hard stage she is going through. Goodnight All. I hope to bring you all better news tomorrow. My mom always told me, "This too shall pass!" I'm holding on to that. Goodnight, all. #TeamBdog

My heart was absolutely crushed when I realized she wiped the notebook clean. I wanted to cry so badly, but I didn't know what that would do to her, so I held it in until I left her room. As I was walking out of the room, I broke down. I cried so hard because I was so diligent about keeping everything on that notebook. The first time she sat up, when she came out of her coma, brushed her teeth, when she signed "I love you"—all of her firsts, all gone. I was so heartbroken I couldn't think straight. All the while, she had no clue what she had done. She thought it was funny, hence the inappropriate stage.

Like I said, she changed at the drop of a hat. She pulled my hair, tried to tear my clothes off, scratched me, and tried to hit me. Her nurse put her in front of the nurses' station after she hit the medications out of her hand when she tried to give them to her. While she was facing her punishment for her behavior, she continued to bang her wheelchair into the nurse's desk and smile every time it hit the desk. Her dad came in to have lunch with her so she could get a break from me. While they were in the cafeteria, she refused to eat. Her dad tried to coax her into eating something, and she just threw her food at him. Then she proceeded to throw the rest of her food off the table and flipped him off.

After her shenanigans in the cafeteria, we were in her room, hanging out, and I saw her hands go under the covers. I asked her what she was doing, and she just smiled. She pulled something out from underneath the covers and handed it to me with a big smile on her face. I opened my hand and realized she had put feces in my hand. When I saw what it was, she actually laughed out loud.

140

She thought that was so funny. I, on the other hand, did not find it so amusing. And five minutes later, she was crying because she was scared. She told me she was dying and that she was not afraid of dying; she was afraid of leaving me. Again, it was all a part of her healing. Inappropriateness has no boundaries, and neither did she. We just had to understand this was all progress and take it as it comes.

October 9, 2017

> PM update on day 46 of Sierra's journey... She is still refusing to eat, even though the tube feedings are making her sick to her stomach. They can't give her medications at the same time because she throws it right back up before they get it all in her stomach. She just needs to eat, we know she can, she just doesn't want to, and we don't know why. It is frustrating for us, but it's much worse for her. She wants to be able to do everything, and she wants it now! Her medical staff asked me to go take a break so they can put her behavior modification plan into effect. We don't know if she's acting out because I'm always here. So I went outside so she couldn't see me. I didn't want to go too far away because she might need me, so I just stayed outside the hospital. When I came back in, I heard whining and realized it was her so I talked to her trying to soothe her, then we called Uncle Tony, Aunt Kristie, and Sarena. When she was done listening to the conversation, she signed "I Love you" to them. After I hung up I asked her if she was crying. She nodded her head yes, and all of a sudden, she was *crying*! It was the first time she has been able to cry and express so much emotion since the accident. She hurt so deeply, and cried so hard. Tears streamed down

her face, and she moaned and cried. She held on to me so tightly I couldn't move. Her chains have been broken. She can cry and release the plethora of emotion that has been trapped inside her. I held her tight and talked to her. I told her that now she doesn't have to be trapped, she can open the flood gates to let the emotion out. While it was extremely sad, it is still forward progress, and it makes me so happy that she has a way to get it out now. I heard her voice louder than we've heard it so far. Please pray for her to get through this stage quickly, and for her to eat so she can get f——g tube out of her belly. Thank you, all, and goodnight for now. #TeamBdog

The brain is so complex, and there are so many things that even the most knowledgeable doctors don't know. She knew she wanted the tube out of her belly so badly and yet she wouldn't eat. The tube feedings she got made her so sick to her stomach that by the time half of it was injected, she was throwing it up. She was losing weight rapidly, and her options were running out. We talked to her about how important it is for her to eat, and she seemed to understand. Then we tried to feed her, and she refused. It was so complicated and so hard doing this on a daily basis. We talked about how much she wanted the tube out of her tummy, and she knew that she had to eat to get it out, and yet she still wouldn't eat.

Until now, we didn't know what she was thinking, if she understood what was happening to her, or where she was. She just appeared to be staring out into space. She wasn't able to express herself, so we had to wonder what she was even capable of understanding. When I walked back into her room and I heard her whining, I wasn't sure what she was doing. I asked if she was in pain, and she said no. I asked her if she wanted to talk to Uncle Tony and Aunt Kristie, and she said yes, so I called, and we talked to them. They told her how proud they were of her, and all the while, she lay on her bed and moaned.

When we got off the phone I asked her if she was crying. She looked at me, nodded her head yes, and all of a sudden, the tears were flowing. She moaned and whined while tears flowed down her face. She held on to me so tightly while she cried and cried. I held her and talked to her so gently, trying to soothe her. The nurse came in and saw her crying. She was happy to see that she finally learned to cry so she could release the pressure that built up in her mind. I hadn't thought about that until she brought it to my attention. While it was incredibly sad to watch her crying so badly, it was also forward progress. This would be the first of so many tears we couldn't begin to count.

October 10, 2017

PM update on day 47 of Sierra's journey. She still won't eat. Her doctors switched her to tube feedings to clear ensure hoping that it would curb her puking, but it didn't help. She's still throwing up everything they put in her tube. We did, however, find out that she has a urinary tract infection which, with a brain injury, can affect her more adversely than a 'normal' brain. It may explain the mood behavior and confusion she has been experiencing, and possibly her inability to hold anything down. So we are praying that we have found a solution to her problems that have been hindering her progression lately. She started antibiotics today, so hopefully by tomorrow, we will see an improvement in her. We also booked a flight for Morke to fly in Thursday and stay until Sunday. We're hoping he will help her progress, and maybe get her to eat again. She has been writing his name in her notebook for days. She also told me that her heart misses Morke. So I will be picking him up Thursday morning then he and I will go check out the rehab in El Paso to get a feel for it because that is supposed to be her next step. Because she has felt so badly, she hasn't participated much in any of her therapies. So tomorrow is another day full of possibilities. Goodnight all, and thank you. #TeamBdog

The fear was starting to overwhelm me. No matter what we did or how much we talked to her about how important it was for her to eat, she was still refusing to eat anything. Her Nino and Nina got her some Naked drinks to help her get some nutrition, and so far, we could get her to drink a few sips of them, but that's it. I told her that I would make her anything she wanted, but she told me no. She just did not want to eat at all, and it was very scary to all of us.

Her temperature was elevated, and her doctor made the assumption she had a urinary tract infection because the urine in her bag was very dark and pungent. They explained to us that when there is a brain injury involved, even a UTI can throw her whole world off-kilter. It can cause confusion, mood swings, pain, and anxiety, which is everything she was displaying the past couple days.

October 11, 2017

PM update on day 48 of Sierra's journey… She took a couple bites of ice cream today. Other than that, she has not eaten nor will she drink anything. I asked her why she won't eat, and she told me, "Because I'm dying!" That was so hard to hear coming from our baby girl's mouth. I thought we were past the point of worrying that she is going to die, and now she believes she is going to die. We don't know why she feels or thinks this, but it is very unsettling because we fear she either knows something we don't, or she's going to give up. Either way, it's a fear that we thought we had gotten past. I explained to her that she's not dying anymore, she fought past that, and now she's getting better every day, but she doesn't believe me. I think the antibiotics are starting to work, so maybe tomorrow will be better. She did manage to lift some weights in Occupational therapy today, but wouldn't do anything except write in her notebook during physical therapy. She just keeps writing that she is going to die and she wants to see Morke. Knowing he is coming has consumed her thoughts, and she thought it was today so I had to reiterate that I will be picking him up from the airport tomorrow. That has calmed her for the moment, but there's a very good chance she won't remember so I will probably have to tell her a few more times before the night is over.

We had another family meeting yesterday and devised a new behavior modification plan, so we ask that visitors come after 5:30 pm so she has no distractions while she is supposed to be concentrating on her therapy, including speech therapy where she is prompted to start eating again. Weekends are open as long as she participates in her weekly therapies. Crying has become a frequent occurrence for her, she is so sad and we have tried in vain to console her, but nothing helps. I just hold on to her, squeeze her tight, rub her, and talk very gently to her. She squeezes me back so tightly and sobs hysterically.

I want so badly to take her pain away but nothing is working. We're very happy Morke is coming tomorrow, and praying his presence will turn her progress around and she starts getting better again. We pray together every night, but she seems to be losing hope, and that's so heartbreaking. Please pray for her. #TeamBdog

Today was a very hard day for her. She cried so many times and was afraid of everything. She continued to tell me that she was dying. I tried to persuade her that she was past that point, but she didn't believe me. She tried to convince me that she was going to die. I asked her why she thought that, but she was not capable of articulating her thoughts, so she just kept telling me she was dying. She talked about Andrew and heaven and dying. It appeared to be consuming her thoughts, and she cried and held on to me so tight that it hurt.

She wanted to see Morke so badly. We told her he was coming to visit her, and we showed her on the calendar, but she had no concept of time, so she constantly asked where he was. We were so excited that he was finally coming to see her, hoping that he could get her to eat or help change her disposition. She was definitely in a valley right now, and we were having a very hard time getting her out of it. Sometimes she seemed to understand where she was and what happened to her, but other times, she seemed so confused about everything. We were hoping that it was the urinary tract infection that had her so confused. We should know by tomorrow because the antibiotics would have taken effect by then.

October 12, 2017

PM update on day 49 of Sierra's journey... Well, I have to say that bringing Morke here was the best decision we could make. As soon as he got here, she popped out of her funk. He fed her, and she reluctantly ate for him. He had to take a bite, and then she would take a bite, all the while gleaming at him. She is so happy he is here, and he is encouraging her to fight again. After she ate all of her food, she went to occupational therapy and worked out hard. She did everything she was asked to do and she did it all with a big smile on her face. It's so nice to see that smile again. She's been smiling ever since he got here. She finally decided to participate in speech therapy

today. This one is her downfall. For some reason unknown to us, her biggest struggle is in her
speech therapy.

After rocking all of her therapies, she went
to dinner and ate almost all of her food. I can't tell
you how happy that made us. Morke is so patient
with her; it's just a pleasure to watch. Him being
here with her turned her around 180 degrees in
a positive direction. After dinner, we went outside to catch a sunset, where she decided that she
was going to start using her voice to speak instead
of her notebook. Her voice is very faint, but it's
there, and it will get better with time. We ended
the day by playing games. She loves connect four,
always has. So she and Morke played and she beat
him, as she does all of us. She was so happy today.
It was a very good day for her which, in turn, was
a very good day for all of us. #TeamBdog

Today, after I went to pick Morke up, we went to the El Paso
rehab to check out their facilities. We took a tour and were given
information of her schedule of events for each day. They had a dining room where all the patients ate; it was more like a family dining
room. They had a chef that prepared the food, and it was more like
home-cooking than the hospital's less-than-desirable food. They had
an all the time menu if she didn't want what they were serving, so I
was hopeful that would encourage her to eat more often. The gym
was small but looked efficient. This was where she would be doing
her occupational and physical therapy. It was definitely smaller, but
I hoped that it would be better for her progression. Less stimulation
was definitely a plus for her.

She would have her own room, which looked nothing like a
hospital room. It was more like a bedroom, and we could decorate
it however we want. After checking it all out, we realized it felt right
to both of us. Thank goodness because we only had a short time to

prepare her for her next transition. We prayed this was the best move for her.

Sierra called us when we were at the rehab in El Paso. She didn't believe I went to go get him, so her physical therapist called me, and we video chatted so she could see that he was with me. It was quite funny. Her therapist said she wouldn't participate in therapy because Morke was coming. So they called and had Morke tell her to work hard so he could see her. That worked very well. Her physical therapist said she worked very hard after our phone call.

October 13, 2017

> PM update on day 50 of Sierra's journey… I just have to reiterate the fact the Morke coming down here to see her was the best medicine we could have prescribed. She is back on track; she's eating and working hard at her therapies again, all the while, smiling that beautiful smile. It was such an incredible transformation. Love is such a miraculous motivator. She has been using her voice to talk to him and she has a constant smile on her face when he is present. This, by the way, is just about every minute since he arrived.
>
> We went outside on the patio to eat dinner because the weather was so beautiful. While we were out there everyone noticed them and how happy she was. Since she is the youngest one here everyone knows who she is and they all noticed her blushing because all eyes were on them. All the patients, staff, and regular visitors were thrilled to see her so happy because she has been so downtrodden lately.
>
> Her physical therapist told her if she rocked her therapy, she could go on a date to the ice cream shop right down the road with Morke. That was very good incentive for her so she worked so hard

and did so well, she earned her reward. Sierra, Morke and I got to drive in my truck down to the ice cream parlor where she enjoyed her first date since the accident, what a tremendous accomplishment for her. I asked her if she was happy and she shook her head yes so hard and tonight she even told me with her words that she is happy, and then she stood up on her own and hugged me. It felt like I entered paradise, she is able to express her emotion. Today was a very good day, and I am thankful. #TeamBdog

As soon as I came back with Morke, her whole demeanor changed. She was so excited to see him that she ignored everyone else and just stared at him with a huge smile on her face. It felt so good to see her smile and know that she was actually happy. Morke stayed with her here at the hospital, and I went home to sleep in my bed and actually got a good night's sleep for the first night since the accident. He got her to use her voice, and she told me she was happy and then said, "Mommy, I love you!" That felt so good, and when she stood up and hugged me, my heart felt like it would explode. When he took her to the cafeteria to eat, she actually ate. She would make him take a bite, and then she would take a bite. By the time they were done, she had eaten about 90% of her food. Yeah!

As soon as we went outside, all eyes were on them. Sierra was so happy, and everyone noticed. They told her she looked happy, and it was very nice to see her feeling so much better. The staff and the patients had all noticed her behavior lately, either by direct interaction or indirect contact. They watched her in the gym doing her therapy, and they watched her throw the ball with us outside, all the while encouraging her, telling her how proud they were of her and how much of an inspiration she was to all of them.

Morke held her hand for the short drive to the ice-cream parlor. She was still afraid of cars, but he calmed her down and told her he would be right there with her. She kept her head down most of the ride and had to wear her sunglasses because her eyes were so light sensitive, but she did it without freaking out. When we got there, she had a big smile on her face. I asked her if she was happy, and the smile on her face said it all. Her heart was finally happy. We couldn't stay very long because she couldn't handle much stimulation, and she got very tired, but she earned her date, and she was so proud of herself for her accomplishment. When we returned, she went straight to her bed to take a nap, and Morke was right by her side.

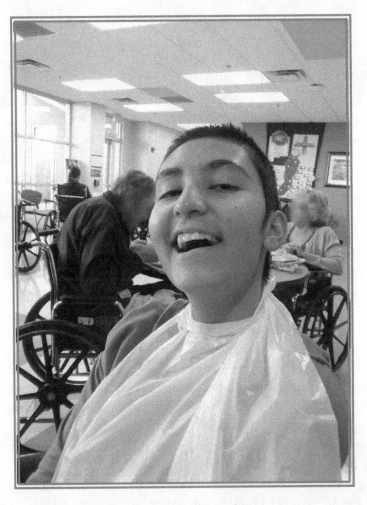

"See, Mommy, I'm happy!"

October 14, 2017

PM update on day 51 of Sierra's journey... She started her day off pretty well. She ate a decent breakfast, and by lunchtime, she started getting a fever. We decided she needed to rest for a while because of the fever and the fact that she didn't sleep well last night. By lunchtime her appetite was even worse than breakfast, so she didn't eat much at all. Then dinner came and she wouldn't eat anything and the nausea started again. We believe she is sad because she knows Morke has to leave tomorrow. We hope that when he leaves it doesn't put her back in the pitfall again. There was no therapy today so she just got to enjoy visitors and enjoy her last day with Morke. Some friends from the Lodge came up to see her, but she had no interest in them because she just wasn't feeling well. We hope that she's not getting a UTI again because it really knocks her off her game.

We had dinner with the family in the cafeteria but it was obvious that she was feeling worse. Her nurse gave her nausea medication in the hopes that it would help her eat. It didn't work for her appetite but it did help her to relax somewhat. After dinner, we left her in the very good hands of Morke so they could spend their last night together alone. He's been trying to prepare her for his departure and she appeared to be okay with it, until tonight when reality hit. I think between her head, her tummy, and him leaving tomorrow, it's too much for her to handle. We pray that whatever she feels, we can get her through it and she doesn't stop eating again because the tube feedings are very hard on her. We need her to keep eating so she can reach the critical seven-day point. If she gets there, she will finally get that dang tube out of her belly. Tomorrow will be four days, but she needs to get to seven days of eating well before her doctor will even consider taking it out. This is so important because she pulls on it because it is so uncomfortable for her and then it gets infected, but she is incapable of understanding the whole process yet so we encourage her to eat as much as possible. I bribe her, I coerce her, I do whatever I can think of to try to get her to eat, to no avail. We pray this will not last and she doesn't quit eating again. So when you pray for her tonight, please pray that she starts eating again. Thank you, all, and goodnight for now. #TeamBdog

We knew she was hungry, but we didn't know why she wouldn't eat. She wasn't capable of telling us what was wrong. She rubbed her stomach with a sad face, so we assumed her tummy was hurting. She had just started using her voice to communicate, but still relied on her notebook to do most of her communication. She also pulled on her catheter, and blood ended up in the bag, so that may also be a reason why she was not eating very well. The fever told us she had an infection somewhere, but it could be from multiple places. It was a change of seasons, so it could be from that, or it could be from pulling on her catheter or from the tube in her stomach because she pulled on that, too, and it got infected on the outside, so it very well could be causing an infection on the inside as well. Because she was incapable of articulating anything, this was all speculation, so her doctors had to give her a broad spectrum antibiotic.

October 15, 2017

To anyone who saw the picture of Sierra and Morke, please do not repost it. It was a mistake that it was posted, and we are trying to protect her privacy. When the day comes that she decides she wants to post her picture, we will. Until then, please do not post pictures of her. Thank you for understanding. #TeamBdog

My friend came up to the hospital to see Sierra and to see Morke before he left. He took pictures. Apparently, I failed to tell him not to post them. My niece called me to tell me that he had posted them, and I blew a lid. I immediately called him and told him to take it down. I feel very strongly about this. I thought I made it clear to everyone that we were not posting any pictures of her until she gave us the green light to do so.

Pm update on day 52 of Sierra's journey... She started her day off fairly well. We have reminded her multiple times that today is the day that Morke has to leave because she forgets so often. She is very sad, but she is talking now. She uses her voice to communicate now. And boy oh boy does she have a lot to say.

Unfortunately, she is also confused because of the stage her brain is in. She believes there is a man underneath her bed and he wants help. Then she tells me he is in the bathroom and he needs help. While we were in the cafeteria eating dinner, she heard him choking and wondered why no one would help him. We don't know if she has a connection to the other side because of the connections her brain is making now, or if this is just her brain confusing her. But it sure seems real to her, and very scary to us. We don't want her to die, and we don't want her to have connections to the other side because it's terrifying to her. She was talking to me about the two other times she has been here at this hospital, which hasn't happened. Also, time, as in past, present, and future are very confusing to her as well. We pray that this stage passes quickly because it is so hard watching our baby girl suffer so badly.

On a lighter note, Morke made it back to school safely. He got her to talk and eat again and made her promise to continue after he left, and she promised that she would. Now if she remembers, that would be great. For now she is talking to everyone, and that is beautiful. She finally found her voice which is great because now she can tell us how she feels and what she thinks. She can tell us if she scared or mad, or if she's in pain and how badly she hurts. In essence, she can communicate everything she wants and feels, and that is such a gift to her and to all of our family. #TeamBdog

This stage was terrifying not only to her but to us as well. The man that she said was in her room was so real to her, so when she told me he was in the room or in the bathroom or under her bed, I had to look to ease her mind. I told her that there was no one there, but she insisted that he was. She told me he was begging for help and no one would help him. She went into specifics and told me that he was in here because he had knee surgery. She woke me up several times a night and told me that he needed help. When we went to the cafeteria today to have lunch, she kept telling me that he was in there, crying out for help. She asked me why no one would help him. Then she told me that he was choking, and she yelled at the staff to help him, but they didn't know what to do because there wasn't anyone there. She wanted me to help him because he was crying out in pain and he needed help.

I tried to explain to her that I didn't see him, and she got mad at me. I had to get up every time she heard him and check under the bed, in the closet, and in her bathroom. It was so real to her, and she was mad at me because I didn't see or hear him. This stage, by far, was the scariest stage she had been in. I felt so helpless. We are going to have a neuropsychiatrist come see her; hopefully, she could help her or at least give us some tools so that we could help her through this stage. So far, all of her stages lasted three to ten days, so we were hoping this was one of the three-day stages and it passed quickly.

October 16, 2017

> PM update on day 53 of Sierra's journey... She is back on track as far as her eating most of her food. One thing I have learned since the accident is that every stage is rewarding, scary, happy, sad, heartbreaking, and almost unbearable at times. But through it all, it is progress. She is at Rancho Level 5, going into Level 6. This is great news, but both stages include confusion, and that is the heartbreaking part.
>
> Now that she is talking, we have found out just how true that is. She hears people that tell her they have died here and they won't leave her alone. She can't rest peacefully at all because she wakes up begging them to leave her alone. I try to explain to her that her brain is healing and confusion is all a part of her getting better even if it doesn't feel like it to her. Our talks don't help much because it is very real to her. She sometimes thinks that Morke is hurt or dead, so we video chat with him so that she can see that he is okay and she can actually talk to him with her voice now. Everyone here is very happy for her now that she found her voice, they love to hear her talk, and it's really big news around the rehab. The staff and patients all know she is talking now and they are all truly happy for her, as are all of our family members.
>
> She is still sad about Morke leaving, but she said she understands that he is building a future

for them. She is working very hard at all of her therapies even though she is not sleeping well. So she literally drags herself through them, but gets them done.

Her speech therapist was exhilarated when she came in today and heard Sierra's voice for the first time. Then her physical therapist came in and said she also heard the great news and asked her to talk. When she heard her voice, she jumped up and down with joy hearing her talk, she was actually on the verge of tears she was so happy. They are truly invested in her recovery here. We hope and pray that her next step to the rehab in El Paso will prove to be just as good as the staff here at this hospital.

Her projected discharge date is October 18th but we are trying to get authorization to stay until the 25th. Her dad and I, along with her team of doctors and therapists believe this is a pivotal moment that we need to get her through before she has another huge adjustment in her life, so hopefully the insurance will authorize her for another week.

Tomorrow will be day six for consistently eating and we're shooting for Thursday to be the day she will get that dang tube out of her stomach. Goodnight and thank you all for your continued prayers. We appreciate all of you taking time to pray for our baby girl. #TeamBdog

This stage was so incredibly hard. It was hard on her because she was hearing voices that were talking to her from beyond the grave. She believed with every ounce of her being that they were trying to get her to help them. She woke up several times a night, begging me to help them, to make them stop, to ask them to please leave her alone. As her mom, I was so heartbroken that I couldn't fix this for her. When she woke me up at night, telling me that they were screaming at her to help them, I had to look in the bathroom, in the closet, and under the bed, trying in vain to find someone I didn't see. I wholeheartedly believe she heard them and she saw them, but I didn't. So while looking for them, I told them to leave my baby girl alone. I told them that they were not welcome here. I actually begged them because they were scaring her so badly. I tried to reason with someone I couldn't see. I told them that she was trying to heal and that they were scaring her. She couldn't help them because her brain was damaged, and she couldn't concentrate on anything but her healing. Then I realized I was talking to the wall, the door, and the bed, but at least it puts her mind at ease for the moment.

On a brighter note, when her therapists came in after the weekend, they heard she was talking now, so they all came in and asked her to talk to them. They literally jumped up and down with exhilaration. They told her she had a beautiful voice, and they were so happy she was using it now. Then they went into therapist mode and told her that she may not use her notebook anymore to communicate. She had to use her voice to let them know what she wanted now, so Sierra smiled and agreed to their request.

October 17, 2017

> PM update on day 54 of Sierra's journey… She started and ended her day with confusion and fear. Fear that everyone she loves is either hurt or dead. She's having a hard time remembering even the simplest tasks. Such as putting her shoes on or standing on her own. She thinks she still cannot stand up on her own, and if she does, she'll fall. Today she told me she doesn't know how to stand. I have to remind her of the things she has already learned again. When I walk in the room she says, "I remember you, you're my Mommy." I tell her, "Yes I am!" I say this with a very grateful heart and a smile on my face. When she sees

people that she encounters every day, she says, "I remember you." The voices are not as predominant today. Today she struggles with forgetfulness more than the voices. The times when she did mention them today, I told her that they're not real that it's just her brain healing. This is one of the stages she has to go through to redevelop her brain and make new connections. I make her repeat it over and over again.

We had a Neuro Psychiatrist come in to talk to her about the voices. She told us that she has an electrical storm going on in her brain right now, which made perfect sense. But then she proceeded to tell us that we need to put her on antipsychotic medications...for a year! I really wanted to tell her to "F" off, but I refrained and explained to her that we are not putting her on anymore medications until we know for fact that this isn't going to pass. I explained to her that she has gone through so many stages in her recovery, and we believe this is one more scary stage that she will surpass. Then she decided to look at Sierra and tell her that she would continue to be like this for two to five years. I about jumped out of my chair to strangle her. Instead, I explained to her that Sierra has overcome every obstacle that has been put in front of her, and she will overcome this one as well, and I made sure Sierra heard me.

I couldn't believe she would say that in front of her. I then asked her where she gets her information. And she told me, "From reading statistics." I told her, "My information is absolute, and she is the amazing young woman right in front of you!" She should still be in the ICU in Albuquerque, but instead she is walking with help, she is eating, breathing, and her cognitive development is way beyond what the medical professionals expected it to be. I am amazed and appalled that someone so intelligent can be so ignorant. Needless to say, Sierra will not be taking antipsychotic medications, and we will never allow that woman to talk to our baby girl again! We will get her through this stage, just like we have helped her through every stage she's been through to get this far. She will prevail! Goodnight, all, and thank you for your prayers. #TeamBdog

Today was a very tough day for her and I both. Last night, I went outside, and when I came back in, she asked me, "Who are you?"

I wanted to cry so badly, but instead, I told her, "I'm your mama."

She looked very confused and stared at me as if she couldn't comprehend what I was saying. I told her about how she got in a car accident, we were in the hospital, and I had been with her since day one. We talked about everything she had been through and why she had tubes protruding out of her body. I literally saw the look of confusion leave her face, and she smiled at me and said, "Oh, yeah, you're my mommy."

I smiled back and said, "Yes, I am."

So, this morning, when she woke up, she looked at me and told me, "You're my Mommy," and we both smiled. It was such a relief to know that she remembered me again.

That was such a fear of mine when she got in the accident, and the doctors told us they didn't know if she would remember us, and that hurt my heart to the core. So when she did remember us, it was such an incredible relief. Now she was forgetting things that we thought she was already past, but the brain is so complex, and it was rewiring itself, so we had no idea what to expect from day to day. When we were getting her ready today, she told me that she didn't know how to stand or how to tie her shoes. It seemed as though she was digressing, and it was so heartbreaking to watch.

The voices were not as predominant today, but they were still there. The neuropsychiatrist that came to talk to her also came with high recommendations from the staff here, so we felt very good about bringing her in to help our baby girl. When she started talking to us, I felt really good about it. She made perfect sense that Sierra's brain was going through an electrical storm. On the other hand, when she started talking about antipsychotic medications and the fact if she gets on them, she can't get off them for at least two years, I felt my blood pressure start to rise. I explained to her that we were trying to get her off the medications, not add to the list, besides the fact that every stage she had gone through to this point had only lasted three to ten days. She was not happy that I had my own opinion about her diagnosis, but I didn't care.

I have stepped on so many toes since August 24, and this was just one more person that I had pissed off, fighting for our baby girl. When she looked at Sierra and told her that she will probably stay like this and hear voices for up to five years or maybe for the rest of her life, it took everything I had not to punch her in the face and shut her up. I did refrain from punching her, but I did tell her to get out of her room and to never come back. Then I made it very clear to Sierra's medical staff that she was never allowed to speak to our daughter again and proceeded to tell Sierra that she had no idea what she was talking about. I told her that this was just another stage she had to go through to get her brain better, and I could see the relief in her eyes.

October 18, 2017

> PM update on day 55 of Sierra's journey...
> Great news is the voices are gone. That definitely
> deserves a happy dance. Now that her brain is
> awake and she can talk, we are realizing just who
> she really is and understand where she is in her
> healing process. She is able to articulate what she

is thinking now, and it is scary. She thinks about the accident. For some reason she also thinks that she got a defibrillator to restart her heart, but that didn't happen. I explained to her that the nurses in the ICU had to do knuckle rubs on her chest to keep her stimulated because there was a very good chance for her to slip into oblivion and never come back to us. She was so close to death when she was on life support, that they knuckle rubbed her chest so hard that it gave her very big bruises. It is an assumption on our part, but it makes sense that's where this memory stems. She's afraid that her whole family is dead, and Morke is dead as well. She asks us fifty times a day if Morke is okay, if he's hurt, if he's alive. She has learned to text him or calls him on her own now, which is nice for her to feel that freedom and some sense of independence.

Her feeding tube is really bothering her but she can't get it out because we still have to push her to eat at least 50% of her food every time she eats, which is a huge task. We try bringing her food from the outside. We will do anything to get her to eat without a fight. She told me that she wanted beef-a-roni and pasta salad, so I went home to make her some. When I came back with them, she had forgotten that she wanted them and wouldn't eat. She wants her tube out so badly, and we want that for her so badly, but she can't make the connection that she has to eat to get it out. The tube feedings are making her sick to her stomach, which makes it so she is too queasy to eat. It's a circle of heartbreak that she doesn't have the capability of reasoning out in her new brain. We asked her if she could have anything she wanted to eat, what would it be. She said Mom's beef-a-roni and pasta salad, so I will continue to make it for her in the hopes that she will remember long enough to eat it. Until tomorrow… Goodnight, all, and thank you. #TeamBdog

We were exhilarated to know that the voices had gone away. That was one of the hardest stages we had to help her through. It was terrifying for her and so very sad for everyone that had the misfortune of seeing her go through it. The news about the voices being gone brought some light to the day. On the other hand, she still put up a fight to eat. We had to prompt her for every bite of food she took. Every time she took a bite, she asked, "Is that enough?" After a few bites, she refused to eat anymore. We tried to reason with her, but that part of her new brain had not developed yet. I was continually taking her hand off her tube. She pulled on it and made it bleed, she rubbed the insertion point all the time, and it got infected, then it bothered her more—and the vicious cycle continues.

October 19, 2017

PM update on day 56 of Sierra's journey… She started off her day very sleepy, actually she has been very sleepy these past few days. Her brain is healing and sometimes it makes her sleepier than others. So, because of this, I have been letting her get off her schedule and sleep more than the half an hour that they allow her. It seems to be helping to get her through the day much better. She is very light and sound sensitive so she has to spend most of her time in her room. When she eats in her room it increases her food intake, but it isn't suggested that she stay in her room all the time. Today she actually ate 100% of her dinner, which hasn't happened since she started eating a couple weeks ago.

She is still confused about many things, and forgets a lot, but she is progressing in every aspect. Even the heartbreaking process she goes through is progress for her, and it's very hard to keep that in mind for all of us. We watch her pain, her fears, her attempt to accomplish the simplest tasks that aren't simple to her, and her struggle to get her life back. We are in awe of the fight this little human being is showing. Speaking of progress, she has been moved up to the Rancho Level 6! In just a few weeks she has jumped up the scale two levels, she is so amazing. Every one of her medical staff is in awe of our little fighting machine.

She wants me to tell you all that it's okay to go home because everything is all set up here. And also, thank you for all of your prayers. "Thank God!" This has become her statement. Those are words straight from her mouth. She wanted me to read what I posted tonight and that was what she wanted to add to my post. That's really cool, she's starting to take interest in her daily posts, which is also progress, and we love progress.

We particularly love it when the progress doesn't break our hearts. Goodnight All and Thank you again for all your prayers. We love and appreciate all of you that take time out of your busy days to read and comment on her posts, I read them to her now and it seems to uplift her. #TeamBdog

After her defiant, aggressive stage, she was put on a behavior modification plan. Part of that plan was for her to only get a half hour nap during the day. I really don't know how beneficial that is because it is the best time for her brain to heal. The doctors in Albuquerque told us that when she came out of her coma. They said to let her sleep because it was the only time that her brain had nothing else to do but heal. While she was going through the stage that she was hearing voices, she was not sleeping very well during the night, besides the fact that with a TBI and after being in a coma, the brain gets confused and the sleep pattern gets off track. So she wouldn't get enough sleep during the night and would drag herself through her therapies during the day, so her team got together and devised a behavior modification plan in the hopes that she got back on track with her sleeping pattern.

Now that she was taking interest in her posts and reading them on her own occasionally, I had to be careful of what I was writing. We loved the fact that she wanted to add to her posts and everyone could get more of a sense of where her brain was and how it thought and developed.

October 20, 2017

> PM update on day 57 of Sierra's journey… Today was a fantastic day! Today she got f——g tube out. This is the first tube that she knew was in her body, and she had control over getting it out. It hurt her every day, and she continuously told us how badly it hurt and how much she wanted it out. Before she could talk, she would pull on it and point to it, she would write in her notebook how much she wanted it out and how much it hurt. This was such a humongous hurdle for her to overcome, and she finally accomplished it. We are all so incredibly happy and proud of her. The wound site is still causing a lot of pain, but at least now it will begin to subside.
>
> She throws the "F" bomb quite frequently, which I found out today, that it was actually a very common word for her. We didn't know because she always had respect for her dad and I so she never cursed around us, she just saved

it for her friends. She walked the whole way to the gym today. Her physical therapist guided her, but she made it the whole way. She held the rails, but she finally did it. After working hard at physical therapy, she walked back to her room as well. What a great accomplishment for her. She is showering herself now, with very little guidance from her occupational therapist or me. This is another great accomplishment. She is jumping hurdles every day, and it is thrilling to watch her drive and passion no matter what obstacles are in her way.

Her whole softball team from Las Vegas came to see her today, and she enjoyed them very much. They pulled up in the bus and I met them at the door to explain what they need to expect when they see her. She is not the same young woman that they knew, but she is still our little Sierra. It brought tears to many of the staff members and patients eyes. Watching her hang out with her team again was a beautiful moment in time that I will never forget. We all went outside on the patio and they hung out and told stories and laughed and Sierra had a constant smile on her face. It was incredibly hard on some of her teammates to see her so they would have to excuse themselves to breakdown for bit, compose themselves, and come back to enjoy Sierra's company. The staff and patients watched all of them from the cafeteria window with happy tears in their eyes, along with all of us. Today was a great day, and we are thankful. #TeamBdog

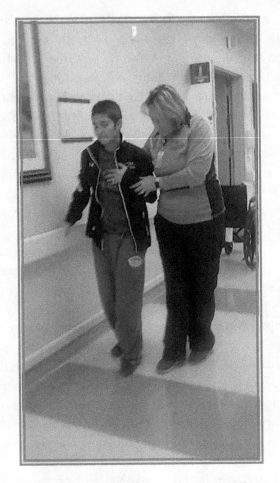

Sierra and her physical therapist, Lisa, walking
to the patio to visit her team.

Today, when the doctor came in, she asked Sierra if she wanted
to get that tube out of her tummy. She lit up, gave us a big smile, and
said, "Yes, please!" Then she proceeded to flip it off, which made us
all laugh. Taking it out was not easy on her because, apparently, there
were several different kinds of feeding tubes. The one that was in
her belly turned out to be the one that had a coil on the inside, and
taking it out proved to be more difficult than anticipated. But, when
all was said and done, it was out, and that was the point. The hole in

the stomach closed immediately, but the one on the outside would take some time to heal.

Her coach called me to tell me that they were on their way back home, coming from El Paso, and asked if they could stop by to see her. I talked to her therapists, and they said it would be okay for her to skip her therapies so she could visit with her team. They drove up in the bus and immediately caught everyone's attention. I quickly prepped them as to what to expect, how she looked, and the fact that they could only speak positive words around her. I also asked that if they had to cry, please excuse themselves so she didn't see. Several of them did break down when they saw her because she was not the young woman they once knew. While they walked through the halls of the hospital on their way to Sierra's room, they caught everyone's attention, so when we went outside to meet them, many of the staff and patients watched them from the cafeteria window with happy tears in their eyes.

It was so emotional and such a happy occasion that it brought tears to everyone that saw them. Her physical therapist helped her walk all the way to them so they could see how far she had progressed. This was the first time many of them had seen her since the accident, so it was very sad for them, but for us that have watched her progress, it was very inspiring.

October 21, 2017

> AM post on day 58 of Sierra's journey… This post is directly from the mouth of Sierra. She will dictate and I will write, so here goes: "Please come see me today because it's visitor's day and I have no therapy today. My Girls from high school, and Morke. All my family too. Thank God and the family for all the prayers because I wouldn't be here without them. Thank you and I love you. Can't wait to see you, and please be very quiet because my ears and my head hurts, and my knee hurts, and my butt hurt when I was showering.

And Morke because I love him so much. Thank God!" #TeamBdog

PM post on day 58 of Sierra's journey… She is extremely happy her feeding tube is out, but it still hurts her very badly. Her post this morning really worked. She had visitors all day long. When some left, others came. She had a happy day today, which in turn, gives all of us a happy day as well. Everyone was so thrilled and teary eyed about her team coming to see her yesterday. Everyone here gets excited for each stage she overcomes, and they love to watch her progress. She is walking with guidance more and more every day. She chooses to walk rather than use her walker or her wheelchair more and more with each passing day. Her wheelchair is becoming more of a tool of the past, if she needs help walking; she chooses her walker rather than using her wheelchair most of the time.

I can reason things out with her more as the days pass, she just forgets five minutes later, but it is still progress. She is very afraid of cars. She doesn't want to see them or hear them, so when we go for walk, we have to stay in the back of the hospital, away from the road. This is just another stage she will surpass, because last week when we went to the ice cream parlor she was okay. Maybe because we were with Morke and she felt more secure. This may not be such an issue if we weren't planning on leaving to the El Paso rehab, and it could be as soon as Monday. So we hope and pray that she will get past this stage before she is transferred to her next step. If not, there are always drugs I suppose. We hate to drug her up, but we hate to let her live in fear more than we hate the drugs. She wants me to read her posts to her now, so we start her day reading the night's prior posts and comments. They seem to be very uplifting to her and they make her smile. Thank you to everyone who came to see her today, you really made her day. It was wonderful to see her have such a good day. Goodnight, all. #TeamBdog

We started every day at 6:30 a.m. I woke her up, got her ready, and went to the cafeteria for breakfast. It was still somewhat of a chore to get her to eat her food. I reminded her that she no longer had the tube in her belly, so it was very important for her to eat all of her food. Sometimes I had to threaten her that the doctors would have to put her feeding tube back in if she didn't eat. Actually, it was not really a threat. That is exactly what would happen if she didn't eat. She would also have to stay here and not move on to the next step of her recovery because the rehab in El Paso would not accept her if she had to be fed through her tube. Besides that, if it does get put back in, it had to stay in for at least six weeks. I explained this to her every time we sat down to eat. She put up a fuss and wouldn't eat, and then I reminded her of the tube and how much she despised it. I asked her if she wanted to go through all that again, and she got a look of fear on her face and shook her head vigorously no! So she reluctantly ate her food.

Her post brought a lot of visitors all day long. Everyone was very understanding of all the "rules" they had to follow to be able to visit. For example, you couldn't talk very loud or wear the color red; she couldn't have too much stimulation, so only a couple of visitors at a time were all she could handle; and we are only allowed to talk positively around her. I was so thankful that people were so understanding about what it took to be able to visit her. It didn't seem to bother anyone, and we were very appreciative that everyone understood. Because of this, she felt so loved all day long. Too many of her days were just she and I along with all of her therapies. So to get so many visitors made her feel loved. She had a continuous smile on her face all day and all night. It was so beautiful.

At the end of the day, before we went to bed, I asked her if she was happy that she got so many visitors. She not only nodded her head yes, but she told me with her voice as well. It was truly an awesome feeling as we drifted off to sleep.

She was so well-known here. All of the patients and even their visitors noticed her, encouraged her, rooted for her, and continually told her how proud they were of her. As she became more aware of where she was and what was happening around her, she was able to interact with people more. In the cafeteria, she wheeled herself around and greeted people. She showed them the hole in her stomach where the feeding tube used to be. She showed them her scars. She hugged them when they looked like they are having a bad day, and she smiled that captivating smile. She wrote notes to patients, telling them they could do it. She was proud of them and told them not to give up. Even in her half dazed state, she was an inspiration.

October 22, 2017

Good morning post directly from Sierra: Thank you for everything and thank God I made it this far. I'm sad because I remember the accident, kinda. I remember there was glass in my foot. I stood up in the shower today and washed my whole body all by myself, and I remembered I needed to breathe. I remember I need water to live, and I remember so much now. Oh my goodness! Thank you to my visitors. #TeamBdog

PM update on day 59 of Sierra's journey... She had another really good day today. She talked to one of the Lodge members that is also an inpatient here. This patient is refusing to eat so Sierra talked to her and asked her to please eat so she doesn't have to get a feeding tube in her stomach. She proceeded to go into the whole story of how much it hurts and she doesn't want her to feel that pain, and she had to show her the hole in her stomach where she just got f———g tube taken out.

After that, she wheeled herself over to another patient who also has a feeding tube in her stomach and they had about a fifteen minute conversation about how much they hate the feeding tube and how much it hurts. Then she made her rounds in the cafeteria and said good morning to the patients and asked them how they were doing. Our little social butterfly is coming back to us, and it's so great.

Her Las Vegas softball team came back to see her on their way back to school. She remembered that they were coming back on their way home, and she had another really good visit with them. They laughed and reminisced about the shenanigans they pulled during their college life. I find out more and more about her college life the more I talk to them. Oh boy! They have had a lot of good times and took full advantage of the college life.

Anthony, Lee and my grand babies brought pumpkins up so we can carve them before she has to be transferred to El Paso. Krystal helped her, well more like Krystal carved her pumpkin while Sierra watched. It was a really nice family time. It brought back some form of normalcy to our lives. And it was nice to be able to keep that tradition going even though she is in the hospital.

She always thinks that people are talking about her. She thinks they are laughing at her about the accident. We explain to her that they are not talking about her; they are just having conversations with each other. But in her mind they are talking about her and the accident. There are a couple of men that are patients here and they are both from Silver City. They always eat together and just hang out together and talk. Well Sierra is convinced that they are talking about her and laughing at her because she was in the accident and had to have her head shaved. She says that they think she's a boy. We explain to her that she is wrong, that no one thinks she is a boy and they surely aren't laughing at her because she was in the accident. Well, that falls on deaf ears. So she tells us that they are f——g annoying and flips them off. One of them looked at her as if to say, "What did I do?" So she proceeds to throw some of the pumpkin carvings at him and flip him off again. She tried to do it again, and we stopped her, so she tried grabbing anything off the table to throw at him, so we had to clear the table.

I went over to explain to them the stage she is in and they were very understanding. They wanted me to tell her that they aren't talking about her and they don't think it's funny at all. She didn't seem to care much about what I was saying, because in her mind they are talking about her. After we were done, we just sat outside and were talking when Sierra started shaking her head. I asked her what was wrong. She told me that those men are annoying and if they don't shut up, she is going to go f——k them up. We couldn't help but burst out laughing. This stage is somewhat funny. It's still terrible what she is going through, but some things are very funny. She flips off any one who shows any sort of authority and we just can't help but chuckle at some of her reactions to people.

She and Krystal with the pumpkin "they" carved.

After her college softball team left, she walked back to her room with almost no guidance from me. When we got back to her room, some of her old teammates from her high school softball team came to visit. It was nice, it sounded like a bunch of teenage girls having a great time. I miss that sound, the sound I took for granted before, and even found to be somewhat annoying before the accident, now

I love it. I love that she is still here and she can just
be one of the girls, doing girl things.

Tomorrow we find out if we're going to El
Paso or staying until Wednesday. The insurance
wants to fight over two days. We are prepared to
go if they decide to deny her those two days, but
we hope that we can stay until Wednesday. When
I know, you all will know. Also, thank you for all
the comments to her on her posts, they are very
uplifting to her. Goodnight, all. #TeamBdog

When her team came back into the hospital, all eyes were on
them. Everyone greeted them with a smile and told them how they
were happy to see them again. We all witnessed the first time they
came and how it made Sierra so happy. Everyone here watched over
her and continually asked how she was doing. They wanted to know
if they could do anything to see that beautiful smile and wanted to
sit with her during meals. It's like they all took her under their wings
and watched over her and celebrated each stage she surpassed.

Now that she was in the inappropriate stage, they all understood that they may be the next victim of "the finger," and they were
all okay with it. When she told us they were laughing at her because
she was in the accident, I was able to tell them, and they went directly
to Sierra and told her how it was a tragic accident and that it made
them very sad to see her there. Many of them tried to ease her mind,
and I spent a lot of time explaining to patients and visitors that she
couldn't control what she was doing, that it was only the stage her
brain was in. Everyone was very understanding and tried to console
her the best they could.

When the two men from Silver City came out onto the patio
where we were carving pumpkins, she immediately rolled her eyes
and started telling us that they are talking about her and they thought
it was funny that she was in the accident. I don't know why she had
specifically picked these two men, but she got irate as soon as she
saw them. She started throwing the "F" bomb continuously. Today,
when we were carving the pumpkins, we put the insides on the table

as we cleaned them out. She decided to take them and throw them at the Silver City men. It hit one of them, and he looked back at us, and she flipped him off. He had a puzzled look on his face; he didn't understand why she had singled him out.

I apologized, and he went back to having his conversation with his friend. Well, this really pissed her off, and she was sure they were talking about her, which they weren't, but she refused to believe us when we told her that they were friends and they're just talking about how they used to work with each other. So she proceeded to roll her eyes and tell us that if they didn't shut the "F" up, she was going to go over there and "F" them up. We tried in vain not to laugh, but it was so funny we couldn't help it. We tried to discipline her for it, but it was very hard when we are laughing at her behavior.

October 23, 2017

> PM update on day 60 of Sierra's journey… She has decided to help me with her update, so here goes… She wants me to tell you all that she is eating really well now and that she misses her family very much. She took a shower all by herself and walked to physical therapy by herself as well. She worked on her knee because it hurts. She graduated out of the diners club because she is eating so well so her speech therapist doesn't have to sit with her while she eats anymore. She wants me to tell you that the nurse has to check her pulse all the time because she is alive. Today in occupational therapy she put colored pegs in the holes and it was hard but she got it. And to thank God for everything and everyone here that helps her. We go to the El Paso rehabilitation hospital on Wednesday and she is very excited because she wants to learn to drive again. And now she wants to go to bed because she is tired, so goodnight everyone and God bless. #TeamBdog

The fact that she was eating was such great news because she was on the verge of getting the tube back in her belly. Now that she was eating, I brought in the food that she has always loved, most of which includes pasta. The pasta would help her gain more weight as long as she continued to eat. She was not very impressed with the selection she had here, so I continually asked her what she wanted so that when I got home, I could make her food that she enjoys. Now that she was eating, we realized her tastes had changed. She liked foods that she didn't used to like, and she disliked foods that she used to like. It was a learning process, but we would learn her new tastes just as we would learn who the new Sierra was with her new brain.

October 24, 2017

> PM update of day 61 of Sierra's journey… Today, she was a social butterfly. When she was in the cafeteria for breakfast, she was socializing with everyone. She stopped at each table and talked to the patients. She told them that she finally got the tube out of her tummy, hugged all of the staff members, and thanked them for everything they have done for her. Then blurts out her favorite sentiment… "Thank God!" She thanks God for everything and tells me "Thank God, Mommy." I tell her that I do every day; I thank him for bringing you back to us, and for giving you the passion and drive to fight so hard to get your life back. I also thank everyone who has prayed for her and continues to pray for her. For they have brought her back to us. Whatever we get back of her, we are thankful. She has come a long way, but still has a very long road of healing ahead of her.
>
> She is still in the inappropriate stage, so tonight at dinner, she saw the same two men. The ones that she thinks are laughing at her because of the accident and because she looks like a boy.

She flipped them and off and told them she is going to "F" them up because they are annoying. Every time she tells us something or someone is annoying, we know that they are going to get the finger. Those are the times when you know you should discipline your child, but it's so darn funny, you just can't. I have talked to the men on multiple occasions explaining her condition and how she can't help what she's doing.

She has no filter to tell her what is considered to be acceptable by society and what is not. She is so genuine right now and what she feels towards anything or anyone is apparent in her words and actions. Since everyone here knows her and have watched her progress, they accept her and the stage she is in. They don't take offense to her flipping them off anymore, they just tell her hi and it's nice to see you talking and getting better all the time. We're grateful they just dismiss her inappropriate behavior.

We leave for El Paso tomorrow around 11am is what we've been told. You all are welcome to see her off if you'd like. We have been trying to prepare her for this for the past week. Anything out of her normal schedule can really throw her off and set her back, so we are approaching this as gently as possible. She says she is ready for the move and knows it is going to teach her to be independent. She is still afraid of cars, so we're not sure how the ride over there will go, but we will do our best to make sure she is comfortable and feels safe and secure. Her doctor said that she can give her drugs if she gets too anxious about it, so we feel better about transporting her. If you do decide to come see her off, please don't wear red, it makes her cry. Thank you, all. #TeamBdog

When she started wheeling herself around the cafeteria and talking to the patients, it made my heart so happy. She was coming back to us slowly but surely. She had a smile for everyone and encouraged them to eat so they didn't have to get a tube in their belly. She encouraged them to keep fighting; she empathized with them about their struggles and hugged them when necessary.

By lunchtime, she was back to being annoyed with everything and everyone. So when the two men from Silver City came out onto the patio where we enjoyed lunch, it sent her into a frenzy. She wanted to go beat them up because she still believed they thought it's funny that she was in her accident, and she said they thought she was a boy. None of this was true, but in her mind, it was, so we constantly told her that it was just her brain telling her things that weren't true. She just rolled her eyes at us as if to tell us that she knew more than we did. We were very thankful that everyone was so understanding about her situation, so when she flipped them off or said ugly things to them, they handled it very well. They told her how proud they were of her and that she had a beautiful voice and love that she was talking now.

While we are all excited for her to take the next step in her recovery, we are also very sad to leave this hospital because they had an extraordinary staff here. This had been the best medical experience we had ever known. Every one of her doctors and therapists had shown exemplary service to our baby girl. After leaving the ICU in Albuquerque and the lack of care she received on the fifth floor, and then coming here to the highest standards for patients we had ever experienced, it was somewhat scary for her to be moved to a new facility. The goal for her next step was to teach her to be independent. Her goal was for her to be able to drive again, so we'd have to keep an open mind and not expect that she would get the care that she received here at the Rehab in Las Cruces. We had been preparing her for this for several weeks, so we hoped her transition went as smoothly as possible.

October 25, 2017

PM update on day 62 of Sierra's journey... We made it to El Paso. They gave her such an amazing send off. We have seen many people leave the rehab and the available staff goes out in the hall as they are leaving to clap for them as they head to their next step in recovery. This was nothing like that. The entire staff and many of the patients of the hospital lined the entire foyer, they all wore her shirts, played her fight song, clapped, and cried for her. It was the most amazing send-off we could have hoped for. They all invested themselves into her healing process and it was very obvious that she touched all of their lives. Her therapists made her a plaque with their names and her fight song on it. They took video of her walking with her physical therapist out of the hospital, ready to take her next step in her recovery, tears in their eyes, and a smile on their faces. Before she made it to the door, she stopped and told them she wanted hugs. They all lined up to hug her and wish her the best, and as each one of the staff hugged her, they couldn't hide the tears rolling down their face. They had tears of joy for Sierra, and tears of sadness that she was leaving. Her story is so sad, but she has defied so many odds, that they all feel a sense of accomplishment for her progress, as they should. They are such amazing people, and we are incredibly grateful for each and every one of them. Their goal was for her walk, talk, swallow, and eat before she left this hospital. She accomplished every one of those goals because of every one of them and the time, love, care, understanding, and compassion they invested into her and her recovery. I cannot even begin to state our gratitude towards these people. We can only hope and pray that her next step is just as good.

We got her to the El Paso rehab safely. Jeff drove and she sat in the backseat with her daddy. The windows are tinted very dark and she wore her dark sunglasses so we think it was easier on her, and we only had to stop one time because she got a little scared. We took the back road so she didn't have to travel on the highway. So we just cruised very slowly on the old highway and got her there safely.

The staff in the El Paso rehab said that we could decorate her room however she wanted so that it feels more like a bedroom rather than a hospital room. I've been decorating for the past three hours, and I am not quite done. We want this to be a very good experience for her and we want her to be as comfortable as possible. She has a lot more freedom here. We get to take her out for ice cream, or the mall if she wants to. We'll probably have to wait on that for a bit, but it's good to know that's an option. She still can't handle very much stimulation at once, but she's getting better with that all the time so we hope it won't be long before she's ready to go out into the world. There is no curfew, but she has to be ready for therapy the next day, so she needs her rest and we can't keep her out too late. She did get sick to her stomach, but we think it may be caused by her nerves, we'll see what happens. She says she likes it so far, and tells us, "Thank God!" She's happy, we're happy! #TeamBdog

Since we got to the rehab in Las Cruces, we had seen so many people leave. The available staff lined up along the hallways and clapped for the person leaving. I had always thought it was such a beautiful sight. Not only that, but the patients had worked hard enough to get themselves better, but the staff took time to recognize their accomplishment. I had truly never seen such care and compassion from any medical facility, and to think that if I had listened to her placement counselor in Albuquerque, we would have never experienced such magnificent care. I feel we would all be indebted to these people for the rest of our lives. The send-off these people gave our baby girl left me speechless. There were so many people in the foyer; there was hardly room for everyone. So many of us were in tears; staff, patients, and family alike were watching such a beautiful event. The smile on everyone's faces said it all. Happy doesn't begin to explain the feeling that everyone in that hallway felt.

When we packed up, her physical therapist came for her because she said she would have her walking out of there, and she wanted the honor of walking out with her. When they came through the doors into the foyer, the look on both of their faces was priceless. Everyone started clapping, and her "Fight Song" was playing over the PA system. Her therapists made her gifts, and the staff gave her cards. It was like she was a star, and they were her fans. After that send-off, I definitely didn't want her to leave. I had tears streaming down my face and was just crying uncontrollably. It was a bittersweet moment in time that I among many other family, friends, and staff members will never forget.

The drive to El Paso was somewhat uneventful. We took the back roads because she was afraid to be on the highway. She sat right next to her dad the whole way while he comforted her. We only had to stop once when we were about halfway there. I was following them, so her dad kept me informed as to how she was doing the whole way. When we stopped, I asked her how she was doing. She seemed really confused and thought that she was okay. We helped her walk around for a bit until she felt she was ready to get on the road again.

When we got to the El Paso rehab, I immediately started decorating her room. We bought her a sheet set and comforter for her bed and filled the walls with all the cards and mementos she had received since the accident. I hung the banner that was made for the benefit softball tournament right above her bed, and, of course, a cross hung right above her head.

October 26, 2017

PM update on day 63 of Sierra's journey… Her first day here was mostly good. She ate breakfast really well. They have a chef here that makes all of the meals for the patients, and she really likes his cooking. It's like having home cooked meals again, and that makes us both happy. They allow me to eat with her the first week so she will feel more comfortable and hopefully not quit eating, which is still a fear we have. We need her to eat regularly without putting up a fight because her medical staff tells her if she doesn't, she will have to get that dang tube back in her belly. Just the thought of it makes her eat pretty well. This afternoon she was nauseated so she missed lunch, but sure made up for it at dinner. She ate every bit of her food tonight.

It seems like such a small advancement, but it is actually her biggest fight at the present moment. After dinner we had homemade éclairs, and oh my, they were delicious. What a difference having a chef as opposed to hospital food. There is also an everyday menu that is available to the patients just in case they don't like what is offered.

She was able to start physical therapy even though her tummy was upset, and her knee was hurting pretty badly, but she pushed through it and worked really hard at her therapy anyways. I have to pick up her medication here. They administer it to her, but I have to pick it all up at the pharmacy. So while I was there picking up her medications, I asked the pharmacist what anti-nausea medication I could give her that won't counteract with what she is already taking. He explained to me that almost all of her medications have a side effect of nausea. Why they didn't prescribe an anti-nausea medication with this knowledge was beyond me. So, again, I had to talk to the doctor and explain my new found information and she decided to go ahead and prescribe an anti-nausea script. I'm not quite sure why I had to bring this to her attention, but the important result is that she now has the medications she needs to give her the best chance to continue her fight.

She has entered a very scary stage. She thinks the cops are after her and that she's going to jail forever. I have to tell her many times throughout the day that they are not after her, and she has not broken the law so there is no reason for the cops to be after her. I explain to her that this is her safe place and the cops are not after her. She tells me, "Thank God!" But then she forgets and I have to reiterate continually throughout the day.

Tonight I walked Jeff outside when he was leaving and when I came back, I saw her in the hallway and one of the techs was putting a blanket around her because she only had a bra and underwear on. I thought she was looking for me because she forgot I was coming back in to stay with her. She also forgets that she's not supposed to walk on her own because she's not quite steady enough to walk without assistance. She actually thought Morke was here and she was looking for him.

Morke is doing really well; he is back to playing baseball and working to get back to

100% as well. They video chat each other almost every night and she carries a picture of the two of them everywhere she goes. Her visiting hours are Monday through Friday from 4pm to 8pm, and weekends from 9am to 8pm. She is settled in and ready for visitors. They said that there are no limits as to how many visitors she can have; it just depends on her tolerance to stimulation as to how many she can have. She said she is ready though and that she looks forward to visitors.

If you do come visit her, please don't wear red. She relates it to blood and it scares her very badly. Her dad and I are the only ones allowed to take her out at this point. This will be trial and error so until we learn what she can tolerate, we have to be with her at all times, especially when she goes out into the world. Thank you for understanding. I have to go now because she is throwing things at me. Goodnight, all. #TeamBdog

I was very happy I talked to the pharmacist. He provided a lot of information on her medications and the fact that a side effect of almost all of them is nausea. Now that they had added anti-nausea medication to her list, we hoped that she would be able to eat without getting sick to her stomach. It was so important for her to eat now that she got the tube out of her belly because it was not an option here. They would not tube-feed her; she had to eat on her own to be here. She was already losing weight, which was somewhat concerning at this point, so I bought a bunch of snacks so that she could have them between meals. Our plan was for her to move forward, and her biggest issue holding her back right now was eating most of her meals. Even though she was nauseous most of the time, she still pushed through with her therapies.

For some reason unknown to us, she thought she was wanted by the police. Every time a staff member walked by her, she said they were coming to arrest her. The only explanation we have for this is that there were so many police officers at the scene of the accident; maybe her brain told her that they were there to arrest her. Otherwise, we have no conceivable idea why she thought that she was going to be arrested. She was afraid all the time and told us that she had to go to jail. It was so sad seeing her like this. I explained to her all the time that she was not wanted by the police that she obeyed the law, and they had no reason to arrest her. It immediately eased her mind, but then she forgot, and we had to go through the whole explanation again. I probably had to explain to her that she was not wanted by the police about twenty times a day. I am thankful that I could ease her mind with an explanation but very sad that she didn't remember, and there was nothing we can do about that. It was where her brain was, and we just had to help her through it.

Now that she was settled in here, she could have visitors, but only after she had finished her therapies for the day because she could only concentrate on one thing at a time, and visitors were too much of a distraction for her. We asked that if people were planning to visit her that they wait for the weekend when she didn't have therapy. Although she enjoyed having her friends here during her therapies, it had proven to be too much for her brain to handle. She related the color red to blood, so when she saw anyone wearing red, she got very scared and cried. She told me there was so much blood, and she thought people were bleeding when she saw them wear red. All of this was trial and error, and unfortunately, the only way we knew what not to do was to do it, and it affected her adversely, but there was no other way. She couldn't predict what she was afraid of without experiencing it, and all of this was a learning experience for us.

October 27, 2017

> PM update on day 64 of Sierra's journey... We are still trying to get accustomed to schedules, rules, and how things work here. The people here appear to be nice, yet standoffish nice, and they are open to listening to me about Sierra. I explained where she is in her mind and how

to deal with each situation as it arises. They are interested in getting to know her so that when I have to leave her in a few days, it won't be such a hard adjustment for her. They have informed me that I can only stay for a week or so because this place is her last step and their goal is to make her independent again, and they feel it is more beneficial for her if I'm not with her 24/7 anymore. It is a very scary thought for me. I have lived with her every day since the accident, and I am her security, her voice, and her advocate. So we don't know how she will react without me, but we have to try.

We are all new to brain injuries and what is best for her, so at this point, we will do what the experts tell us is the best for her. If it has adverse effects on her, we will figure out something else to make it as easy as possible on her. We will do whatever is best for her, and I will give them the benefit of doubt for now, but we will continue to monitor her progress. If there are any indications that it's not working for her, we will change the situation so that it benefits her.

She still thinks that the cops are after her and that they are here to take her to jail forever. So when she sees any of the staff members, she asks them if they are cops and if she's going to jail. She thinks that her family and Morke are dead. She thinks that she is dying and I have to check her pulse multiple times a day. She asks me, "Am I dead?" I tell her that she's not dead, I tell her to look in the mirror and to touch her chest and feel her heart beating and that soothes her for a few minutes until she forgets again, and we have to repeat all the motions again. We check her pulse, feel her heartbeat, feel her breath coming out of her mouth, have her look in the mirror, and try reasoning it out with her.

She writes on her hand, "You can do this!" And also, "There are no cops here!" So she's really trying to do whatever it takes to make herself remember. She is obviously confused, but she's right on task with other things. Her fine motor skills are getting better, but her critical motor skills are lacking. They had to put an alarm on her bed and I am teaching her to pull the nurses string if she needs anything so she doesn't get up on her own.

The thought of me leaving her is really weighing heavily on me at this point. Her dad and I think that she still needs me, and are very weary of leaving her overnight at this point in her recovery. I am only allowed to stay with her until Sunday night, Monday she is on her own. I will be staying here in El Paso for a while so if she needs me, I will be about five minutes away. I've been trying to prepare her for this, but she forgets and she gets scared when I leave. She told me she doesn't want me to leave, and I don't want to leave either, but I have to try to convince her that this is what's best for her. I also need to convince myself as well.

One of the softball parents was gracious enough to get me a motel room to extend my stay here. I'm still not working and money is tight, but I have to do what is best for our baby. If I have to stay out in the parking lot in my truck, I will do that too, but I am not going back to Las Cruces until I know she is okay without me sleeping with her.

Aunt Susan and Uncle Bob got her a phone because we still haven't gotten her phone back

from the police yet. This way she will have a
way to contact me if she needs me, or she just
wants to talk. She has homework over the weekend because there is no therapy over the weekend here. So she has a list of speech and physical
therapies she has to accomplish over the weekend
so she can earn her rewards, such as going for
ice cream and eventually getting passes to come
home for the weekend. Visitors are welcome to
come see her over the weekend, but I have to
reiterate. Please don't wear red. Thank you and
goodnight, all. #TeamBdog

Every day, she and I woke up, and together, we went over what
she had to do for that day. I explained to her where she was and what
the purpose of her being here was. We continually went over the fact
that I would no longer be spending the night with her because she
was here to learn independence again. We didn't think she was ready
to be on her own, but we were willing to give it a try as long as I felt
she was getting the care and attention she needed. I taught the staff
about her, what her needs were, what her fears were, and how to
counteract her fears. I hoped that they would take care of her. I didn't
want male techs to help her shower. I wanted her to be checked on
continuously. I want the next best thing to me.

She still believed the police were looking for her to arrest her.
Every time someone in scrubs walked by her, she stood up and put her
hands behind her back. She told me that they were here to arrest her.
The staff looks at her like she is crazy. I didn't think they understood
brain injuries near as much as the staff at the rehab in Las Cruces. They
were very understanding and informed us of each stage she was in and
what to expect as she went through it. Here in El Paso, they didn't seem
understanding or compassionate at all. This was my first red flag.

She was also in the stage where she thought she is dying. We
had to check her pulse every time this fear arose. I told her that her
heart was beating strong, and then I put her hand to her mouth so
she could feel her breath, and I put her hand on her heart so she

could feel that it was beating. Finally, I had to ask one of the nurses to check her pulse. They acted like I am putting them out, but I didn't care. My main focus was for her to be at ease, and I really didn't care what they thought about it. After all the reassurance we gave her, she said, "Thank God." Until five minutes or an hour from now when we had to do it all over again because she forgot. We would do whatever it takes to help her find some solace.

October 28, 2017

PM update on day 65 of Sierra's journey... She's been getting dizzy these past few days, but today it caught up with her. She was so dizzy it affected her eyesight and made her nauseous. Her doctor is thinking it may be vertigo, or possibly another UTI. She tried using her eye patch today because she tells us she sees "different," but she doesn't know how to articulate exactly how she sees different. She switches her eye patch every couple hours to try and strengthen her eyes. It seems to be helping so she didn't have a problem using it today. Her nurse gave her Dramamine for the nausea, and it seemed to help her. It's very hard to focus when she is feeling good, let alone when she isn't. Everything she gets is amplified because of her brain injury.

Anthony, Lee, Zo, Sebby, Jeff and I all took her to the Sunland Park outlet mall today. We thought since it is an outside mall, that she may be able to handle it. She said she wanted to try it, so we packed her up and went shopping. Zo and Sebby love to push her wheelchair and Zo is very protective over her, so she doesn't leave her side. We got her a pair of pants and three shirts because all of her clothes are still in Las Vegas. She thought everyone was laughing at her, so we had to explain to her that they aren't laughing at her, people just laugh, they have conversations with each other and sometimes they laugh, but it has nothing to do with her. No one thinks it's funny that you're in a wheelchair. She actually did very well, until we went into the food court. That proved to be way too much stimulation for her, so we had to leave abruptly. It was very nice to take her for a small family outing, and she was very grateful to get out. She has been in hospital beds for over two months, and she was definitely ready for a change.

Her dad, Izzy, Charlene, and the boys came up to see her and hang out with her until she got tired of the boys, and kicked them out of her room. When she is done dealing with people, talking or interacting, she decides she's done and points to the door. That's her signal to get out of her room. She's done it to every one of us, and we just respect her space and give her some distance to regroup.

Apparently I have not explained about the cops, and the color red. We assume she is afraid of the cops because she has such vivid recollections of the accident and remembers all the police officers on the scene. In her very injured brain she assumed if there were so many officers there for her, she must have done something very wrong. We also assume that the fear of red is because there was so much blood all over her face, hair, and body, that it is a reminder of, and the fear of the accident. She tells me that she hopes no one ever has to be in an accident like that. We totally agree, this has been one of her dad's and my hardest battles we've ever had to endure. She still asks me to check her pulse multiple times a day. When she is not asking me, she is asking one of the staff members to check it.

We are compiling a list of assurances and a list of fears so we can tackle them as she feels them. I have to put them right next to her bed all the time so she knows she's alive and the cops aren't outside her door. Today was a chill day, so no therapy, just her weekend homework. Tomorrow is her last easy day. They have been letting her get accustomed to her surroundings before they added too much to her plate, so tomorrow is the day where the hard work begins again. It is also the last night that I will be allowed to stay with her overnight. I'm not too sure which one of us is more scared of this transition. But, like I said before, I will stay here in El Paso so I can be close if she needs me, and I will still be staying with her every day from 7am to 9pm when it's lights out. Goodnight for now. #TeamBdog

When she woke up this morning, I immediately realized something was off. As soon as she sat up in bed, she felt dizzy and was swaying back and forth. I tried to get her up, but she was very unsteady. I felt her head to see if she had a fever because she may be getting sick. If she was, the doctors told us that everything she went through, such as illness, could get amplified tremendously in an injured brain. She had already proven that when she got a urinary tract infection from the catheter she had.

I was not looking forward to leaving her alone at night. I didn't feel she was ready, and they didn't check in on her enough to ease my mind. Hopefully, it would be different when I was not here all the time. Thank goodness Aunt Susan and Uncle Bob got her a phone so she could contact me any time she needed me. I would show her how to navigate her phone, and most of all, how to call me if she needed me. I had also been showing her how to push the nurse's button and keep pushing it until someone came. I didn't care if it irritated them; I only cared if they took care of her properly.

When we went to the mall, she brought her bee, so when she started to get overwhelmed, she played with his antennae. I taught her this when she was in the Las Cruces rehab. I could see she was getting scared, so I told her to rub her bee's antennae. It seemed to calm her down. She also hugged her bee and put her feet up on the wheelchair when she needed security. She had him since she was about two years old, so we brought him to her as soon as we could. So far, he had helped her tremendously. She took him everywhere she went. He sits in the wheelchair next to her, she laid him on the table next to her when she ate, he slept with her, and he stayed in the wheelchair right outside the shower when she was showering.

She was so excited to see both of her brothers and her nieces and nephews today. They all talked and laughed, and then all of a sudden, she was done with them and pointed to the door. I had to explain that she did that when she wanted people to leave. She did it to me all the time, so I just went outside for a bit and let her have some space. But, before long, she was calling me back into her room.

October 29, 2017

> PM update on day 66 of Sierra's journey… Weekends are nice here. She gets to sleep in until 8am. She goes to breakfast with four or five Interns who are getting to know her. They give her so much attention, and they already love her. That doesn't surprise us at all; people are always drawn to her. We narrowed her nausea down to the medications they have her on. There is not a full time Neurologist here so we have to wait until she comes in on Tuesday so we can talk about switching her medications, or even weaning her off some of them. We want her to feel the best she can so she can crush her therapies. She is still eating, even with the nausea, but it's hard not to want to eat the food here.
> She actually remembered some things today and we were very happy about that because she has hit a wall since she's been here. Between the

nausea, dizziness, and her knee, she hasn't progressed much since we got here.

We got the phone Aunt Susan and Uncle
Bob got for her up and running, so if you want
her number, please text me or her dad and we
will give it to you. If you are not programmed in
her phone, she will not be allowed to answer. If
you send your number, we can enter it into her
phone so she can talk to you.

There is a nursing student here that was in a
very similar accident with his girlfriend. His girlfriend didn't remember anyone when she woke
from her coma. Great news is that she is a year
down the road of recovery and she is a full time
student and working again. It gives her hope.
He told Sierra his story and it really inspired her.
It was very emotional for Sierra, and the young
man, but I think it was good for both of them to
talk about it as well. Thank you again for all your
prayers and kindness. Goodnight, all. #TeamBdog

Every weekend, there was a group of interns that came to help
the staff with the patients. Immediately, they were drawn to Sierra
because she was the youngest one here too. They talked to us about
her story and what brought her here. As we were telling them, one
of the male interns told us that he and his girlfriend were in a very
similar accident. His girlfriend incurred a TBI, was in a coma, and
on life support as well. When he started telling Sierra about their
story, she really perked up and listened intently. The parallels in their
story were astounding. He told her how his girlfriend received the
worst injuries of everyone in the car, just as Sierra did. Now she was
enrolled in school full-time, and she was working, and that is what
brought him to this rehab. After their accident, he decided to go to
school so he could learn to help people with brain injuries.

Once we got her phone working, we proceeded to program all
of our family and her friends in it so that she understood who she

could answer it to. I had already gotten so many people trying to scam me because they saw her story online and obviously knew my defenses were down, so we didn't want any unwanted people calling her. She knew that if her phone rang and she saw a name, she could answer, but if it was a number, she is not allowed to answer. I monitored her throughout the day to make sure she understood. So far, when she saw a number on the screen, she handed me the phone.

October 30, 2017

> PM update on day 67 of Sierra's journey… She is definitely in her fight mode again. The staff is still evaluating her abilities. They are having her do exercises that she is already accustomed to, and today she had her game face on and kicked some butt. Her physical therapist told me that she stood for seven minutes as if that was a great feat. My thought was that she not only can stand longer than that, but she can walk longer than that as well. They don't let her walk here, and we are concerned about that. We don't want her to feel as if she is going backwards. She worked harder on the hand bike than I've seen her to date. She is actually starting to catch the softball with her glove on. Her left side is starting to come back slowly but surely. Sometimes she can squeeze her glove enough to keep the ball in her glove.
>
> She is still in the stage that she thinks the cops are here and she is going to be arrested. When people walk by her, she stands up and puts her hands behind her back. She tells me the cops are here for her so she is going to jail. I try my hardest to reassure her that she hasn't broken the law and she is *not* going to jail. It's so sad, we want to help her, and we can for the moment, but then she forgets. And in five minutes, she

might remember. We never know what to expect, we just take it as it comes. We believe her filter is developing because now when she wants to give someone the finger, or throw the "F" bomb, she tells me, "Mom, you say it" with a big on smile on her face. The manner in which she holds conversations is cool, and funny, and sad, and scary all at the same time. But we are having conversation, and for that we are thankful.

They decorated for Halloween here, which reiterates my concern about their knowledge about brain injuries. Everyone here has some degree of brain injury. Some people are not able to state their fears, but I would bet if they could, they would not like the Halloween decorations. I know for a fact Sierra does not like them, they scare her. There are spider webs with giant spiders all over the place and they give me the creeps, I can't imagine how it makes someone who is unable to communicate feel. It definitely doesn't feel like a safe place. I am absolutely getting more apprehensive about her being here. The employees are not trained in brain injuries obviously, and her dad and I are not happy about that one bit! Goodnight for now, please keep her in your prayers.

Tonight is the night. I will be leaving her to sleep on her own and all I can do is pray that my baby girl will be okay. Please, please, please pray that she is safe and secure, that she is not afraid because I am not with her. I think I will stay until she has received her night time medications and has gone to sleep before I leave. #TeamBdog

Although she was more progressed at the rehab in Las Cruces, the rehab here had to test her abilities. So when her physical therapist told me that she stood for seven minutes, I was not very impressed.

I didn't show Sierra my disappointment, but I was. Her therapist in Las Cruces had her walking a lot. We didn't measure it in minutes; we measured it in distance. Most days, she walked to the gym, crushed her therapies, and then walked back to her room. I feel like they are holding her back here. They didn't let her walk on her own at all, so I walked next to her with her wheelchair.

The nurses had told me that she was a fall risk so they didn't want her walking, but again, I didn't care. If she had the drive and passion to walk or do things on her own, I'd let her. Now don't get me wrong, I made sure she was safe, but I let her push the limits they set on her. I had always let her take risks, and most times, she achieved whatever it was that she embarked on. Sometimes she failed, so I told her to get back up and do it again until she achieved it. Because of this, she had overcome every single obstacle the doctors put in front of her. She was much further in her recovery than all the professionals told us she would be.

Her brain was still playing tricks on her. She still thought that the police are coming to arrest her. She told me about twenty times a day that she was going to jail. When the staff members walked by her, she stood up and put her hands behind her back and told them, "I'm ready to go." They just looked at her and then looked at me like they were confused. It really bothered me that they didn't seem to understand. It appeared that the staff here was just here for a job, not because they understood brain injuries in the least. In Las Cruces, every one of the staff members understood brain injuries. So when she did "crazy" things, they explained to us that it was okay, it was just a part of her healing. They understood the Rancho Level Scale and the stages her brain had to go through to get better, and they didn't even know about the Rancho Level Scale here. I felt like I was constantly explaining to the staff here what she was going through and the stages of her progress.

I didn't tell Sierra about my anger and frustration. I would just wait for her dad to get here, and I unloaded on him, and then we'd go state our concerns with the administrator. She did get frustrated and wanted me to flip them off. I explained to her that it was not acceptable for me to do that, no matter how much I wanted to. But

I also told her that if that's what she felt, then do it, and it could be easily explained because of her brain injury.

October 31, 2017

> PM update on day 68 of Sierra's journey... I started off my day with a phone call from Sierra. She wanted me to know she had a really good night, that she slept well, and today is a really good day. As she says: "Thank God!" It was so beautiful. I waited for a phone call all night. It's so hard leaving her and spending the night somewhere that she is not right next to me. But she said she slept well and I was so happy, it relieved so much tension in me, I hated to leave her and I felt like I left my heart with her.
>
> She worked so hard in her therapies today. Her left side is getting better all the time. It's stronger and she is starting to grasp things with it and not drop them. This is great because it means the blood in her brain stem is dissipating and she's regaining the use of her left side. And the best part of that is she is crushing the odds against her ever walking, talking, or using that side of her body. She has amazed every doctor in her wake.
>
> She laughed so much today. Some of the things she laughed at were inappropriate to the subject, but it doesn't matter, she laughed and that does matter. On the other hand, she cries. She cries because she thinks the cops are going to take her to jail. She cries because she thinks her family is hurt, she thinks Morke is hurt, or dying. Then she just cries for no apparent reason. I know there is a reason, but she doesn't know how to express it, and that is very sad. I just hold her and tell her that this is her safe place, and we call

our family and Morke so that she can hear them and know that they are okay. Still everything is trial and error, and her dad and I are trying our best to make her as comfortable as possible. Yet neither of us knows exactly what to do for her, and it hurts our hearts. We tell her to repeat that she is not dying, that her family is fine, and that the cops are not coming for her because she didn't break the law. It seems to soothe her for the moment, at least until she forgets again.

She wrote her own post today on her Facebook page. We made her a Bitmoji, and she used it on her page. The post itself was beautiful, but the look in her eyes and the emotion she was able to express from writing it was priceless. She and Morke are still video chatting but for some reason, we can't get the video to work on her phone. So she uses her phone to text him and the smile on her face when she receives texts from him warms my heart. He is doing very well. He's back to playing again with very little pain. Thank God. He's working very hard to get as many days as possible for Thanksgiving. Today she video chatted with Morke, Uncle Tony, Aunt Kristie, and Sarena. They all got to see how much progress she has made and they are so very proud of her. We all had such big smiles. Today was a good day, and we are grateful for that. #TeamBdog

What I didn't say was that I stayed up all night waiting for her phone call. I cried because my heart hurt so badly. I really didn't know if I was doing her a favor by leaving her overnight. She had so much anxiety about me leaving, as did I. But I had to hide my emotions from her; I had to put on a brave face every day. I had to help her through her struggles, fear, and grief. I had to reassure her when her fears arose, even though whatever she felt I also felt. The emotional roller coaster she was on was exhausting.

Sometimes when she was talking to me about her fears or when she said she is going to jail, I wanted to break down and cry. I wanted to scream to the heavens to please take it all away from her, please let her be at peace and be healed. But I didn't. I didn't because I think God may misinterpret what I was asking for and take her home like he did with my mom when I prayed for her to be healed and at peace. I wanted her to truly be healed. I didn't want to see her suffer anymore. I wanted all of this to be past us. I want to watch her on that pitcher's mound throwing fire again.

Today, I saw a difference in her. I saw a glimmer of the passion and drive her old brain had. She worked so hard in her therapies. We were working on her left side, trying to get it stronger. I put the glove on her left hand and tossed her the ball. Most times, she didn't catch it, but every once in a while, she did, and we both smiled and enjoyed her accomplishment.

She enjoyed making her own posts. They didn't seem to make much sense a lot of the time, but the effort was there, and the people who were reading them understood where she was in her recovery. Sometimes they had to call me and verify the things she posted, but all in all, she was doing a great job for someone who was three months post-traumatic brain injury, diffused axonal injury, four brain bleeds, and one in the brain stem.

Today, I had to reassure her that our family and Morke were not hurt or dead. I had to check her pulse about twenty times. I had to reiterate that the police were not coming to arrest her and wipe the tears she cried today. But I also laughed with her, I watched her laugh, I listened to her laugh, and my heart was filled with joy and gratefulness.

November 1, 2017

> PM update on day 69 of Sierra's journey... She had another good night. We talked to her about why I can't stay with her anymore. She seems to understand, and she really wants her indepen-

dence back. I stay with her until 9pm and I make sure she has her pain medications before I leave so if she's not asleep by the time I have to go, she is well on her way. The staff said she is doing well at night so far, and that really eases my mind. I might actually start to get a good night's sleep without worrying if she needs me.

I feel so bad when I walk down the hallway to leave her for the night; it makes my heart sink into my stomach. But knowing that she is doing okay without me here really helps. She had a nightmare that she died and she thought it was real when she woke up, but we talked about it and she seemed to accept that it wasn't real. Although, we did have to call the nurse to check her pulse and her heart to make sure it is still beating. Her memory is very short-term so we have to reiterate everything we tell her, every time her fears come back. Then she retorts with her, "Oh, thank God!"

At physical therapy she thought her therapist called her a boy and now that she's back on the 'F' bomb kick, she flipped him off, then she proceeded to tell him. "You called me a boy." He looked shocked, his eyes opened wide in disbelief, he explained to her that he didn't think she is a boy, he knows that she is a girl. It took some convincing on my part, but it seemed to pacify her for the moment, until she forgets again in five or ten minutes, maybe an hour. Later in physical therapy, she unlocked the wheels on her wheelchair and rolled herself over to him and lifted her shirt and told him, "See, I'm a girl!" She didn't have a bra on and his jaw about fell to the floor, as did mine. Her shaved head makes her believe she is a boy and she also thinks that other people think she is a boy. She looks in the mirror and tells me she is a boy. I explain to her that she is a girl, and I show her girl anatomy to her and it eases her mind for the moment.

She laughs, she gets mad, she smiles, and she cries, and it is all progress. We help her through her anger and her fears, hold her when she cries, but most of all cherish those little moments when we laugh. We are just so thrilled that she has emotion and is learning to express it instead of being trapped inside her own mind and body. #TeamBdog

When I stayed with her all night, I didn't get much sleep. I thought when I wasn't waking up to the sounds of alarms and people walking around, I would get a good night's sleep. That was not the case. I think I got less sleep without her by my side. When I was with her, I could hear her breathing, I could soothe her when she was restless, and I could know immediately if she tried to get out of bed instead of the nurses getting there as soon as they could after the alarm went off. It didn't feel right leaving her. She was not ready. She still needed me, and it hurt me to leave her. I would give it a week or so, and if it was still affecting her adversely, I would stay with her until she felt like she was ready.

This morning after her shower, she looked in the mirror and asked me, "Mommy, am I a boy?"

I abruptly told her, "No way!" I told her what a beautiful young woman she was; I asked her if she wanted her makeup done. I told her that Auntie or Lee could come and put her make up on if she'd like. She smiled and said she liked that idea very much. Her brain fooled her into things that weren't true. If she thought it, she believed it to be true. So when she went to therapy and thought she was a boy again, she also thought that her physical therapist viewed her as a boy. Just as the cops were after her, people were laughing at her because she was in an accident, her loved ones were hurt, and her heart wasn't beating. We all went through so many emotions in one day, so when we got to laugh, we enjoyed the heck out of that moment.

November 2, 2017

PM update on day 70 of Sierra's journey... She is getting into the swing of things here. She has a notebook that is with her wherever she goes. It has her schedule, her menu for the week, a calendar, and all the information she needs in it. She is learning that this is her go-to book so that she knows where she is supposed to be and when. She's learning to recall new things, which is awesome. She still forgets a lot, but she is recalling new events and people.

Today she is having a conversation with someone in her mind. I was watching her and she would nod her head, or shrug her shoulders to someone. I asked her who she is talking to and she just tells me to be quiet and close my eyes. It kind of freaked me out, so I watched her for a few minutes and asked her again if she was okay. She got very aggravated with me and wheeled herself away. I was about a minute behind her. I thought she was going to her room, but she went to the nurse's station and got out of her wheelchair and just stood there doing the same thing. Like she was having a conversation with someone standing right next to her, but there was no one there. There was one of the techs behind her, he asked me a question, so I answered and Sierra looked at me and told me, "I told you to be quiet! Go outside! Go somewhere!" So I did. When I came back, she was happy to see me again, but she didn't want me to talk. After being with her for a short time, she wanted me to leave again. It's all a roller coaster ride, but it's also progress, so we'll take it. Everything new, and each stage she goes through, brings her one step closer to healing so we are thankful for all of it.

She is often aware of what she used to be, the life she used to have, and the fact that she has brain damage now. But more importantly, she believes she will get back to 100% again, and that's the important part. Goodnight, all, and thank you. #TeamBdog

When she got here, her therapists created a notebook for her. It had specific tabs, such as Menu, Calendar, Schedule, Speech, Occupational, and Physical therapy. Every night, we went over it to see what she had to do for the following day, and when she woke up in the morning, we'd go over it again. I could see she went through her day in her head as I read. When I was done reading, we talked about her concerns or fears, and then I'd do my best to counteract what weighed heavily on her. Then we talked about how she was going to give it her best so that she could achieve 100%.

She seemed to be going through a stage where she was in and out of touch with reality. Or maybe with her new brain, she was able to communicate with the other side. She said she was talking to the dead when she was at the rehab in Las Cruces, that they always asked for her help. Was it possible that she was truly talking to people who had crossed over? She wholeheartedly believed it to be true. I believe that our environment teaches us that we can't communicate with people who have died, but what if we weren't taught that? Her new brain hadn't been conditioned by society's standards, expectations, and obstacles. Watching her have conversations with someone that I couldn't see had taught me to be more open-minded about accepting things that my mind had been taught wasn't possible.

November 3, 2017

PM update on day 71 of Sierra's journey… This morning, she immediately started with "The cops are after me." She thinks the staff members are cops, and when she sees them, she stands up, puts her hands behind her back and tells them to take her. She has to have a babysitter now because she is impulsive, and she thinks her babysitter is a cop as well and she's under watch. All the staff has told her that they are not here to arrest her, and we have told her that they are there to help her, that they are doctors and nurses. That seems to ease her mind for a very short period of time.

This is an ongoing fear with her, and it makes us very sad that we can't diminish her fears, so we try to think of ways to make her understand and continue reiterating that. I asked her what I could do to help her to remember that the cops are not after her. She couldn't think of anything. So I came up with an option that I hoped would help her. I asked her if I brought some police officers to her and they told her that she is not wanted, if that would help her. She looked at me with her eyes wide open, and said, "Oh my gosh, yes!" So I went to the police station. While waiting in line, two police officers came in. I asked them if I could talk to them. They said sure, so I proceeded to tell them about Sierra's story, and her fears about cops arresting her, and her fear of going to the electric chair. I asked them if they would be willing to talk to her and tell her that everything is okay and she is not wanted by the police. First they had to run her name to make sure that she is truly not wanted, and then they gladly accepted my invitation to go talk to her at the rehab. So these two officers dropped everything they were doing, and followed me to the rehab so they could talk to her and try to ease her fears. It was so beautiful. They had about a twenty-minute conversation with her. They were so patient and kind to her, they explained that she is not wanted by the police but maybe she remembers a lot of police on the scene of the accident, and they were there to help her, not arrest her. At the end of their conversation, she felt really good. It looked like a weight was lifted off her chest. When it ended, I asked if I could take a picture of all three of them so when she forgets, I can show her the picture. They agreed and I took several pictures of the three of them. To watch her glow sitting next to them made my heart feel so good. After they left, she went to therapy with a big smile on her face and confidence in her heart.

Coach Lucas also came up to see her two days in a row. He brought her some Under Amour sweats, and they talked about her singing again. That always makes her laugh. He's here to sign girls for softball so he got to see her both days he was here. He went with her to therapy, and pushed her through it and got her in her groove. I say again, she's an athlete and she needs a coach to push her. Even though it's not so easy when she's being stubborn, but he managed to succeed. When she was done for the night she decided to write a letter to everyone, her writing is much better and easier to read. This is an example of how she writes and how her thoughts are put on paper. #TeamBdog

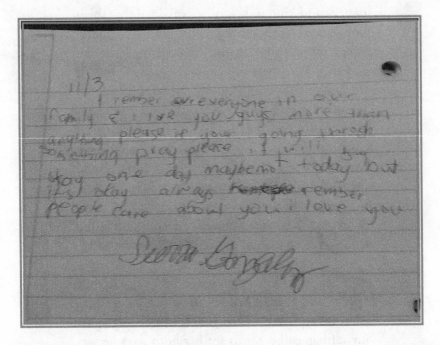

A letter to everyone. With love from Sierra.

I don't usually brag on myself; however, the idea to bring those officers to talk to her was brilliant. It took some convincing on my part to the administrator of the facility, but he finally agreed. He was afraid of the adverse effect it may have on the other patients, but he also knew what a tough time Sierra was having.

The adjustment from being in the Las Cruces rehab hospital to this one has proven to set her progress backwards since she has been here, so we thought it may help her to start moving forward again. They provided us with a small room in the front of the hospital so we could have privacy and it wouldn't disrupt the other patients. Sierra asked the officers questions, and they patiently explained away every fear she was experiencing. I cannot say enough good things about these two men, and I cannot build a pedestal high enough to place them in the highest regards we hold them. They asked her about her therapies and told her how proud they were of her, as was everyone that met her. They talked about their job and how important it was to them to help people as much as possible. She listened intently to every word they said with a huge smile on her face.

I told them she had to get to her therapy, and she asked to hug them and take a picture with them. They happily agreed and wished her the best that life had to offer. When they left, she thanked me and hugged me so hard. She told me how happy she was and that she wasn't afraid anymore. "Oh my gosh!" I was on top of the world. This had been such a gigantic obstacle for her, and I prayed that today was the end of that fear. We would face the next one as it arose, but for today, it was a great day, thanks to these two beautiful men.

Heros!

We can't thank these two beautiful people enough. Officer Orlando Hernandez and Officer Albert Machorro really turned around her fear that the cops were after her. She is no longer afraid of police officers because they took time out of their busy schedule to ease her fears. These men are two more heroes in our lives.

She was also very happy that she got to see Coach Lucas two days in a row as was I because he always made her laugh. He asked her if she wanted to sing, and she smiled and told him, "I suck." He agreed but explained she was still his singing partner. They used to sing together when they were traveling to games, and even though she is tone deaf, they both enjoyed it anyway.

November 4, 2017

> PM update on day 72 of Sierra's journey... She is still really confused. She thinks she's going to die and she cries so hard, telling me she can't do it anymore. She tells me she can't breathe and she doesn't know anything. I try to ease her mind as much as I possibly can. I hold her and tell her she's living, and she's breathing. I told her that God has a plan for her that's why he brought her back. I can see she thinks about it and then tells me, "Okay." Then she cries again. We couldn't possibly begin to understand where she is in her mind, but we want to so badly.
>
> Aunt Susan and Uncle Bob got her that phone so she can get a hold of me at night if she needs me, and she's learning how to work it more and more. Today she decided to call 911 when she heard people outside her room talking. I caught her and took the phone when she told me she dialed 911, I explained to them that she has a brain injury and she doesn't know better. They cautioned me not to let her have her phone if that's what she is going to do, so I assured her that it wouldn't happen again.

Tonight when I got back to the motel, she called me and told me that people were talking outside her door again. She told me that she was going to call 911 again. I tried to talk her down, but she wasn't having it. So, needless to say, I had to go back to the hospital and take her phone away from her so she wouldn't call again. After we hung up, I was getting ready to leave and she text me and told me to hurry or she's calling them. Little stinker is learning how to manipulate me, and I love it.

She played games with the students today, the ones that just dote over her when they come on the weekends. The young man who was in the accident like hers said his girlfriend wants to come see her when she gets Thanksgiving break. Sierra is very excited about that and is looking forward to meeting her. She's heard their story, and knows it is almost identical to hers and Morke's story. I hope the young woman can give her inspiration. #TeamBdog

This morning, when I got her out of bed, she told me that she didn't know how to stand, then she looked at me and asked, "Mommy, do I know how to stand?" I told her that she did, and I showed her videos of how she stood and walked. While she was watching it, I could see her confusion unraveling, and finally, "Oh yeah, I do know how to stand." Then she told me that she didn't know how to tie her shoes. She did know how to tie her shoes. It was one of the many things that we had to teach her again. She chose to tie them differently than her old brain did it, but she got the job done, and that is what I had to remind her of.

I don't know where the thought of calling 911 came from, but this was her new thing. I showed her how to push the nurses' button if she needed help when I was not there. When I asked her why she was calling 911, she said the nurses didn't come to her room quickly enough, so she had to call 911 to tell on them. Besides wanting to call 911 on the nurses, she threatened me that if I didn't get there fast enough, she was going to call on me as well. We often wondered where her brain was as far as healing, and we were definitely realizing there may not be any rhyme or reason to what she did, but we also didn't know what it was like to think from a very injured brain. As long as she continued to make new connections, we would continue to be grateful for her progress, even though we had no idea as each day arose and what it would bring; the fears, insecurities, obstacles, and hardships we would have to help her through.

She was teaching the students that came to see her many lessons as they embarked on their careers working with people who had brain injuries. They spent most of their time with her. They asked her questions about her brain injury. They asked me questions. They were like sponges soaking up every piece of information they could to help them in the field they were studying, which for most of them was the brain.

November 5, 2017

PM update on day 73 of Sierra's journey… In so many ways, she is extremely confused, and on the other hand, she is completely focused in some situations. She is very sure that she wants out of here. She wants to go home so badly, but doesn't understand that she is not ready for the world we live in. She is still unable to handle stimulation and she thinks that everyone looks at her and laughs at her because she was in an accident. We explain to her that people in public don't even know about her accident, but she doesn't believe it.

When it's time to go to sleep, she thinks she's going to heaven. Since her brain "woke up," it exploded with thoughts, feelings, fears; lots of fears, and anxiety about it all. October 5 is very significant to our family, so the fact her brain woke up on that day, reassures us that our loved ones that have passed still give us signs that they are in our lives, guiding us.

After the explosion of thoughts and fears comes forgetfulness and she doesn't remember again. It's a roller coaster ride with its ups and downs, and twists and turns, peaks and valleys. But through it all, its progress and we are thankful.

One recurring memory is that she needs to work hard for her overnight pass. She wants to sleep in her own bed with familiar surroundings where she is not getting woken up to take medications or do therapy, just sleep in until she decides to wake up. I continue to tell her therapists to act like a coach and treat her like the athlete that she is. That's what she knows, she's been an athlete her whole life and it's familiar to her. She tells me all the time that they don't push her hard enough and let her work as hard as she wants to. They get excited when she walks twenty steps, and she no longer wants to use her wheelchair. She wants to walk, and pitch and play catch. They want to cover their assets, and she wants to soar. I will be talking to her therapists again tomorrow because they are not working her hard enough to her liking. #TeamBdog

Another day, another battle. This had become our new normal. Every day, I woke up and I wondered what the day had in store for us. She may wake up in a great mood, ready to fight, and at any moment, she may break down in tears. She went through so many emotions in one day. It was exhausting. Seeing as how I was with her every minute of every day, I got to experience everything she went through, and as her mom, I felt all the pain, anger, frustration, fear, depression, and helplessness she felt. On the other hand, I was also the one that got to be with her during her moments of happiness, drive, and passion she experienced as well. It was a double-edged sword, and I was extremely blessed to have the opportunity to be by her side through it all.

When she told me that her brain woke up on my son's anniversary, I knew it was not a coincidence. I knew it was him guiding her and his way of letting me know that he was with us. We also know that coincidence is when God remains anonymous. She had been talking about Andrew quite often lately. She never got the chance to meet him, but she knew him. I had talked about him her whole life, so she felt as if she did know him. She told me that he was guiding her and that he was her biggest cheerleader. She talked about him and how he was helping her every day. As she was more and more able to tell me her feelings and articulate her thoughts, I realized they were full of him. By the way she talked to me about him, I had to believe that she was having or had conversations with him.

She told me, "Andrew said" or "Andrew wants" or "Andrew thinks." It gave me goosebumps to hear her talk about him just as she did her brother, Anthony, Andrew's twin brother. The only difference was that Anthony didn't die. Anthony had been here since she got in the accident, and she had many of her "firsts" with him. He understood how to get through to her, and she listened to him when he was trying to teach her things she knew before the accident, such as walking or talking. He figured out how she thought and explained to us how he got through to her because we didn't understand.

One thing she was sure of is they didn't push her hard enough here. They were so worried about protecting themselves for insurance purposes, and she wanted her wings so she could fly. I was constantly getting in trouble here because I let her walk by herself. When she was pitching to me, I let her stand by herself with her wheelchair behind her, and I pushed her like I had always done. I walked her around the hospital without her wheelchair. I just let her hold my arm to guide her, and if she faltered, I was right there to help her. Apparently, the "driven" old brain is still a part of her new brain.

November 6, 2017

PM update on day 74 of Sierra's journey...
When I got to her room this morning she was
crying uncontrollably. She thinks she's ugly, she's
ready to go to jail, and she thinks she's going to
die. She has listened to her "Fight Song" over and
over today, and cried every time she plays it, yet
she insists on listening to it. After listening to her
song, we found a video called "You're Awesome!"
She listens intently and cries profusely. We're
hoping the change in her emotions is because of
the change in her medications. We feel like she's
a guinea pig because apparently they are trying
to find the right combination of medications
to help her, but the only way to know that they
aren't helping is for her to go through emotional
roller coasters and it's just sickening to see her
going through so much turmoil.

We will talk to the doctor about this tomorrow because we get our one day a week to see
the doctor, which has become very frustrating.
Before now we had doctors available 24-7, and
now she has one doctor that only shows up once
a week. The longer she is here, the more we question if this is really a good fit for her to excel.
This is heartbreaking for her, and for her dad
and I. We feel overwhelmed with the rules and
regulations they impose here to cover themselves
more than to help her reach her goals. The compassion she gets here in comparison to the compassion and care she had at the hospital in Las
Cruces is lacking to say the least. Here they seem
to care more about covering themselves for insurance purposes, but in Las Cruces they were more
concerned with her recovering and advancing in

every way possible. They invested themselves in her recovery, and here it seems they are coming to work and getting a paycheck.

Just weeks ago I was able to console her, to reason things out with her so she could understand, but now, no matter what I do or say, she is inconsolable. She is combative so when I tell her that she is not going to die, she argues with me that she is. She tells me, "Mom, you don't know!" She continues to tell me all day long that she is going to die, and tries to prepare me for her death. She tells me that I will be okay. I tell her no way any of us will be okay without her. She tells me she's not worth dying for, that she is ugly, and puts her hands behind her back and tells me that she is ready to go to jail now. Then I show her the picture of her and the police officers that came to see her and she remembers she's not going to jail. But then just starts on her rampage about how she is going to die and that her father and I will be okay. She tells me that she'll be okay; she knows she's going to heaven again. She tells me how beautiful and peaceful it is, and how her brother said she had to come back to me, but he will be waiting for her when it's her time. I'm definitely beginning to believe that she left us for some amount of time, went to "the peaceful place" where her brother is, and came back for me.

I talked to her therapists today about working her harder and they agreed that they would. So today when she went to therapy, they worked her harder than they have since she's been here and she responded very well. She was still crying, but she worked hard as she cried. She did stop long enough to pitch me some balls, and they are actually starting to sting a bit. So, needless to say, I have to start wearing a glove to be her catcher now. She actually stood up to pitch today, it was great! I put her wheelchair behind her, locked her brakes in case she had to sit down, and let her fire away. #TeamBdog

As the days go on here, we are less and less impressed with this hospital. It seems as though every time we try to help her progression, they put obstacles in our way. One example is that she wanted to walk, and instead of encouraging her to do so, they told her she couldn't walk by herself because of insurance purposes. They didn't seem to understand the stages she went through. They just looked at her like she was crazy, and they didn't bother trying to ease her mind about her fears at all. There was very little compassionate interaction here.

Now that I couldn't stay with her at night anymore, I made sure she got her sleeping medications about an hour before I left because I didn't feel comfortable leaving her here, knowing that they didn't bother to console her. They just let her cry, and that pissed me off. I had told them that it wouldn't hurt them to show some compassion. I had questioned all the staff if they understood anything about brain injuries because they just didn't seem to understand.

I was already making a name down here because I refused to accept the conditions and obstacles they put on Sierra. I had become argumentative, and when they told me, "She can't do that," I retorted with, "Yes, she can!" I would fight for her no matter how many people didn't like me in the wake. I was not here to be liked; I was here to fight for my child's life back. Now they walked on eggshells around me, and I could see them talking behind my back. I had also heard them talking about Sierra, and when I walked up to them, they'd quit talking and looked at me as if they were guilty. I didn't like the feeling I got here, and I was starting to listen to Sierra more about wanting out of here. I was starting to believe that we could do the therapy they gave her here better at home. But taking her home at this point was very scary. We just wanted her to go back to Las Cruces Rehab hospital.

I was truly beginning to believe that she did cross over into heaven's gates at some point in her journey. She told me she talked to Andrew, but her thoughts were so scattered, sometimes it was hard to understand what she was trying to convey, but now it was becoming hard to deny.

Now that she was in the stage that she believed she was going to die, she had been telling that she was ready and how her dad and I would be okay. She had started telling me how she saw her brother, Andrew, that he sent her back because I couldn't make it without her. She told me that she knew she would be fine, and Andrew would be there when she crossed over.

It was too much to hear. She'd come way too far to give up now. I told her in a very stern voice that she was not going to die, that we would not be okay without her, and that she would continue to fight. Giving up was not an option. It never was with her old brain, and I refused to let her new brain be a quitter. Then I sent her to her therapy, tears and all, and told her to go work hard so she could get the heck out of here, and that's exactly what she did.

November 7, 2017

> PM update on day 75 of Sierra's journey… As soon as I walked in this morning I heard her crying in the dining room. She is still in the stage of "I'm dying," "I'm ugly," "I'm a boy," and "I can't fight anymore!" It's very upsetting because the staff here doesn't console her. Apparently they can't touch or hold her in any way that may be construed as inappropriate, so they just look at her and it really upsets me.
>
> I hold her, talk to her, and try to redirect her attention, but her attention span is so short that it makes it difficult to steer her away from her thoughts. Daddy came down here today because

she is having such a hard time. The staff has a very long name for what they believe this is, but I couldn't remember it to save my life. It's a medical term for why she cries all the time, but we really don't care what it's called, the only thing we care about is how to help her. The point is that her brain cannot figure out what is real and what is imaginary. We all have fears, but our brains can decipher what is real and tell us that the monsters in the closet are not real. But her brain can't do that. If she has a fear of anything, it is as real as the absolute truth.

Her evening got much better tonight. We all had dinner together, and even ate dessert. The best part is that she got through it all without crying. After dinner, she decided she wanted to go for a walk. So she used her walker to walk around the entire hospital, without crying! It was such a relief. She wore herself out enough to want to go to sleep early.

When it was time for me to leave, I told her I had to go and she actually said "okay mommy." It felt much better to leave with her blessing as opposed to how it's been since we started letting her sleep alone at night.

We had a family meeting today, and apparently the rehab received a letter from the insurance company stating her projected discharge date is November 20. She is far from being ready to be released, so her dad will have to fight the insurance company *again*! Oh joy! Goodnight for now, and thank you all for continuing your prayers for her. #TeamBdog

Apparently, she was in a crying stage. She cried and cried from her stomach, from her heart. It took everything I had to watch our baby girl go through this. My anxiety level was through the roof because I couldn't help her. I hugged her, I held her, I talked to her very gently trying to ease her fears to no avail. Somewhere in her mind, she created these farces, and they amplified until they became truth for her.

At this point in her recovery, she was unable to decipher reality from fiction, and no matter how many times we would tell her what was true, her brain wouldn't let her believe it. She was going through her own hell in her mind, and it wouldn't let us redirect her train of thought, so she suffered with them, trying to overtake her every day. But, again, I refused for this to happen to our baby girl! I would figure out a way to get her brain on the right track. Tomorrow, I would put positive affirmations all over her room. I would make her read them with conviction, and we would redirect her negative, self-defeating thoughts into positive, reassuring thoughts. This was a new brain, and we would reprogram it to think positive.

November 8, 2017

> PM update on day 76 of Sierra's journey… She wants to help me write her post tonight, so here goes: "In the morning I ate breakfast really good. I had a better day at breakfast today. After I ate, I went to the Neuro Ophthalmologist, he put drops in my eyes and it made them feel freaky. Now I feel like I'm tripping. But I want to say that I love Morke and I miss him and can't wait to see him again. Even though my eyes are messed up I worked real hard at therapy today. I couldn't really walk much because my eyes were messed up, and still are. But the doctor said my nerves and muscles are good so I should be able to see after my brain heals, and I may not even need to wear glasses. He gave me medicine to help calm my eyes down because they always jump up and down and it makes it hard for me to see. So

tonight I get that medicine and I hope it helps my eyes.

"My daddy spent the day with me so Mommy could go to Las Cruces today because she has an appointment. I know that I broke many laws, but I'm not ready to pull the cord. I thought I was, but I'm not ready. I know I have to write so many people letters, I know I have to get a job, but I don't know how because I'm a felon (not true of course, just a fear that she believes to be true). It was loud in the dining room tonight and noise really, really bothers me. I've never liked narcotics and told my friends not to take them. I really love you guys and I'm sorry for everything I've done wrong (this is not true either). I bit myself today because I was so worried I couldn't say what I needed to because of all the money spent and all the work put into trying to get me better, and time. I put my life on the line for this and I want you to know how sorry I am. I'm not ready to live life. You don't know how hard I've worked, and now I'm living. Goodnight, I love you." #TeamBdog

She had been reading my posts lately. When she saw them, she asked if we could read them together and if I could explain them to her. So this was our newest thing. We sat on the bed, and I read what I wrote the previous night and all the comments from her many followers. She smiled when I read the comments. Sometimes she cried because they are very touching, but that was a good cry.

So many people were praying for her and sending encouraging words. I think this is just what she needed to pull her out of her funk. After reading posts and comments, we talked about all of them, and I told her what an inspiration she was to so many people. She asked me, "I am, Mommy? Really?"

I told her she was definitely an inspiration, and we go through the list of everything she had overcome and crushed the obstacles the doctors put in her path. They only had science as their guide; we had God.

Unfortunately, much of her days were still filled with "I'm ugly" or "I'm a boy" or "I'm not worth it" or "The cops are after me because I'm a felon" or "I'm not worth the money you are spending on me" or "I can't do this" or "I'm going to die" and so many other negative thoughts that were so unjustified. We had not surrounded her with any negativity since the accident. We knew a whole new brain was making all new connections, so we didn't want any negativity around her; yet so many of her thoughts were negative, and we couldn't find the reasoning behind it all. Nonetheless, we would find a way to reprogram the negative into positive and insist she keep fighting to get her life back.

She was happy that her dad could spend the day with her, but it proved to be a bit much for him. I was usually the one that stayed with her, so when he got the chance to spend the whole day with her, he realized how exhausting one day with her could be. He was extremely glad to see me when I got back. He actually told me how much he needed me to be with her because he couldn't do what I did on a daily basis. He had been here since day one, but I was the one that spent every hour of every day with her, and it was much different than just visiting her for a few hours at a time.

November 9, 2017

> PM update on day 77 of Sierra's journey… Good news is that she may be through her crying stage. Her doctor switched her medications so now she just feels strange. She tells me that she's in a state of confusion most of the time, but she really pushes through it. She walked for fifteen minutes on her walker even though she was dazed and confused. The medication the ophthalmologist gave her to calm her eye muscles down hasn't kicked in yet. Her eyes jump up and down con-

tinuously, which makes it very hard for her to see or focus on anything.

If she tilts her head to the right she can find a point of focus for small periods of time. She told me today that she is ready to live and she knows she has to fight more. Thank God for that! It is so hard hearing your child trying to prepare you for their imminent death. As she was walking this morning she kept repeating over and over, "I can do this!" And a short time later, she tells me that she is going to "the chair" because she is bad. We want so badly to get her out of her head for a while just so she doesn't have any fears, only security and peace. I remind her of her police officer friends. How they ran her name and she is not wanted by the police. I show her the picture they took together, and she says, "Oh yeah" with a very confused look on her face.

Auntie Von and Cole came to visit today and did her make-up. They laughed and had snacks and walked around. They got to see her walking with a walker now as opposed to a wheelchair. They were very impressed with her. She improves a little every day, and we all get to witness our miracle. I came back home for some down time and to recharge so hopefully I will be able to sleep being an hour away from her. Goodnight All. #TeamBdog

Now that her medications have been changed, she has stopped crying. We can only hope and pray that was the reason for her crying stage. That stage was so exhausting to see our baby girl constantly crying, and nothing we did or said helped her to feel any better. But, today, she had a completely different attitude. She informed me this morning that she was going to fight, no matter how hard things got for her throughout the day. She said, "I can do this!" Her persever-ance was unrelenting.

By lunchtime, she was telling me that she was going to "the chair" because she was bad. And then she continued with her trying to prepare me for her death. She continually told me that she'd be okay and that Andrew was waiting for her.

The neuro-ophthalmologist told us that she tilted her head because her eyes were not connecting with her brain properly. He believed all of her nerves and muscles were intact, so eventually, she would regain her ability to see as a healthy eye saw. She also damaged her brain stem, and there was blood in her optic nerve, so it affected her sight and ability to see anything correctly, even with glasses.

When Auntie Von and Cole came to hang out with us, they were putting her makeup on, and she thought that was so funny. As she would laugh, she would bounce up and down because she was laughing so hard, which made it very difficult to put her make up on and made all of us laugh. It felt so good to laugh, even if for just a short time.

November 10, 2017

> PM Update on day 78 of Sierra's journey… She still feels like she's tripping on drugs. She said she's never felt like this before, which makes per-fect sense because she's never done drugs so it is very hard for her to handle. Yet, she still pushes through her therapies, she still walks every chance she gets, and chokes down her food even though she doesn't want to eat.
>
> She asks me all day long, "What's happen-ing, Mama? What is going on in my brain?" She tells me everything is confusing and she can't have a straight thought. We are reasonably sure that it has to do with her medications. The doctors keep changing them, trying to find a happy medium for her, but as of yet, they haven't succeeded. It

really upsets her dad and I. We feel like she's a guinea pig and they actually have no idea what to give her so she can feel somewhat normal.

She's writing letters to me in her speech therapy. They are sad, and beautiful. She apologizes for being such a burden, and she tells me how thankful she is that I have been with her since the accident. She is very empathetic towards everyone. If they are sad, so is she.

She knows that tomorrow is Veteran's Day, so she walked around the hospital asking people if they were veterans. If they are, she shakes their hands and tells them how grateful she is for their service and how much she appreciates them. There is a nurse here that she calls "The Wounded Warrior." He got blown up by and IED in Iraq, incurred severe brain damage, and was in a wheelchair for fifteen months while he was recovering. He tells Sierra the story of his fight to survive and how some days he just wanted to give up but he had people that loved him and wouldn't let him give up. Now he is a nurse helping others who have sustained severe brain injuries. She is truly inspired by him, and every time she sees him, and the scars on his head, she tells me his story of how he came to be here, helping others who have brain injuries. She named him the "Wounded Warrior" because she realizes that he is truly a warrior.

When her spirits are down and she just wants to give up, we talk about him and his story to get his life back. She tells him how sorry she is for him and he tells her, "Don't be, you'll get there, and then you will have your own story of inspiration to help other people." It's very nice to have someone for her to look up to; someone who understands exactly what she is going through because no matter how much her dad and I want to help, we have no clue the turmoil in her brain. She apologizes to me all the time for being such a problem, for being bad, and says she needs to go to "the chair." It's so gut-wrenching, and no matter how much we tell her the contrary, she won't believe it. We are just so incredibly thankful she is alive, we tell her how we feel so blessed for the opportunity to be here for her and want her to know that above all else. Hopefully by tomorrow her new medications will start to level out so she doesn't have to feel stoned out of her mind and riddled with guilt because we have to take care of her. #TeamBdog

The doctor changed her medications again, and although they don't make her cry, they do make her feel like her head is tripping on hard drugs, and she does not like that feeling at all. Since she has never done drugs, she can't understand why people like the feeling she is experiencing. We will watch to see if it evens out; otherwise, we will have the doctor change them again. There's got to be a happy medium.

When we were looking at her calendar, she realized tomorrow was Veteran's Day, and obviously, her new brain held them in high regard too. She constantly asked the man that was wounded in Iraq questions about his injury, and he told her his story so she could have faith in the process. He explained to her that he knew it was hard, but she could do it. He had become somewhat of an idol to her.

In speech, her therapist wanted her to write letters, so she chose to write them to me. They were the most heartbreaking, yet inspiring, loving, thoughtful, and were scattered with contradictions, fears, love, and gratefulness all in one. They were hard to decipher sometimes, but if I asked her, we could usually figure out what she was trying to say. Every day, I am amazed watching a new brain form in front of my eyes. The brain is so complex, and even the best doctors are barely touching the surface of its capabilities.

November 11, 2017

> PM update on day 79 of Sierra's journey... Today is not much different from yesterday, she's still extremely confused. We try to distract her mind from what she's thinking, but she is so clouded that it doesn't sink in. We were walking down the hall today and she stopped, looked around, and asked me, "What are we doing?" It's so heartbreaking to see this on a daily basis, but the worst part of it is that we can't help her. We have to accept where she is and somehow get through each day.
>
> Today she had it in her head that Morke was coming to see her so she asked me every five minutes where he was. Then she wanted to go outside and she took me to the parking lot and we just stood there. I asked her what we were doing and she informed me that we were waiting for Morke. I tried in vain to tell her that he's not coming today, but she wasn't having it. She believed he was, so we just stood out in the parking lot waiting for him to arrive.
>
> She's having a very hard time distinguishing between reality and fiction. On a brighter note, she didn't talk about the cops coming for her all day. That was definitely a bonus. She's just scared all the time and she doesn't want her dad or I to leave her because she thinks we won't be back. Of course we tell her nothing could keep us away from her, but she thinks if we leave her that we will die or be injured to where we can't come back. What she doesn't understand is that either

one of us would take her place in a heartbeat so
we don't have to watch our baby girl suffer like
this every day. #TeamBdog

Today she questioned everything she did. Her head was so
cloudy she couldn't finish a thought. Everything was a battle for her
anyway, but now with the drugs that she was on, she found it impossible to focus on anything. I could see the confusion in everything
she did, so I just tried to lead the way and have her sit as much as
possible. But on days like this that she was convinced that Morke
was coming, I could only try in vain to convince her that he was not.
I finally did coax her into going back inside to call him. I knew he
wouldn't answer because he was at practice, but it got her out of the
parking lot and redirected her brain.

It was a sigh of relief that she didn't tell me she was going to jail
at all today. Not only that, but she didn't tell me she was going to die
or prepare me for her death once today. Even if the rest of the day
was bad, I would hold on to that because that cut very deep, and I
felt like I was going to run out of energy every time she spoke of her
imminent death. She did talk about her dad and I being on the road
and having to drive to El Paso to come see her. She was very afraid
that we would get in an accident and die. The sad part was that I
couldn't promise her that wouldn't happen, but I tried to ease her
mind and tell her that God was watching over us when we got on the
road. Then she retorted with, "Oh, yeah, just like he was with me in
my accident?"

"Absolutely, honey, absolutely!"

November 12, 2017

PM update on day 80 of Sierra's journey... When
I came in this morning she was crying. She said
she was scared because she thought I was never
coming back. I reassured her that there was no
way that would happen. It is very bothersome
that the staff here has no compassion for her

and doesn't seem to understand her brain injury. When she is hurting, she needs comfort. But the staff here just looks at her like she's some kind of freak. They don't hug her or have any compassion for her. She is supposed to learn to be independent while she's here so they just leave her to cry and we're really getting upset with the lack of kindness or humanity she is receiving here.

We miss the rehabilitation hospital in Las Cruces so badly; they truly understood brain injuries and worked on her with compassion, kindness, and understanding. They also took the time out for us and our family, to teach us about her injury and what to expect. She asks me if she is Forrest Gump. She wonders what is happening all the time. Her newest thing is, "I'm not DNR, I don't want to die!" Again, her dad and I explain to her that she's past that point, that now she is living and fighting to get her brain better. Her brain is trying to make so many new connections, with that comes emotions. That's always scary because we never know what to expect. As of yet, they haven't been positive emotions. When we prayed for her to be able to express emotion, we had no idea how much pain would surface. She laughs at inappropriate situations, she cries all the time, she throws things at us and off her bed, and she thinks she's caused us so much trouble. It's so very sad. #TeamBdog

She wanted to go home so badly. She yelled out in the halls that this place sucked. She told the staff that they just wanted a paycheck, and they didn't know what they were doing. She said if she had to stay in the hospital, she wanted to go back to the rehab in Las Cruces. We all understood that the care she got there was above and beyond anything we'd seen or experienced here. When she was acting inappropriately, they just looked at her and then looked at me with a confused look on their faces because they didn't know how to interact or address any of the stages she went through.

Seeing as how they only had one doctor to treat the patients here and she only came on Tuesdays, we had to make a list of questions and concerns throughout the week so we could address them when she did come. This was very bothersome to her dad and I because we had experienced multiple times when we needed her doctor's advice, but they only called her and had to wait for her to get back to her nurse so we knew what to do.

So when she went through stages, we had to research and see if it truly was a stage she had to go through, if it was her medication, or if she was getting sick. When she got a urinary tract infection, she started getting really confused and forgetful. It seemed like she was going backward until, finally, I realized her urine was cloudy and asked the nurse to check it for infection. Sure enough, she had one, and once they started giving her medication to treat it, she started coming around. Her memory and confusion started to subside.

November 13, 2017

> PM update on day 81 of Sierra's journey… She can't seem to get out of her funk. She cries all the time, and she's scared of so many things. Her fears are mostly unrealistic, like going to prison or going to the electric chair. She continuously tells me that she is going to die. She tells me how I'll be okay without her and how she has to go back to the peaceful place. She has just begun to tell me about her time in another place where it was so peaceful and beautiful, where she talked to her brother Andrew and he told her she has to come back. He told her that our Mom wouldn't make it if she stayed with him. He explained to her that it's going to be hard, very hard, and it's going to hurt a lot, but she can do it and he will be with her the entire way. Now she wants to go back. She

said it's too hard, too scary, and too painful. Her dad and I are at a loss. We don't know what to do to make her feel better, the more we try, the more she cries.

We're trying to figure out where she is going after the El Paso rehab. We don't feel as though she is ready to come home, and frankly, we are scared to death that we don't have enough knowledge to take care of her and help her get better. The insurance already has a projected discharge date. All we can do is continue to fight the insurance company and get her more time. She is not ready to come home and deal with the outside world. We are trying to get the approval to go back to the rehab in Las Cruces. We know the people and staff there. We know that she soared there, and she did get the best treatment and care.

It makes such a difference when the medical staff cares about your recovery and shows each patient compassion and humanity. Just in case the insurance denies her further treatment, we are starting to prepare her to come home. For now, we have to play the game, and see how it turns out. She wants you all to know thank you for everything and God bless you. #TeamBdog

Now we realize that she did, in fact, cross over into heaven. She called it "the peaceful place," and she wanted to go back with her brother, Andrew. She said it was too hard here, and she wanted to go back where it was peaceful and nothing hurt. While I didn't want my baby girl to be in pain, I surely didn't want her to die and go back to heaven. She put up a good argument. By the way she explained it, I wanted to go there too. But my brain was not injured, and I understood that I had to wait until it was my time to cross over. She, on the other hand, wasn't capable of thinking past any thought that was at the forefront of her mind. She was also angry with her brother, Andrew, for convincing her to come back and angry with me because I was the reason she had to come back.

She told me that she wanted to stay because it was so beautiful and peaceful, but her brother told her that she had to come back to me, so she blamed me for the pain that she had to endure every day. She said it isn't worth it, that she was not worth it, that it was too hard and too painful, that she just wanted to go back with her brother because he said he would be waiting for her when the day came that she had to pass on, but he also told her that it was not her time, that I needed her. He was right. Just as I told Jeff on the way to Albuquerque right after she got in the accident, I would not make it if she died. I knew in my heart and, unfortunately, from experience, how very excruciating it is to lose a child, and I knew that there was no way I could do it again.

I feel like we were roped into coming to this hospital. The lack of care and compassion was definitely wearing on her dad and I, but mostly on our baby girl. I watched her fight every day, and when she surpassed each obstacle, none of the staff was happy for her or rooting for her like they did in Las Cruces. They just looked at her and acted like it was no big deal. When I was allowed to join her for her therapies, I rooted for her and clapped for her every time she accomplished the task at hand while they just looked at me as if to say, "Calm down." I believe the atmosphere here also contributed to her sadness and crying episodes.

A lot of the times when we were excited that she was making accomplishments, the staff came to tell us that she was not allowed to do what she was doing. For example, when she was walking on her own and we were both so happy for her, the staff came and told us she couldn't walk by herself because of insurance purposes. Or when I had her outside, pitching, the nurse came outside and told her that she couldn't pitch because she had to be in her wheelchair. I was aggravated with all the rules that didn't allow her to progress, and I saw it wearing on her. They were taking away her passion and her drive to fight so hard.

November 14, 2017

> PM update on day 82 of Sierra's journey… It has been so overwhelming on all of us that I need to take a break today…will post again tomorrow. #TeamBdog

This was the day, the first day since the accident, that I doubted myself. I was out of steam. I had nothing left to give, no fight left. I was exhausted, I had lost so much weight and lost so much sleep that I was running on empty. I was tired of living in hospitals and getting woken up all hours of the night. I was tired of being on a schedule that they controlled. I wanted a home-cooked meal, and most of all, I wanted my mom. She always knew the right words to get me through the dark times. My mom had passed over twenty years ago, and although I had my son, Anthony, I still felt all alone. I prayed that she started to make a turn for the better while I tried to recharge myself. I needed to be there for her. I had to find a way to get my head back in the game so I could be the best me for the benefit of her.

I had to go home and sleep in my own bed, take a shower in my own home, watch my own TV, and even had a home-cooked meal. It was so great when I lay in my bed, just the Lord and I. I prayed with everything I had. I prayed for strength to help Sierra. I prayed for Sierra to have better days, and I prayed for the staff in El Paso that they may find compassion and understanding so they can be better for her.

November 15, 2017

> PM update on day 83 of Sierra's journey… I am very happy to say that today was a better day for her. She still cried several times, but she also smiled. Thank God for that! We were all so maxed out that doubt starts setting in. Doubt as to whether we are strong enough to be strong enough for her. She is our only focus and at times we feel backed up against a wall. Everything we

do or say doesn't seem to help her, and that is the hardest part for her dad and me, let alone for Sierra. We just watch it, but she has to live it.

She thinks her social worker here is very pretty, so she asked if she could do her make-up. Christy told her that she would be honored to do her make-up, and that made her smile, which in turn made me smile. She said she doesn't want to look like a boy anymore and she knows I'm not good at all when it comes to putting makeup on, so she asked Christy. They sat on her bed while Christy talked to her and told her how pretty she is. She put her make up on exactly how Sierra wanted it, and when she was done, Sierra shined. She looked at me and told me how pretty she was and how happy she is. What an incredible weight off my shoulders, she's happy and that makes me so happy. Everyone in the hospital told her how pretty she looked and she smiled every time she was complimented. Then she would cry, but when she looked in the mirror, she smiled and said, "I'm pretty!" I told her, "Yes you are!" And that made her smile even more.

Her medications still make her feel like she is tripping, and she still believes she is Forrest Gump or at least mentally handicapped like him. I do my best to comfort her when she is scared, reassure her when she has doubts, and enjoy the heck out of the moments of laughter and smiles. She's choosing to walk a lot more now, but it's hard for her to focus. There are so many people here all the time, which makes it hard for her to concentrate on what she is doing. It is imperative for her to focus in everything she does. If not, she can fall when she walks, choke when she eats, and forget what she's doing on a regular basis. She is reconnecting a new brain, re-learning everything so we continue to feed positive into her brain in the hopes that we can change the negativity that seems to plague her brain now.

She is starting to remember who and what she used to be so it is very frustrating and confusing for her. The doctors told us that she would never play softball again, but she has proven time and time again that she doesn't let their guidelines hold her back. She has more passion, drive, and determination than anyone I've ever known. Through it all, she continues to work diligently in her therapies because she is determined to earn her overnight pass and learn to play softball again. #TeamBdog

Almost every day since she got her hair shaved off, she told me that she was a boy. I pointed out her female attributes. She looks at them like she was confused and finally came to the conclusion that if she had breasts, she must not be a boy. I was constantly telling her how beautiful she was and how her short hair looked great on her. She didn't believe me or anyone else when they told her how beautiful she was, even with short hair. She told me that people thought she was a boy, so I was constantly trying to contradict what her mind was telling her.

When Christy did her make-up, it made all the difference in the world. She walked around the hospital with a big smile on her face, and all the patients and visitors told her how pretty she looked. Then she would tell me she was ugly, she was Forrest Gump, and that people laughed at her because she was a boy. It was a never-ending cycle that we had to repeat continuously. She had no short-term memory, so we had to constantly repeat ourselves while trying to counteract all her negative thoughts. I know this is all progress, and her brain was still healing, but I just wanted my baby girl back. I didn't want her to fear anything or cry because of the thoughts that plagued her mind.

She was starting to remember her past. She remembered she had been working since she was sixteen. She remembered that she was in college, studying to be a trauma nurse, and that she had a full ride to college because she was an awesome pitcher. Fortunately, she didn't remember the accident. She knows she was in a terrible accident, and that's why she was in the hospital, but she didn't remember any of the details of the accident; thank God for that. I have heard many of the details, and it sickens me and makes my heart drop into my stomach. But she is alive, and that is the most important thing to take away from all of this—she is alive!

She had a whiteboard in her room to help her remember what she needed to do each day and give her inspiration. We wrote affirmations and inspirational quotes on it each day, and I made her say them out loud each day when she woke up. We also wrote her goals for the week, and this week was "Work hard for your overnight pass!" That was her main focus right now, and she repeated it multiple times a day. "I will earn my overnight pass! I will lie in my own bed! I can do this!"

November 16, 2017

> PM update on day 83 of Sierra's journey… We can finally breathe a sigh of relief. These past couple days have been a little better. We have been working on her a lot. We only allow positive out of her mouth. I'm not sure if this is the correct way to handle her situation, but when she starts her negative talk, which is almost every thought so her words follow suit. So when she starts, I shut her down and make her say positive affirmations about herself. If her fears are too overwhelming, I say them for her, and then I make her repeat them. I tell her how beautiful she is, and how she is the biggest fighter I know. How she is such an inspiration to so many people and she is my hero. Sometimes she has to repeat them

through her tears, but she does it. She's such a big fighter. No matter how hard her stages of recovery are, she doesn't give up.

She went on an outing today with some of the other patients. This is a reward for her hard work. There is a woman here that is also a patient, she watches over Sierra when I can't be with her. We call her Mama Mimi. Because she is here to learn independence, they don't let me participate like I did in Las Cruces Rehabilitation hospital, so Mama Mimi watches over her when I'm not around. She stayed by Sierra's side the entire time they were on their outing. She said that Sierra handled it very well, and when she started getting overwhelmed, they got away from the stimulation and Mama talked her down enough to get through it all. Now that she handled that, the staff is thinking about a pass to go home for Thanksgiving. She knows we have to sign her out, so now she goes to the nurse's station to sign out. When they tell her that she can't sign herself out, she looks at them and rolls her eyes. Then she wheels herself away with a disgusted look on her face. Her dad told her that he was going to talk to the staff about getting her a three-day pass. When he came back, she was ready to go. She had packed her clothes and essentials and was ready to go. He explained to her that he was only going to inquire about getting a pass for a later date, not today. She was very disappointed to hear that so she went back to the nurse's station to try to sign herself out again. Of course they didn't let her, but it was really cute watching the effort. Today was a better day, and we are thankful. Her coach sent me this picture and wanted me to show it to Sierra so that she knew they were playing for her. #TeamBdog

Playing for #18

This picture is of her college softball team before a game. They released balloons and hung Sierra's picture by the dugout, then they played their hearts out for #18.

I realized it was extremely rude to cut people off when they were talking, but I had come to the conclusion that there was no other way to redirect her brain from her negative thoughts. So when she started talking negative, I interrupted her and told her that there was no negative talk allowed. She tried to argue with me, but I wouldn't have it. I would not even let the words come out of her mouth. As

236

soon as I realized she was about to spout off with negativity, I shut her down and told her to tell me something positive. If she couldn't think of anything, I helped her. I made her talk about the obstacles she had overcome. We went through the list one by one. I told her how she was beautiful and what an inspiration she was to so many people. Then I made her repeat after me. She rolled her eyes at me and reluctantly followed orders.

Her new thing was to try to sign herself out of the hospital. She knew that every time we took her out, we had to sign the daily log. So now every time she wanted to leave, she went to the nurses' station and tried to sign herself out. When they told her that she couldn't sign herself out, she gave them a dirty look, rolled her eyes at them, and wheeled herself away. One recurring memory was that she wanted out of here. She wanted to go home and continue therapy at the rehab hospital in Las Cruces where people cared about her and her recovery.

When Coach Lucas sent me this picture, I broke down and cried. He told me that his team played for Sierra. They played their hearts out for her. They felt so helpless, but this was something they could do for her. They could play their hearts out for her, and that is exactly what they did.

November 17, 2017

> PM update on day 84 of Sierra's journey... I remember when I decided to call this Sierra's journey back in Albuquerque. It seems so long ago, but it's only been 11 weeks. In that amount of time she has come back from knockin' on heaven's door and actually entering the gates of heaven to talk to her brother. She has had tubes removed from so many parts of her body, stitches removed, surgeries, and IV's giving her the nutrients and medications she needed to stay alive. She has dealt with fears beyond most of our comprehension. She has conquered the voices in her

head, broken bones, an extremely swollen brain, several brain bleeds, around her brain, in her brain stem, and shearing of her brain. She had no use of her left side, tore tendons and ligaments in her neck and her knee; she also had a collapsed lung, twice. She battled through pneumonia and beat it at one of her lowest points in recovery. She has endured more than most of us can even conceive. Through it all, she has been such a trooper, such a fighter, and the most inspirational person I know.

Art and I, along with our family, are very blessed to have her in our lives, she is truly our Miracle. She still has a ways to go, but she *will* get there. Thank you all for so many prayers for our baby girl, and for us. We are very grateful for all of you that have helped us in so many ways so I can be here with her 24-7.

The information we received about her projected discharge date was incorrect. Her dad called the insurance company and they said she has 100 days, and if needed, they will approve more time. This is one less thing for us to worry about. #TeamBdog

She had some downtime between therapies, so she asked me what she should do. I told her it would be a good idea to write what she was feeling, so she asked me for some Post-its. She had a big smile on her face, and I was wondering what she was up to. She started writing affirmations and sticking them all over her room. Another strange fact about her brain injury: when she came out of her coma, she knew how to read but no longer knew how to spell. I didn't want to discourage her, so I didn't point it out. I just let her write, and I read it without judgment. Most of it I could decipher, some I needed help with, but I had to be cautious how to present it to her so she wouldn't lose interest in her writing.

November 18, 2017

AM update on day 85 of Sierra's journey… When I walked in this morning she asked me if she needed a spinal tap because she has meningitis. I'm not exactly sure if that has to do with the fact that she has had it four times, or if she heard that the tubes in her brain could cause meningitis.

The young woman that was in the car accident just like hers came to visit her and told her about her struggles, her fight, the fact that she had to trust people that loved her because her brain was playing tricks with her. She made Sierra laugh, and cry, but after their conversation was over, I think she gained inspiration and determination.

She now believes that she's not stuck where she is, she can get her life back. She keeps telling us that we don't know what it's like, and she is completely correct. We have no clue what it is like for her every day. So we thought if she could talk to someone who has been in the same position, it might help her and give her something to look forward to. It really seemed to work, she definitely gave our baby girl hope.

Now she tells me negative things about her and her recovery, and stops to think. Then she looks at me and says, "But I have to stay positive." It's a small start, but it's a start nonetheless, and it's in a good direction. That's a good reason for us to be thankful. We are working on getting her knee healed, and we're taking her to a neuro-ophthalmologist specialist to see if he can stop her eyes from jumping all over the place.

I'm back home now, making the commute every morning so I can be with her during her waking hours and at night after they kick me out. We'll see how this goes, but for now it's necessary. Thank you to everyone who pitched in to get me the motel room for the past three weeks so I could be close to her while she was adjusting to her new surroundings. #TeamBdog

Now that I was back home, I had to get up extra early so I could make the hour-long drive to be at the hospital by 7:00 a.m. when she woke up. She didn't like it if I was not there to wake her up. She thought that I was hurt or dead, so it was very important that I was there when she woke up. She didn't want anyone else to help her shower and get ready for the day, so it was imperative to me that I get there before she woke up.

This morning, when I came to wake her up, the first thing to come out of her mouth was, "Do I need a spinal tap?" She may have had a dream or her brain may have told her that if she was in the hospital, she had meningitis. It was all speculation on my part, but the fact that she had it four times may have something to do with why her brain thought of that.

When the young woman that was in the accident like hers came to talk to Sierra, we made a list of questions she wanted to ask her so we wouldn't forget. She sat down with Sierra for about an hour and told her about her accident and how she didn't know any of her family when she woke up, so she had to have great faith in the people around her and came to trust them. She had to believe in them and know that they knew what was best for her because her mind played tricks on her. She told Sierra that she was a year and a half down the road of recovery and she was back at school, working and driving again.

Sierra's eyes lit up, and she asked, "Do you think I can do that?"

We both spouted in unison with, "Absolutely!" We all got a kick out of that. She damaged her brain in different parts than Sierra, so they had different disabilities, but she knew Sierra's struggle. That is why we thought it was imperative for Sierra to hear her story from someone she could relate to because she was right; we didn't know what it was like for her, but this young woman did.

After their conversation, Sierra learned the parallel events in each of their accidents. They were both with their boyfriends when they got in their accidents, they were both in a coma for two weeks, they both had to relearn everything, such as walking, talking, eating, all the things a healthy person takes for granted, and best of all, neither of them remembered their accidents. She told me, "Mommy, she gets it." Ah, that's exactly what we wanted—someone who understood her entire story.

PM update on day 85 of Sierra's journey... She had a much better day today. She didn't tell me she was going to die once. That's such a great day if we get through it without her preparing us for her death while she cries and tells us that she's ready. She has decided she wants to walk everywhere. She still has to use her walker, but she has learned to maneuver it very well. If we can get her knee fixed, I'm sure it will help her to walk on her own. She is still a little unstable, but the walker helps her keep her balance.

Eating, on the other hand, is still a big issue. Every time I tell her it's time to eat, she tells me she doesn't want to. So I reiterate the fact that she'll have to get the tube back in her stomach if she doesn't eat, and then she eats almost all of her meal after that. That is such a huge fear for her. She remembers the tube in her stomach and how much pain it caused her, so all I have to do is mention f——g tube, and she eats. Her medication curbs her appetite so she doesn't want to eat much. But the fear of getting the tube back in her stomach is enough for her to push through it and force the food down. She's down to 97lbs, so we have to make sure she eats all of her meals so she doesn't continue to lose weight.

She misses her family so much so we decided to have a bar-b-q with both sides of her family tomorrow here at the hospital in El Paso. She is so excited; she won't quit talking about it. She talked to me all day about it with a big smile on her face, it was so beautiful. Not only to see her smile, but because it shows her recall memory is getting better as well. She did think it was today a few times, but I had to remind her it will be tomorrow when Uncle Tony gets here. The fact that he will be here tomorrow for the bar-b-q makes its extra exciting for her. She is still working hard to earn her Thanksgiving pass, so if we don't hear anything by Monday, I'll have to start pushing the staff here to make it happen. Goodnight for now and thank you, all. #TeamBdog

Today, we started our day like every other day. I woke her up so we could get her in the shower and brought her wheelchair to her. She looked at me and said, "No, I am not using that. I am walking!" We settled on her walker because of the rules they had here. She still needed assistive devices because she was unsteady and more so now that she was on these new medications. So for the rest of the day, she used her walker, and I walked behind her with the wheelchair for when she got tired. She did have to sit in it a few times, but she did really great.

We believe the cookout with the family was just what she needed to give her a taste of family life again. Not only was she excited about the barbecue, but Uncle Tony was coming tomorrow as well, so I could see the anxiety building up. Since her dad and I had been divorced for fifteen years, we hadn't had both sides of the family together for family events, so this would be interesting.

She had been telling me she was going back to heaven for many weeks, but it felt like years. It broke my heart every time she told me that, yet I still had to be strong and continue to deal with every situation that may arise during the day.

November 19, 2017

AM update on day 86 of Sierra's journey… This morning, when I walked into her room, she told me, "We have a big day today" with a big smile on her face. Again, this is recall memory, which is extraordinary. Her ability to recall events is increasing every day. She didn't eat breakfast because she wasn't hungry, and when lunchtime came around she told me she didn't want to eat because of the cookout. I explained to her that our cookout isn't for several more hours so she reluctantly ate lunch. She has already lost six pounds since we arrived here so it is very important for her to eat as much as possible.

We had our family cookout and it was great. Both sides of her family came, except Aunt Susan and Uncle Bob because they had prior commitments. We missed them very much but it didn't hold us back from having a wonderful time. Uncle Tony arrived safely and he was here so she was very happy that he was able to join us.

She did get a little overwhelmed at times so we would just pull her aside for a bit, let her collect herself, and go back to the patio with the family. This is the most stimulation she has had since the accident, and even though it was a bit much for her at times, she handled it very well. She realized when it started getting overly stimulating for her and she would let me know so we could get away from everyone for a bit, she would breathe through it and then let me know when she was ready to join her family again.

She danced the two-step with Auntie Von and "I Got You, Babe" with her dad—that was priceless! She held the babies Brody, Sebby, and Sebastian; it was so beautiful. Thank you so much to all of my family and to all of her dad's family for coming out to make this day special for her. She said she wanted her family to have a cookout, and that's exactly what she got. She was so happy that everyone did this just for her. She knows her dad and I are divorced and we haven't had both families together since our wedding, but today was different, today was only about Sierra and it was beautiful! She smiled so much the entire time that everyone was there. After a couple hours, she was ready to go back to her room and informed me that everyone can come say goodbye to her one at a time.

After everyone left I asked her how she felt. She said she was very happy but it was a little too much stimulation for her. Again, it's progress. Not only being around so many people, but also the fact that she knew when it started to be too much for her and asked to get away from the situation until she could breathe through it, and when she was ready to join us again, she let me know she was good. She didn't cry or get mad, she just asked if she could go back to her room when the stimulation became too much to handle.

This far exceeds the amount of stimulation she has been able to handle since her accident, and we were delightfully surprised at how well she handled it seeing as how just last week she couldn't handle sitting in the dining room with ten people. Today was such a great day, and we are so thankful. #TeamBdog

Mommy and Bee

What a beautiful day we had today. A day we all desperately needed; a day of laughter, family, food, good times. This was a day that we never knew if we would be able to experience with her again.

Uncle Tony made it here just in time for the cookout, so that was an added bonus for her. We also had several of the inpatients here join us because they didn't get many visitors. Today, we were all family, and it was magnificent. It almost felt like our old lives, the lives we lived before she was in her horrific accident, the life we never knew we would have again. We did get it again, and we all felt so blessed that we were given the opportunity to do this again.

Although I was very worried about how she would handle being around so many people, I knew this time I wasn't alone. I had many people there to take some of the constant weight I alone carried on a daily basis. Today was the best day yet—the day we celebrated our MIRACLE.

November 20, 2017

> PM update on day 87 of Sierra's journey... She woke up and had a great day; she was positive, happy, and ready to go. By afternoon, she was crying and scared about everything again. I let her tell me all of her fears and then she cries, and I tell her, "There's no crying in baseball!" And she sucks it up, takes a breath, and moves on. Her focus is increasing every day. She is starting to get back on track, and it's a wonderful sight. This is a peak, and we love peaks! They get us through the valleys.
>
> I just found out we're going home for Thanksgiving! We had a meeting with the staff and my brother Tony went in with me to help me argue her case. It went Very well! It was a very positive outcome after having to fight for what she wants. She has been focused, and driven. She has been working so hard for this pass, and she *earned it*! We're so proud of her. #TeamBdog

Today we had a meeting with her entire staff. I felt that they were not as positive about her progress as we were. I sat and listened to them telling me how she wasn't doing this or that right, of how she isn't supposed to walk on her own, and they didn't want her pitching, etc. I really didn't care what they had to say. I cared what Sierra had to say, and I was here for her best interest. They aren't happy that I argued with them about almost everything. They were very reluctant to let Sierra come home for Thanksgiving because it would be a lot of stimulation for her.

She wanted to walk on her own, and her staff was more worried about getting sued than for her to progress at her own pace. I felt if she stated interest in wanting to improve her abilities, then we should listen to her and take the proper precautions for her to advance at her own pace. Of course, we took her brain injury in to account; however, when she stated the same desires for weeks, then her staff also needed to take that into account.

Her medications were still not the right balance for her because she was still having bouts of crying. It could go on for ten or fifteen minutes or it could go on for hours. It wore her out, and she couldn't understand why she couldn't quit crying. She told me she was so sad and it wouldn't go away. I told her about the things that made her happy or made her smile, and sometimes it worked, sometimes not so much. When it was all over, she slept. She slept so hard that the constant chattering, alarms, and people didn't wake her up. I sometimes had to check to make sure she was still breathing because she was sleeping so hard.

November 21, 2017

> PM update on day 88 of Sierra's journey… Today she has made the choice to reveal herself. As I stated before, I would not post any pictures of her until she gave me permission to do so. I am happy to say that today is that day. So, for the first time since her accident, here she is in all her glory. Beside her is her very thankful and proud family. The adage "A picture is worth a thousand words" rings so true for us today. #TeamBdog

The First of Many

This is the first of many pictures to come. However, this one is the most important because she has healed enough to make the decision to reveal herself. Here is the beautiful young lady that you all prayed so hard for. Had it not been for all of your prayers, we truly believe this picture would not be possible, so thank you to all of you for your prayers.

What a beautiful day for all of us to share this tremendous milestone in her recovery. We were so blessed just to be ABLE to have this family time. When she saw it, she asked me if she looked like a boy. I told her, "No Way!"

She was actually the one who asked me if we could take a picture of all of us and post it. I was delightfully surprised and immediately obliged before she changed her mind because at this point in her recovery, she changed her mind from one minute to the next.

November 22, 2017

> PM update on day 89 of Sierra's journey... She woke up this morning and wanted to pack so we could leave. I explained she still had to do her therapies. So she rolls her eyes at me and says, "F—k" under her breath. So, repeatedly, she asked if it was time to go. Finally, the time to go came. She decided it was okay to come back on the highway, which was a very big step for her. We got her to her dad's and we could see the sense of relief on her face. She's a little confused about what's fact and what's fiction, but that's why we're here for her to help her distinguish between fact and fiction.
>
> We wanted to wish a Happy Thanksgiving to all. And thank you for your prayers so we can be truly thankful. Our baby is not only alive, but she is doing so well that she gets to spend Thanksgiving at home with her family where she belongs. #TeamBdog

Today was the first day that I saw her halfheartedly work on her therapies. The only thing on her mind was going home. She had a list of things that she wanted to do, and just lying down in her own bed was at the top of the list. She was so anxious to get home she decided she wanted to take the highway. Her dad and I looked at each other with a puzzled look but decided to go with it.

We got home safely, and the first thing she did was go to her room and lie in her bed. She told me it was the best day ever in her own room, in her own bed. Then she smiled at me and said, "I'm so happy, Mommy" and went to sleep. She slept soundly for about four hours, and when she woke, up she reiterated how happy she was to be home. Her dad and I couldn't help but feel the same exhilaration.

On the other hand, I was also a nervous wreck. I was afraid that something may happen to her. I was afraid she won't wake up. I was afraid she might hit her head or fall down. I wanted to keep her in a padded room and protect her from anything that could hurt her. My security was gone.

November 23, 2017

> PM update on day 90 of Sierra's journey… Day 90! This is the day that the doctors said she would be getting out of ICU. When we got to Albuquerque 90 days ago, they told me to expect 90 days in ICU, at least, and up to a year. They also informed me that I should count on being in Albuquerque at least six months to two years if she lived.
>
> Today she walked around holding our hands, she held conversation, she sat with us in her own chair, she eats, she pitches, she catches with the left arm (the affected arm), she has no tubes in her body and she is down to only two medications. She is so amazing, and she wants out of the El Paso rehab so badly. The fact she can think about that is a really good sign. It gives her focus and a goal for her to achieve. She did very well at the family gathering. All of our family understands where she is in her recovery, and we just accept everything as it comes. Aunt Susan and Uncle Bob's house is the most secure place she could be, besides her bedroom. She had to go out on the porch swing for a little while because the stimulation was a bit much for her, but she came back in and joined everyone after a short break.
>
> She did finally get too overwhelmed and told me she wants to go. I told her she has to go back to El Paso, so she rolled her eyes, sighed, and decided against it. Then about ten minutes later she was really ready to go. So we got her back early, but safe. She was completely worn out by

the time we got back so Morke put her to sleep. She was asleep by the time we had to leave, which makes it so much easier to walk down that very long hallway. It's really not that long, but it feels like a mile having to leave her at night. Good night All, we are so very thankful for you all.

We wanted to wish all of you a Happy Thanksgiving, which also includes the massive amount of friends that have joined us on our journey. Sierra says… "I couldn't thank you enough!" So this Thanksgiving we are not only extremely thankful that we still have our baby girl, but to all of you! To the people that started this journey with us since day one and everyone who has joined her journey along the way. We are truly thankful for all of you as well. We are thankful for all your prayers, support, kindness, and love. #TeamBdog

Ninety days in the outside world goes by in a flash. Ninety days living in a hospital seems like an eternity. Although I am not the one who had to live in the hospital, I was the one who chose to live in hospitals for the past ninety days. I absolutely refused to leave my child alone day after day. I was a huge part of her recovery. She told me that she needed me every day since she could speak. I was the one who decided to quit my jobs and stay with her until she was able to come home. After getting a taste of the lack of health care, there was no way I could leave her alone.

Today was Thanksgiving, and we had so much to be thankful for, mostly for Sierra and her path to recovery. She is our miracle, and we would never forget that. We all love our children with everything we've got, but when you almost lose that child, you understand how very blessed you are to have one more day, one more smile, one more breath of that child you love so much.

We were also very thankful to have Aunt Susan. She had started chemotherapy and was responding well to it. She was the most

251

beautiful woman I had ever met. She was the epitome of kindness, thoughtfulness, acceptance, and love, and we were so thankful she was our family. We had our family dinner at her house as we did every year. The house was full of love and laughter as it had been most of my life and every year of my children's lives.

Sierra did so well with so much stimulation, and when she started getting overwhelmed, she just stepped outside. That may not sound like a very big deal, but it was. It meant her brain continued to heal rapidly, and she knew what she needed to do to feel better. She didn't cry or feel helpless because she didn't know what to do; she just did what she needed to do.

I enjoyed a beautiful sunset that night with my children and grandchildren, and I can't think of a better way to end our night. When the sun went down, she was ready to go. I told her she had to go back to El Paso, and I could see the wheels turning, and she finally decided she didn't want to leave; she wanted to spend more time with the family. We went back inside, but I could see that she was getting really worn out. I decided to wait and see what she would do instead of telling her that she needed to go.

I went to go sit in the living room, and next thing I knew, she was hugging everyone and saying her goodbyes. We got her back to El Paso, and she fell asleep almost immediately, which made it so much easier to leave her for the night.

November 24, 2017

> PM update on day 91 of Sierra's journey... As you can see, she is making her own posts now. Her thoughts are clearer, more often. Yesterday, she went to see her coworkers at Albertson's, and they were very impressed and very happy to see her; lots of tears, and lots of smiles. Today, when I got to El Paso, they asked me how it went. I explained to them that, with the support of someone's hand, she walked everywhere; she recognized unsafe situations and chose different

options. She is back on the high road again. So she worked really hard at her therapy today and the Administrator came in about 5pm and told us she gets a weekend pass. Woohoo! She and her daddy packed immediately and were ready to go in a couple minutes. So we are all home for the weekend. She wanted nothing more than to chill in her room, and that's exactly what she did… with a big smile on her face.

She can have visitors but not too many at once so you can contact her, Art, or I to make arrangements so we can keep her stimulation level low. I broke my phone so Sierra and I both got new phone numbers. If you don't already have our numbers, please contact me through messenger. If you are not programmed in her phone, she can't answer. That way we can monitor who is calling her, and she understands if it doesn't come up with a name, we don't allow her to answer. Goodnight and thank you again for your understanding. #TeamBdog

Exhilaration combined with fear and anxiety were some of the emotions we experienced bringing our daughter home. We were so happy to finally have her home, even if it was only for a couple of days. However, we were afraid because she hadn't been home for more than a day since the accident. She needed twenty-four-hour care, and we were unsure if we were capable of taking care of her on our own. What if she fell? What if she had a seizure? What if she entered a stage that we didn't know what to do for her? There were so many questions and so much anxiety that came with bringing her home. So we decided to take one minute at a time and deal with whatever presented itself.

She was so incredibly happy to be home. Many people contacted us to come visit her. We all understood how very close we were to losing her, so having the opportunity to visit was truly a godsend. It was very nice because one or two people would come visit, and when they left, more would come, and it was like that most of the weekend. There were some times when we would have to turn people away because it was just too much stimulation for her. But everyone was very understanding of her situation. We overcame our fears, dealt with each situation as we were faced with them, and we were able to just be thankful.

November 25, 2017

> PM update on day 92 of Sierra's journey… She is very happy to be home. When we got here she had big plans of what she wanted to do, but instead she has just enjoyed being home and slept a lot. She walked to the park about a block away with Morke today and no walker. She is adamant that she does not want to use the wheelchair or walker, she wants to walk. Now she is telling us that her pelvis has been hurting as well as the knee, which upsets her because it hinders her walking.
>
> She had several visitors today and, for the most part, she handled it pretty well. She had to go into her room a couple times, but the fact she knew that, is progress. She tells us she's so confused, she doesn't know what's happening, so we are trying repetition to help her memory. Morke is leaving tomorrow morning and she is very sad about that of course. She thought he was going back to Panama, which he isn't but she knew he was leaving. It's just one of those things where she knows bits and pieces of a story and fills in the rest, the medical term is actually confabulation. She's also bummed about having to go back to El Paso tomorrow and rolls her eyes and tells us I know I have to get better, but I just want to be home. We want that too, but are very thankful for where she's at in her healing process. #TeamBdog

When we got back home, she told me of all the things she wanted to do and people she wanted to see, but as soon as we got here, all she wanted to do was stay home and hang out in her room. I believed her security was gone as well, and the only secure place she knew was home. We didn't wake her up here; we just let her sleep as much as she wanted. The doctors told us in Albuquerque that her brain healed when she was sleeping, but they didn't let her sleep as much as she wanted. It was a catch-22, I suppose. She couldn't sleep all the time because she needed her therapy to improve, but her brain needed sleep to heal. Somewhere, there has to be a happy medium.

When we brought her home, we didn't make her use her wheelchair or walker just to walk around the house, and if she was walking outside, we could let her hold on to us for stability so she could walk on her own. We still had to pay very close attention because she tended to try to push herself too much, and her pelvis and knee had been hurting, so we surely didn't need her falling down. She wanted to push herself, but we were not quite sure if she understood her limits yet, so we had to set them for her. She had a revolving door of visitors. When one set of people would leave, another would arrive. It made her very happy, but it also wore her out, so we continually asked her how she was feeling, and she would say, "I'm kind of worn out." So we had to ask her visitors to leave because she didn't quite know her limits just yet.

November 26, 2017

> PM update on day 93 of Sierra's journey... She had a fantastic weekend at home. When we got there she had plans to do things. But she was so comfortable in her surroundings; she decided to stay home the whole weekend. We watched movies, worked on puzzles, and just got to hang out. It felt so good, so right to have her back home. Morke cooked all her meals for her because he is an amazing cook and she loves his cooking. Actually, we all love his cooking. Speaking

of Morke, he left today and he will be going to Panama, for a well-deserved family gathering for Christmas. His parents have not seen him since the accident and my heart goes out to them. She took it hard, but didn't cry as much as I thought she would. She was definitely bummed all day, but her attitude is to get back to El Paso, kick some butt, and get home!

She has a white board on the wall as you walk into her room at the rehab and we have her write her goals on it. She sees it every time she enters and every time she leaves her room. They seem to be working, I write them every week, and every day when we leave the room first thing in the morning, I make her read it. When the negative thoughts try to surface, I make her read it again.

We listen to her fears, help her ease them, and remind her of her goal of the week. It's obviously working because tonight she asked me if we have to change it for next week. This week I will let her choose her own goal and write it herself. I'm interested in what she will come up with after reading her posts. She's back in El Paso, I had to walk what I've deemed the long mile but apparently she's still awake because she's posting on line and texting me. She's on a peak, and we're very grateful for it. One Day at a Time. I've had that imprinted in my brain most of my life. Thank you, Dad, it has been my saving grace through this. If today is good, we're thankful. If it is not, we know we only have to do this today. So, today is good, and we're thankful. #TeamBdog

This is the first of many goals she will write for herself.

November 26, 2017—From the mouth of Sierra

She decided she wanted to write her own post tonight: Thank you God for the life I've been given and guiding me through the good and bad times. I'm so blessed, thank you Lord. You keep me positive even if it seems impossible, nothing is impossible with you God! I cry sometimes, but it's okay. My Mommy helps me when I'm sad. I remember some things and some people. I liked Thanksgiving at Aunt Susan and Uncle Bob's, I love them. I had to write I'm capable to remind me because I forget, and I forget I'm not going to the chair because I'm a felon. The nurses have to check my pulse to make sure I'm alive because I'm dying.

This was her first post that she wrote all by herself. It was such a blessing for our family to see this. It was such a simple post, yet so profound. She was *not* a felon, and she was obviously not going to "the chair." That was just a constant fear that we had to continually redirect her brain from. We also had to ask the nurses to check her pulse to ease her mind and reiterate the fact that she was alive.

November 27, 2017

> PM update on day 94 of Sierra's journey… She had a really hard time getting up this am because she stayed up late posting and texting, so I had to put a curfew on her. Then I saw her recent post and I realized she was on her phone way after her curfew. It's somewhat of a rock and a hard place because I have to leave her phone with her until I make it home safely and call her, but then she has to stay up late enough for me to get home and call her.
>
> One of her many fears is that we are all in harm's way or that we are dead, so it is imperative that I call her every night when I am safely home. That also goes for all of her friends and family, if you come visit her, she needs you to call her and tell her that you're safe. If we don't call her, she will cry and convince herself that something is wrong and we must be hurt or dead.
>
> She is no longer on their one on one program because she is more aware of safety issues; this is a definite improvement from last week. However, that gives her more freedom to stay up late and she doesn't have the ability to understand if she stays up late and has to get up early, she will have a rough day.
>
> We don't have to turn the alarm on her bed anymore and one of the techs doesn't have to stay

with her every time she's alone now. Her goal for the week is "Slow and steady, I'll get there!" and "Pray!" Her dad taught her that this weekend when she was at home. When she walked against the wall by herself, she kept telling herself, "Slow and steady, I'll get there."

She's not asking near as much about being wanted by *America's Most Wanted*. We only had to check her pulse about five times today so that she can be sure she's alive. Some of the staff is very good about it, others are not. Every time she asks them to check it, they check all her stats to ease her mind, then they tell her what the numbers are. Seeing as how she's studying to be a nurse, they show her every reading and she says "Okay," with a huge sigh of relief, then she takes a breath and continues what she was doing.

The negative thoughts are subsiding for now and she prays a lot. She prays for everyone, all of you, people here, and people from all the hospitals, and of course, her family. She still apologizes for being so much trouble and she writes me letters in speech telling me she's sorry for the immense pain she has caused me. It breaks my heart that she thinks like that. I tell her thank you for her immense fight she has shown us, and for not giving up, and giving me this opportunity to go through this with her. Then she cries, takes a breath, and continues on. Wow! We could have never dreamed of the roller-coaster ride, but we are so thankful for this opportunity. Goodnight for now, and thank you. #TeamBdog

Baby steps. She took baby steps forward all the time. Every day was something new. It may be a very bad day when she was afraid of everything or it could be a great day when she smiled a lot. Either way, it was all progress. Peaks and valleys was what the doctors told us in Albuquerque, and that's exactly what it was.

She could go through peaks and valleys all in one day or she could be in a valley for a week or she could be on a peak for days. The one thing we had to keep in mind was that it was all progress; even the bad times she had to go through was her brain making new connections and healing every day. We were truly happy that she was only having her pulse and heart rate checked a handful of times each day now. We had to check it about thirty times a day just a week ago, so five times today was a great relief.

I told her when her fears tried to take over her thoughts to pray. So she had taken up prayer in everything she did. When she cried, sometimes she didn't even know why she was crying, but she prayed through it. She prayed for God to get her through her therapies, to help her eat; she prayed for her family, friends, and the staff that took care of her.

More than anything, I wished that I could make her understand that she was not a burden and not to worry about money being spent on her or to take care of her. When I read the letter she wrote for me in her speech therapy, I just cried. It hurt me so badly that she was worried about being a burden to us when we were elated to have the opportunity to help her come back to us.

I was happy to quit my jobs to have the honor of staying with her every day and every night since the accident. I had been given the opportunity to watch an entire new brain form, and it was the most awe-inspiring phenomenon I have ever experienced.

November 28, 2017

> PM update on day 95 of Sierra's journey… I got there early today to wake her up and, of course she didn't want to get out of bed. That also happened many times with her old brain as well. Her old brain and her new brain don't like mornings. Speaking of her old brain, we are learning the differences in old brain and new brain. One interesting fact is that her tastes in food have changed.

Foods that she used to like, she no longer does. An example of this is green chili, she used to love it, now she wants nothing to do with it. On the other hand, foods that she wouldn't eat before her accident she likes now. We have no clue how or why but we know it to be fact.

She had a rough day in her mind today. She apologized multiple times for spending so much money on her to get better, for taking up so much of our time, and for causing so much trouble. We don't know where these thoughts are coming from because we never even talk about these things around her, and by no means do we feel like that.

She asked me many times today if she was one of America's Most Wanted. Again, we have no clue where this is coming from. She doesn't watch it now, nor has she ever watched it. We also had to get her vitals checked about ten times today, and every time they were all good, yet she continues to ask at least once an hour. After the nurse checks her vitals and she hears that they are good, she breathes a sigh of relief as if it's the first time she's heard that.

Her newest thing is that she is paranoid about people stealing her things. She wants me to lock her door every time we leave her room. I explain to her that no one goes into her room and she just rolls her eyes and argues with me.

Today she was very sensitive to any form of stimulus. We were working on a puzzle in the dining room today and there were only a couple people in there talking but it bothered her so much that we had to go back to her room.

She cried a lot, but through all of her struggles today, she would stop, take a breath, and tell herself, "I can do this!" She is truly amazing! With every emotion and hurdle she faces each day, she won't give up her fight and perseverance.

Her dad will come spend the day with her tomorrow because it is his birthday and Aunt Susan has surgery, please add her to your prayers tonight as well. Thank you for keeping us all in your prayers. Goodnight All, until tomorrow. #TeamBdog

I asked her why she was crying today, and she said she didn't know. She was just so sad that she had to cry. This made it so much more difficult because I didn't know how to help her if I didn't know the cause of her tears. The only thing I knew to do was to hold her, rub her, and talk very gently to her. I told her it was okay because she wasn't trapped anymore. She could cry and release and emotions that built up in her and move on to fight another day. It wasn't too long ago that she didn't have that ability. She was trapped within her own body and didn't know how to cry.

What seemed to soothe her most was when we went through the list of obstacles she had overcome. With that in mind, I told her to go through the list, so she told me all the hurdles she had jumped through, and I helped her when she couldn't remember. That comforted her for a while, but then she just cried again. She told me she was scared and she didn't know why she was crying. It got so overwhelming sometimes that my only defense was to cry right along with her; the only difference is that I knew exactly why I was crying. I was crying because I couldn't help my baby girl, and I wanted to with every part of my being, but nothing I did could soothe her, and it hurt me to the core.

When she was in one of her crying episodes, I told her to pray, so she did, and I prayed right along with her. We begged God to please help her get through this stage so she didn't have to feel so incredibly sad. I begged God to please give her emotions to me and let her mind be at peace.

She was looking forward to spending time with her dad for his birthday tomorrow. She made him a bracelet in occupational therapy today, and she was excited to give it to him.

November 29, 2017

PM update on day 96 of Sierra's journey… She spent the day with her daddy today. She painted him a picture with a heart and wrote to him on the inside of the heart. She also made him a bracelet in her occupational therapy and, of course he loved it. He said she cried many times today. She's stuck on the accident now. She wants to know how it happened, why it happened. She wants to know who saved her life, if everyone in the car is okay, and so on. So we go through the whole story and she cries, and lets it out then she breathes and says, "Okay, that's why I'm in here because I have to get better!" Then she proceeds to tell us that if God wants her to stay like this, then so be it. If he doesn't want her to walk right, she will deal with it. We explain that she isn't stuck, that she's getting better all the time.

We still have contact with one of the ICU nurses in Albuquerque that saw her brain scan. He got an update on her and said, "No way!" They could not believe that she has come so far, so quickly. They calculated this much progress in a year, maybe. So those stories help her get through the moment. She went on an outing today to the history museum with some of the other patients. Mama Mimi was by her side the entire time. She texted me and told me, "Mommy, it was a little too much for me, but it was fun, and Mama Mimi took me away from everyone when it was too much for me." It seems contrary, but it just means that she worked through it enough to have fun. That's pretty big, considering her sensitivity to stimulation lately.

I've been trying to push her a little more, and Daddy just says, "Okay, honey, if you don't want to, you don't have to." That hasn't changed either; he's always been wrapped around that little finger. We had birthday cake tonight after dinner and sang Happy Birthday to him, it made her really happy. Tomorrow she goes back to the eye doctor so they can check her eyes again. Her eyes are not jumping around near as much as they were, and we can definitely see the change when you look her in the eyes. The doctor said it was like trying to read when your hand is shaking. It is getting a little better, but it's very frustrating for her. She still has to look closely to read and her right eye floats around. So, hopefully tomorrow we get some answers to help her vision.

Thank you for prayers for Aunt Susan. She came out of surgery okay and will be staying overnight. If you would like more info on that, please get a hold me on messenger. I'd also like to send a special thank you going out to the Georgia, her coworkers, and family for raising enough money for me to stay in El Paso for another two weeks. Thank you, and goodnight. #TeamBdog

She had a wonderful day spending time with her dad for his birthday. He loved and appreciated the card and the bracelet that she made for him. It meant a lot more this year than it ever had before. I did have to go back to El Paso after Aunt Susan's surgery. While she loved being with her dad, she felt like she needed me to be with her all the time.

She knew now about Aunt Susan and her cancer. One of our family members mentioned it at our Thanksgiving dinner, so I had to explain to her what was going on. We tried to keep it from her because she was so close to Aunt Susan. We didn't know how it would affect her recovery. That was the main reason she was okay with me going to Las Cruces and not being there when she woke up today. She and Aunt Susan had decided to fight together. I told her that some of the parents chipped in so I could stay at a motel close to the rehab, so she was very happy now that I was able to stay in El Paso longer. She told me, "So if I need you, Mommy, you'll be close?" I told her I would only be about five minutes away, so she gave her approval, which made all of us feel much better.

November 30, 2017

PM update on day 97 of Sierra's journey… We took her to a different eye doctor today, he specializes in neuro-ophthalmology. He wrote her a new script for glasses and we're very hopeful that he can help her get her sight back to where it should be. Her right eye is very bad right now and the left is 20/40. However, a month ago, it was her left eye that she had problems with because the left side was the affected side. Now her left eye is getting stronger all the time.

We have been playing catch and she catches the softball regularly. She uses her very 'broke in' glove and the light softball, but she's actually squeezing the glove shut to keep the ball in. She told us that her pelvis doesn't hurt, but it doesn't feel right when she walks, so her occupational therapist checked it out and it is definitely swollen, but also it seems to be shifted. That's where she had surgery to fix it, so we are wondering if, at the time she had surgery, which was the first night, that there were a lot more pressing issues like her brain and saving her life. So we have to wonder if that didn't get fixed as well as it should have. She has an MRI for her knee on the fourth; so hopefully, they can check both the pelvis and her knee the same day because of her reaction to stimulus in public.

Speaking of stimulus, she has been struggling with that a lot. We had to eat dinner in her room tonight, and she wanted to get away from everyone today. I realized how hyper-sensitive her hearing really is today. We were sitting in the dining room with the social worker, having her Thursday meeting and my phone rang, but I had it on the lowest possible volume and in my pocket. So she tells me mom your phone is ringing, but I was sure it wasn't. I looked at it, and sure enough, it was ringing. I couldn't hear it even when I took it out of my pocket, neither could the social worker.

She appears to be going into a valley. She's sad and she cries all the time. She cries because she's scared, and she's scared because she thinks everyone is either hurt or dead. So it is very important to keep your word to her when you tell her something because it really throws her off if you don't. It's simple to us but it consumes her. An example is, "I'll let you know when I get home." However, if you forget, she thinks you're hurt or dead. I try to reassure her continually that whoever is the target of the night is okay. We have to face time people, call them, or text them so they can let her know that they're okay and they made it home safely.

She wants to know why she's so sad. We talk about the great things SHE has accomplished and I make her repeat wonderful things about herself to bring her out of the funk she gets in. We talk about the obstacles she's overcome, from the tubes in her brain and no reaction to stimulus to where she is now. She eats, she talks, she walks, she works on deduction puzzles and logic problems, and she is able to reason things out more often. So we are thankful for all the hurdles she has fought with everything she's got to get where she's at and I tell her how we are all in awe of her strength. Goodnight for now. Thank you for your continued prayers. #TeamBdog

This was so very hard on all of us. We wanted nothing more than to take away her pain and her fears, but we couldn't. We had to watch her go through unimaginable pains and fears. We tried so hard to relinquish all of her pain and help to diminish her fears. We talked to her about her fears and explained why they are not true. We tried to reason it out with her, but the part of her brain that reasons things out had not reconnected yet.

She cried so much that she exhausted herself and she just wanted to sleep. Since I was with her all day, every day, I got to witness her pain continuously, and it was so heartbreaking. I held her and tried my best to comfort her, and she cried. She cried from the core of her being. I held her so tight and told her how proud we were of her. I told her that I had no idea what she was going through, but I was not leaving her. She would never have to go through this alone. I would be here with her every step of the way. I prayed to God to give me the right words to help her. I prayed to God to help her and take away her fears. All the while, I prayed that by answering my prayers, he didn't decide to take her home.

She had come so far, and the fear of her dying was constantly in the forefront of our thoughts and our fears. Most days, I couldn't eat because my stomach was so upset because of what she had to battle on a daily basis. As a mom, the hardest thing we ever have to do was see our child in pain, but to know that we were helpless in taking it away was extremely hard. We could be by their side and talk to them and hold them, but they were the ones that had to go through it to get on the other side. I would give anything to take her place and give her life back, but I couldn't. Her dad couldn't, her family couldn't; only she and God could get her through this. It was such a helpless feeling that didn't go away. It was our life now, and we couldn't do anything to change that. We took one day at a time and dealt with whatever we were handed each day as it came.

December 1, 2017

> PM update on day 98 of Sierra's journey... Well, it was quite an eventful day. She sent her dad a text last night that had us questioning a lot of things, particularly where her brain is at as far as progress. There are two terms they have for what we believe she may be going through. One is *confabulation*, and the other is *perseverance*. In layman's terms, it means that she may hear a piece of information and her brain will create stories out of that piece information. Or she recalls memories, most of the memory anyways, and her brain just fills in the rest. Example: "The cops are coming for me." Because there were so many police officers at the scene of the accident, her brain damaged mind thought that they had to be there to arrest her. When, in reality, they were all there for her because she was on the brink of death. We have to check her vitals all the time because she thinks she died and needed the defibrillator, which she didn't. She had to have knuckle rubs on her chest to try to get some kind of reaction from her so she wouldn't slip into oblivion in the beginning so it put a huge bruise on her chest and apparently caused great pain that she remembers from being in the coma. So, in her mind, her chest was sore because of the defibrillator. She fills in the blanks with whatever pops in her mind, and her mind is still overpowered by negative thoughts.

She is definitely in a valley, but she prays a lot, takes a breath and says, "I can do this!" We had to put more restrictions on her phone now that she's got the whole social media thing down again. What she doesn't have down, is the filter and capacity to understand she can't post everything she thinks, particularly at the stage her brain is at. So, from now on, she cannot send or post anything until we okay it. I repeated it to her several times today and she remembered so I feel better about that. If, for some reason, you do receive a message from her that makes you wonder 'what the heck?' then please contact us to determine its validity. Thank you and goodnight, all. #TeamBdog

This was the night I received several calls and texts from concerned family members. She was in an inappropriate stage, which included sexually inappropriate, unfortunately. She posted several sexually explicit posts. She didn't understand how inviting her posts may be to the wrong audience, besides the fact that sexual encounters were a private matter.

I explained to her that there were a lot of people out there that may see her posts but not understand her story. They didn't understand she had a new brain forming, and this was one of her many stages she had to go through. From this point on, she was not allowed to post anything until her dad or I approved it. This was also one of the many stages that I did not go into depth when I posted her progress because they were of a sexual nature.

She was struggling with so many emotions, fears, and obstacles. She was also reading my posts now, so I didn't want to humiliate her. This experience was already so humbling for her and for us that we had to use some discretion when posting her stages and progress.

On top of all that, she was also suffering from perseverance, which meant she remembered part of a story, and her brain filled in the rest. So she told us some stories that were doozies. Now that she was posting on social media, she told all of her readers some as well. That's why I had to post to everyone to please ask us before you take her posts as fact.

December 2, 2017

> AM update on day 99 of Sierra's journey… I came in this morning, and her nurse asked me if we're taking her home because she has an overnight pass. Again, we had no clue. They just spring this on us. But, all in all, we are thankful that we get to have her home again! Visitors are welcome of course, but please call first. Her stimulation tolerance is low. However, the softball girls are always welcome; she said it's okay because she gets to see a few of you at a time. When she's done with the ones in her room, she tells them that they can leave and then the next set of girls comes in. We just don't want to overwhelm her because that will put a damper on her getting overnight passes. She has to earn her passes, and the way she does that is when she goes back to the hospital, she has to get up for breakfast on time, perform well in her therapies, and show initiative as far as chores and hygiene. With what her mind has been going through this week, we believe some home time, family, friends, and her own room is exactly what she needs. So we'll see you soon. We love you. #TeamBdog

This week, she had undergone so many fears she was trying to conquer. She still stood up and put her hands behind her back and told the staff that she was ready to go to jail. She also believed she was going to the electric chair, so when she stood up, she put her hands behind her back and told them, "I'm ready!" What she was actually telling all of us was that she had contemplated her death a thousand times, and she mentally prepared herself for her imminent death. Again they looked at her like she was crazy.

She told us that she was going to die; she tried to prepare us for her death. She explained to us what it was like in heaven, where her brother was waiting for her, and we would be okay when she went home. She cried inconsolably. A lot of the time, we didn't even know why. I just held her, hugged her, and told her how amazing she was and how she had overcome so many obstacles. Then I made her repeat them. We went through the list of what she had overcome. Sometimes she could repeat after me, and sometimes she was crying so much that I went through them, and she just nodded her head in acknowledgment.

On my drive home, I cried. I begged God to please heal her. It was my time when I could actually be weak and break down. I told him how hard it was on me to hear my baby girl trying to prepare me for her death. I felt so helpless and hurt so deeply, but I couldn't do anything with it. I absolutely had to continue to be strong for our baby girl. So I cried on the way home, and I prayed for God to give me the right words to help ease her fears and dry her tears.

> PM update on day 99 of Sierra's journey… This am when I went in, they asked me if I was going to take her home today. I was surprised because no one gave us a head's up, but I told her, "Heck Yeah!" So I packed up all her stuff and waited for her dad and Krystal to get here and we got out of there. She has to have someone sit next to her every time we get in a vehicle.
>
> We went to pick out her glasses, and her only concern was that she didn't look like a boy. Her hair is growing out very quickly. Six weeks ago it wasn't 1/4 in long; today it's about three inches long. She put a tiny little pony in it, but it didn't stay. I'll be braiding it before she knows it. She got home and she went straight to her room to lay in bed. We could see the relief in her eyes;

hear the relief in her voice, and her whole general attitude.

She walks around the house with no walker; all the while she tells us how the El Paso rehab is holding her back. They still don't want her walking around without her wheelchair or walker, but she wants to, so we let her walk her around everywhere now. We just stand next to her and she puts her hand on our shoulder for balance. She doesn't want to use the walker because she said it's stupid and she doesn't need it. So we are listening to her and letting her walk everywhere, as long as it's safe for her. We are there in case she falls or gets tripped up, but she is doing it on her own.

She is responding much better to her restrictions on her phone as well. Every time she uses it, she asks us if what she wrote is okay before she posts or texts. And when she goes to bed, she knows her phone goes to the nurses' station now because she was sending inappropriate texts and posts. She is starting to argue more about things she believes to be true. So if she gets something in her head, like close my door so nobody steals anything, we explain that's not going to happen and she argues. So we reason it out so she gets it and it gets her through that moment.

She has homework over the weekend and part of it is to do puzzles, which she loves so it's not a fight to have her work on them. All three of us worked on one for about two hours. That's two hours of being able to focus, that's pretty incredible.

We also went to Auntie Von's for her birthday and had cake and ice cream. The kids were playing and the baby was crying while we were talking and she smiled at everything around her. She tolerated it for over an hour. Having our family back together means the world to us. When we went back to her dad's house, he had made green enchiladas and rice. It was so nice to be home and have a home cooked meal. It really is the simple things we miss. Family time and home cooked meals, it was great! So we get to spend the day here tomorrow and have her back tomorrow evening.

She wants to do word problems and math tomorrow because she wants us to challenge her. She also wants her therapists to challenge her more because she remembers she used to be smart. She doesn't think she can do calculus yet, but she said she'll get there again. Today was a much better day for her and we are grateful for today. Goodnight, all, and thank you. #TeamBdog

Sierra, Krystal, and Art getting ready to bring
her home. That smile says it all!

Since the day she got to the El Paso rehab hospital, they had
been holding her back. Lisa, her physical therapist from the Las
Cruces Rehab Hospital, had her walking by the time she left. Now
that she was here, they wanted her to use her wheelchair or walker
everywhere she went.

She was supposed to be here to learn independence, but they
were holding her back, and she knew it. She got very frustrated and
yelled when we were in the dining room where everyone could hear.
She yelled that they didn't care about her, that they were only there
for the paycheck, and they were holding her back. I had told her therapists to treat her like an athlete and they were her coach. She had
been an athlete her whole life, and she responded to being coached
better than anything else they had tried. Her physical therapist told
me with a big smile on his face how he got her to take fifteen steps
by herself. I explained to him that Lisa had her walking by herself for
two weeks already. She was walking from her room all the way to the

gym. We stood beside her with the wheelchair in case she got tired, and we helped her with balance, but she walked on her own, only using the handicap bars on the walls.

December 3, 2017

> PM update on day 100 of Sierra's journey… She would like to post for her 100 day mark: I appreciate where my past has lead me, and I'm praying that I get a pass for Christmas, and I got to sleep in my own bed and got to see my family. This is what I came from…tubes in my brain and tubes throughout my whole body. My remembrance of nothing, to where it is now. I'm thankful God has guided me to this day because my life's been a little rocky lately. But I'm learning to accept what happened to me and ready to move on to the next part of my life.
>
> That's all I really feel, I'm just thankful. And I can remember I'm a girl and I know how to shower by myself. And cops are my friends and my vitals are a little fast, but please don't worry about me, I'll be okay because I have the man upstairs and my family, and even though what happened to me is really sad, I'm fighting to get back and be 120% because Mom said I'm going to be better than what I was because I didn't give up, and giving up is an option, but I don't choose that path, I choose to keep fighting. Me and Aunt Sue Sue are warriors together now. I Love you guys and you're not wasting your time or money on me because I don't give up! Goodnight. I love you. #TeamBdog

Writing this post was heartbreaking for me. On the other hand, it made me so happy that she was able to get her thoughts out. These fears were constant; they didn't leave her mind, and that's what we dealt with on a daily basis. She thought she was a boy. We had to have the nurse check her vitals every day, multiple times a day. She feared getting arrested, she feared taking showers, and she didn't want to be here anymore.

Aunt Susan was fighting breast cancer, and they decided to fight together to get their lives back. While it was extremely sad that Aunt Susan had breast cancer, it was great that they could fight together, and neither of them felt alone in their journey to get better. They had made a pact to help each other through the bad days and enjoy the heck out of the good days.

Sierra and Aunt Sue Sue—the two biggest fighters

December 4, 2017

PM update on day 101 of Sierra's journey... So last night's post was fun. She just went on and on and I had to slow her down because she gets on a train of thought, and she goes with it. She was not happy to go back to El Paso, but we explained to her that her brain still needs to heal. Even around family, she has to take a break and get away from everyone. We continually explain to her that if she can't handle just family, she can't handle the outside world.

There are so many things we can't talk about when she's around or she cries and gets very scared. It sticks in her head, and the negative thoughts come rushing out. So, for now, we watch everything we say so we don't set her off, we monitor everything she watches on TV, and we don't let anyone talk negative around her. She and I were talking about that today. I told her if she can't handle ten people in the dining room, there's no way she can handle the outside world. There is so much negativity and self-centered people when we go out. They stare at her, and bump into her when she tries to walk out in public.

She's still not eating very well either. She definitely needs to tolerate a lot more stimulation and start gaining weight, before we can consider bringing her home. If she continues to refuse to eat, she will have to get the tube put back in her stomach to give her the nutrients she needs. We talk to her and tell her if she doesn't start eating, the doctor is going to put the f——g tube back in her stomach.

It makes me so sad to threaten her like that, but we don't want that tube back in her belly, and she definitely doesn't want it back in so we use that to remind her how important it is for her to eat. She will reluctantly take some bites, and with every one of them she asks if that's enough to not get the tube back in her tummy. Right now, the doctor told her she has to eat at least 50% of every meal. So far the only way I can make her eat enough is to go home and make her pasta dishes. She loves beef-a-roni, pasta salad, spaghetti, and fettuccine. So when I come home, I make her one of those dishes just so she'll eat some without fighting it as much, even then, it's a chore to get her to eat.

She also reads all my posts now, so that's a whole other issue. I give pertinent information to all of you; pay attention to what is appropriate for her and careful about issues that are not. I told her now that her brain is better, she can say what she feels, and understand the point she is trying to make. So I told her that she needs to make it clear to her therapists that they need to push her. She feels like they aren't doing a good enough job of doing that. So we talked about it and I told her to state her mind and tell them what she wants. She said she doesn't want to cause trouble, so I told her this is your life, so tell them! It means a lot more coming from her rather than her parents.

She got an MRI today and she did amazingly well. It was loud and huge. So I sat with her and she kept looking at me telling me "I'm okay Mommy." She also chose to ride in my truck, with no chaperon, and we took the highway. Big accomplishments today! Daddy came in to eat with her this evening, so I left them to enjoy their time and take a couple hours down time. Today was progress, and progress is good. Goodnight, and thank you, all. #TeamBdog

Our biggest obstacle for her right now is trying to get her to eat. There is nothing that looks good to her. I have told her to pick anything, and I will get it for her in the hopes that she willingly eats. I don't like having to push her, coax her, and threaten her just to get her to eat some of her food. We're assuming it is the medication they have her on that is curbing her appetite.

She was still in danger of having grand mal seizures, so she had to take medication for that. She was extremely depressed, so we put her on antidepressants and several other medications to help her brain heal. We were also starting to wean her off the medications and introduce vitamins as a supplement in the hopes of getting her off all of her medications.

The hardest obstacle we were going through now was listening to her tell me how she was dying and she was ready to go home. She wanted to go back with her brother, back to the "peaceful place." We had to check her vitals multiple times a day to make sure she was still alive. She didn't quite understand that if she was talking or breathing that she was alive. She told me every day that she talked to her brother, Andrew. This scared me tremendously because I didn't want her to have a connection to heaven. I wanted her to understand she was alive and she was going to fight to make all new connections in her new brain.

She wanted to come home so badly, but I was terrified to take her home while she was talking about dying and talking to her brother who lives with Jesus. I didn't know how to handle or how to react when she told me that she was talking to Andrew. She told him that he had to come visit me, and she asked me every day if he had come to visit me. When I told her no or not yet, she told me that she was going to tell him that she wouldn't talk to him anymore if he didn't come visit me. I would love him to come visit me more than anything I could ever imagine. Her brain had not been programmed yet, so I truly believe she didn't know the obstacles that are ingrained in our brains as we grow up. Maybe if no one ever told us that we can't talk to people who have crossed over, we could achieve the unimaginable. No one has told Sierra's new brain that it isn't possible for her to have conversations with people that have died, so her potential was endless. One of the many times she had written for her brother to come visit me.

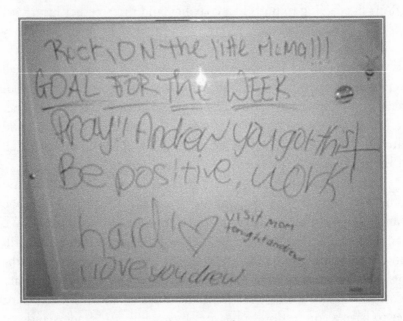

Talking to Andrew

December 5, 2017

> PM update on day 102 of Sierra's journey... Today was a great day! Probably one of her best days yet. She went to therapy today and came back with body odor because she was sweating when she worked out on the stepper. We made a bet about the infused water they were serving, I said that it had lemon, and she said lime. If I won, she would eat 100% of her food, and if she won, she only had to eat 50%. She laughed and said, "Okay, Mommy!" And we shook hands. Well, I won and she shook her head, smiled and said, "Okay, a bet's a bet, and I said I would, so—" and

she proceeded to eat 100% of her food. That's the first time she ate all of her food in quite a while.

We had our family meeting today and Sierra has several concerns, so I told her to write them down to prepare for the meeting. We went over what she wanted and how she would present it. I explained to her that her dad and I can fight for her and it won't matter until *she* shows them her progression.

They work on her body and I work on her mind, and she's really responding lately. It's so beautiful. Anyways, we walked into the meeting, and I mean walked. I let go of her hand and let her walk in. She sat down and informed her whole team that she has a list of requests. I love it! So they let her speak her mind, and it was one of the most poetic debates I have witnessed. She informed them she wants to walk, and she not only wants to walk, but she wants to walk normal, so if it takes surgery, so be it, whatever it takes. She continued with she wants to listen to music when she's doing therapy. Also, she wants the alarm off her bed because she is aware of her safety. She knows that she can't get out of bed without someone there to watch her as she gets up. There are other requests she made that have to do with her other wounds and she stated those precisely as well. They all listened intently and when she was done, they contemplated all of her requests and…She will be walking without the walker and also with no assistance when she feels she doesn't need it. The alarm is off her bed, she gets to listen to music in therapy, even speech therapy, and she needs to go back to the doctor for the other issues, which they will set up an appointment. Wow! She stated her case, and I was in awe of her, with her body language and assertiveness, I was so proud of what I was witnessing.

That's the young woman we raised to be independent and state her mind, as long as it's with respect. That strong willed young woman who goes after what she wants, and always gets it because she works hard and *earns* it. She's coming back! And today was the most I've seen of her since August 24th. As we left the meeting she held her head high, maybe not as high as mine after what I just witnessed, but pretty high.

We went back to her room and I told her how very proud I am of her and she was in a really good mood, smiling and laughing. It felt so good. She found some post-its and decided to write herself notes all over her room, and on her door she put one that says, "God Bless! True believer inside! I can do it! And keep fighting!" She also posted them all over her room and bathroom. Then she wrote one that said, "God's miracle!" and put it on her forehead so I took a picture, and all you can see is the post it and a Big smile under it. The spelling may not be correct, but the meaning is clear. Today was a fantastic day, and we are so thankful for that and for all your prayers for her and our family. #TeamBdog

Absolutely true!

Today was the best meeting we have had with the staff by far. We had meetings every week to discuss her progress and make a game plan. This week, I prepped her so that she could state her requests so her medical staff would listen to her and understand that she did know what she wanted. Every time she had an idea or stated what she wanted and didn't want, I had her write it down so she would be prepared for the meeting. She was not only prepared, she eloquently stated her requests, backed them up with facts, and came out of the meeting with everything she had asked for. It was so beautiful. I was so proud of her. I saw so much of our old Sierra today in that meeting; my heart was so full of pride for my baby girl. She is truly our miracle. She told them what she wanted, and they granted her request…that's my baby!

December 6, 2017

PM update on day 103 of Sierra's journey... She had another really good day. I woke her up at 7am and she was ready to go. She refused her medications last night because she said she didn't like how they make her feel. The nurses said she has the right to refuse them now because she is aware of what she feels and how to state it. She said that she slept well, she even had a dream, and she woke up much better.

We will pay attention to her behavior and moods to see if it affects her adversely. For now, we're going with it. She went on an outing with other patients to the museum at the university, and Mama Mimi, the woman who has taken Sierra under her wing, said she handled it very well. At times it was a little overwhelming for her, but when it got a bit overwhelming she just got away from the crowd and composed herself. I was very glad to hear that.

We started another puzzle, a 550-piece puzzle and she is able to focus on it for over an hour every time we work on it. That's beautiful. Her ability to focus for much longer periods of time is showing great progress. I told her I was going to leave early because the roads were probably going to get bad because of the weather, and she pulled out her phone to check El Paso weather and calculated what time I would have to leave depending on the temperature. She informed me that I should leave around 6pm because the temperature was going to drop quickly and it's been raining all day so the roads will get icy. Wow! I Love her ability to reason. So I left and she was going to have girls' night in her room where they are going to do each other's nails. I'm interested in seeing what they came up with when I go in tomorrow. Goodnight for now, and we are thankful for another good day. One day at a time, and today was good. #TeamBdog

When she told me that she didn't want her nighttime medications, I tried to reason with her to take them, but she wasn't having it. She actually made a very good case against taking them, but I was fearful of her not taking them. The only way I could leave her at night and not worry about her was to know she had her nighttime medications that knocked her out. I was afraid if she woke up at night and I was not with her that something bad may happen to her.

She still had moments of confusion, and the nurses were not exactly speedy in answering the nurse's button. They didn't check on her regularly, so anything could happen. She could fall out of bed, she could decide she was going to walk around when she was sleepy, which could be very dangerous for her; she may not pull the nurses cord when she got up, and no telling what she may do if she thought no one would come in. She was still so impulsive; I feared what may happen to her.

When the staff told her that she earned the pass to go on an outing with them, she was very reluctant to go. Mama Mimi told her that she was going and told Sierra that she would watch over her. We both felt much better about that. Once they got there, Mama Mimi never left her side. She kept a constant eye on Sierra to make sure she was okay. She seemed to have a better understanding of Sierra's condition than the staff did. When she saw that Sierra was starting to have a hard time, she brought her away from everyone until she was calmed down enough to join the group again. The outing itself was a success; however, when they were driving back to the hospital, Sierra decided she wanted out and tried to open the door while they were driving down the road.

That's exactly what I feared; the staff would not keep an eye on her because they didn't understand her injury. Thank God Mama Mimi did, and she had a close eye on Sierra the whole time, so when she tried opening the door to the van, she stopped her and explained to her how dangerous that was. When they got back, the staff informed me of what she did and obviously had no understanding of Sierra's injury; they just acted like she was a bad kid that didn't follow the rules. They had no comprehension that she was impulsive and didn't understand consequences. I felt so misguided by the people that came to see her in Las Cruces. They came with smiles and assured us this was a good move for her. Now we were seriously doubting our decision to let her come here to continue her healing process.

Sierra and Mama Mimi heading to the van for their outing.

December 7, 2017

> PM update on day 104 of Sierra's journey...
> Before I write her posts every night, I contemplate what to write...and what not to write.
> There is a level of privacy we have to respect for

Sierra, such as the pictures. We decided that when the day came that she wanted to show herself, we would determine if she's capable enough to make that decision, and if she is, we would go with it. She did, and it happened to be when Uncle Tony came to visit.

Today she informed us of a memory that is very disturbing, which completely sent her off course. Disturbing memories can slow, or even stop her healing process. The Administrator told us that we have to redirect her brain because it can get stuck there. Of course this is very disturbing news to us, after how far she's come, and the immense struggles she's overcome, this was hard to hear. We can only pray that the road we take to remedy this is the correct road for her new brain. It's worked up to this point as far as we know!

She still thinks she's a boy sometimes, which is odd because she knows much more complex issues, it's hard to understand. But it is amazing watching new connections being made all the time. Sometimes when we have conversations, I look at her and forget, just for a moment, that she was knocking on heaven's door three months ago.

This morning when we were walking, with no walker and no hand to hold, she started laughing, and because of the knee and pelvis, she limps so she has to think to walk, so laughing and walking is out of the question. But she tries. It makes me laugh too, and then she laughs harder so I have to help her walk, while she's laughing, which makes everyone around her laugh. Anyone who knows her knows exactly what I'm talking about because she has a very contagious laugh. She has become quite popular around here, which is also no surprise. She loves to hug everyone, and she has a big smile for them. She's also an inspiration to many of the patients here.

Her second Mom, Mama Mimi watches over her when we're not there. It makes me feel really good because I don't think the staff here cares about her near as much as Mama Mimi. It also makes her feel good because Sierra always has a smile for her and a word of encouragement for her. Besides Mama Mimi, Sierra is an inspiration to many of the other patients as well. They tell her that they want to sit with her and hang out with her because she makes them feel better and they want to fight for their lives just as she does.

Everyone here has a brain injury and they fight their own battles every day. Sierra inspires all of them, she tells them how she believes in them and she knows they will get better. She also informs them that she will fight with them and for them if they would like her to. She's like a mother hen here, even though she is the youngest patient, she is still helpful and inspirational to all of them. She holds them and talks to them about how they are going to get better and how she will help them any time they feel down or defeated.

I watch her and I smile so big. I listen to her talk to the other patients and I am in awe that she is not only able to talk with them, but to capture their attention and their hearts the way she does. The closest person in age is about ten years older, yet they listen to her and her words of wisdom so intently. She makes them smile and gives them hope for a better day. I truly believe she is better for them than the staff here. They administer medications and continually lay down the law, but they don't offer compassion and understanding. I am so incredibly proud of her, she's coming back to us and it's beautiful. Goodnight and Thank you all for your prayers, we see them in action every day. #TeamBdog

Our little social butterfly was coming back to us. First thing in the morning, all the patients met in the dining room for breakfast. They all had certain tables they sat at depending on their comfort level. Sierra always chose the first one as you walked into the dining room. In the beginning, it was just she and I. Now that we had been here a while, the patients had come to know her and chose to sit with us at her table. They told her how inspiring she was to them, how they wanted to have her incredible strength because they had seen her go through very bad days and come through them with grace and dignity.

She had dubbed her table "the positive table." So the patients knew when they sat with her, they had to be positive about their healing. On the other hand, when they were having a hard time progressing, she asked them to sit with her so she could encourage them. Even the people who seemed the hardest to get through softened up around her after hearing her story. Now she and Mama Mimi were the patients that everyone looked up to. They had also decided to fight together to get their lives back, so they helped each other when one of them was feeling discouraged.

December 8, 2017

PM update on day 105 of Sierra's journey... We got the results back from the MRI today, she has complete tear of the ACL and the meniscus in her knee. She needs surgery, but we don't know if her new brain can tolerate it yet so we'll be going back to the orthopedic doctor to figure out when she can withstand the surgery. Now the limp definitely makes sense. She's compensating for it but her therapists believe that's what is tweaking her pelvis as well, because she's over compensating for the knee.

She's getting really aggravated that she has to be here in the El Paso rehab. She argues with us, telling us that she's ready to go home. Until we remind her of what she will face when she's in the outside world. We tell her that she told us she was ready two weeks ago and ask her if she was really ready then? She agrees that she wasn't. Then we talk about where she is as far as her recovery. We tell her she has to trust us because we want her home as much as she wants to be home. Our fear is that her getting out too soon can set her back. Right now she is improving rapidly and we'd like to keep it that way.

She's still refusing her night time medications but she's starting to cry again. She just keeps saying, "I don't know why I'm so sad, why do I keep crying?" She's easily irritated as well. We had to leave the dining room tonight because a guy that was visiting a patient was talking too loud and she told me, "If we don't get out of here I'm gonna tell this guy something, and he's not going to like it!" After the incident at the Rehab in Las Cruces when she told the man who irritated her that she was going to f——k him up if he didn't quit talking, I thought it was a very good idea to get her out of the situation, so we went back to her room and hung out until bedtime. It's so hard to know what is good for her at any given moment. Sometimes she is okay with a room full of people, and the next minute, she wants to hurt people because they are talking. We just continue to take it as it comes, and remember that it is all progress, and progress is good whatever form it comes in. #TeamBdog

The trip to the orthopedic doctor was interesting. I knew she was going to get an MRI, so I tried to prepare her for that. We were beginning to realize the obstacles and the struggles that a disabled person in our society faced. When we went out, she still needed her wheelchair. The handicapped spaces to park were almost always taken, so we had to park at the end of parking lots so I could have enough room to get her in the wheelchair. She had to wear dark sunglasses because she was so light sensitive, her head was shaved, and she had to have her bee everywhere we went for added security. When we took her to the doctor's office, we had to schedule her appointments at their slowest time of the day because she couldn't handle being around a lot of people. When we got to the doctor's office, I checked her in, and then we had to go outside or find a quiet place for us to wait until they called her back.

People looked at her as if she was an ogre. They stared at her and then whispered to each other. They bumped into her and didn't even acknowledge when they did. This did not help her paranoia about people talking about her. She still thought people were talking about her, and they thought it was funny that she was in an accident. I'm sure that they didn't think that at all, but it was very hard to convince her of that. I explained to her that people feared what they didn't understand, that we had a natural curiosity to know what happened to someone when we saw that they were not "normal," so they just stared at her everywhere we went. The fact that she realized what is happening in her surroundings was progress for her, and although it was scary and sad for her, it was all necessary for her to understand how to be in the outside world and also for her to understand she was not quite ready to leave the hospital yet.

As for me, I wanted to punch people in the face when they bumped into her or talked about her because she was not "normal." It was so hard for me to keep my cool sometimes, but I had to keep in mind that I needed to be here for her no matter what, so I had to bite my tongue and let people's ignorance roll off my back. I'm sure that my intolerance comes from the fact that I was sleep-deprived, was still not eating well, and I had to watch her cry just about every day because of fears she created in her head. She also cried because she was so sad.

She asked me about everyone that was in the accident all the time. She wanted to know if they were okay or if they were hurt like her. I told her that they were all okay, that the passenger had to have surgery on her wrist, but she was okay.

She was beginning to understand her life now. She knew she was in a terrible accident, that she died and saw her brother in heaven, and that he told her she had to come back and fight the hardest fight of her life. She cried and she cried. She tried to prepare me for her death daily. She knew how beautiful it was on the other side, and she wanted to go back there because it was too hard here. When we had our family meeting and the staff asked me what I wanted as far as her recovery went, just one thing: I wanted my baby girl to stop preparing me for her death. I needed a day when she didn't tell me that she was going to die every hour. I needed to regain strength, and I couldn't do it when she told me she was going to die. It broke my heart every time she told me, and I had to muster up the strength to distract her from those thoughts.

December 9, 2017

PM update on day 106 of Sierra's journey... This morning, as soon as she woke up, she called me and told me she was ready to go. I stayed in El Paso last night because I knew she has a pass to come home today so I was only about five minutes away and when I got there, she was not ready at all, she still had sleepy eyes. She was so anxious to come home that she didn't think about brushing her teeth or washing her face, just the basics that a healthy brain knows to do. So we washed her up a bit, put her in the truck, and got her home safely. She is able to ride in my passengers' seat all by herself now. When it's too much for her, she just puts the seat down, puts her bee over her head and holds my hand. I've noticed the more traffic, the more anxiety, but she's also able to soothe herself more often. We got home and she went straight to her room and lay on the bed. She didn't sleep, or turn on the TV; she just laid there and soaked up the experience of her own room.

She has homework over the weekend and part of it was to complete a Sudoku puzzle. It was fairly easy for her. I helped her with which lines or boxes to work on, but she figured out where to put the numbers. She wanted to get her eyebrows done so she called Auntie Von and she was over there in about ten minutes and away they went. It was hard to see her in another car driving away; part of my heart went with her. She did really well and she was very happy to have them done.

She wanted to spend the night with her brother so she can wake up there for Zo's birthday. Zo was very excited to have Auntie Sierra back. She hasn't seen her in quite a while so she is extremely happy to see the progress she has made. Sierra's trying to figure out all the details of the accident and why Morke was in the car. She thinks it's her fault that he was hurt. She has a very intrinsic personality now, but her old brain was very extrinsic so it's hard to watch the burden she carries for everyone and everything bad that happens.

We explain to her exactly what happened, Leslie spilled her drink, looked down and veered off the road, when she looked up she realized what happened and over corrected to try to get back on the road, it was just a terrible accident. Maybe inexperience played a role in the outcome, but it's the past and this is the present that we have to deal with now. The fact that she can even ask these questions is progress. By next week, hopefully her brain will make the necessary connections to come to an understanding for the questions and concerns she has this week. Then there will be a whole new set of questions that she will have to figure out, and she will! Goodnight, and thank you, all. #TeamBdog

When I got back to the hospital, I went straight to her room, expecting her to be waiting at the end of the bed for me. Instead, I saw her eyes just peeking out of her covers and messed up hair. I pulled down the covers, and what I saw was a big smile that asked me, "Are you ready to go, Mommy?" I couldn't help but laugh. I told her that we had to get her cleaned up before we went, and she reluctantly washed her face, brushed her teeth, and combed her hair. She didn't want to change out of her jammies because she said she was just going back to bed when she got home. We agreed that was okay, so we packed up her things, grabbed her bee, and headed off. The roads were busy, so she took the initiative and put her seat down and covered her head with her bee, then she reached over, grabbed my hand, and breathed a sigh of relief. After a minute, she muttered, "I'm okay, Mommy." It was so sweet; she was learning how to soothe herself in scary situations.

After lying in her bed for a while, she decided she wanted her eyebrows done, so she called Auntie Von, and she came over immediately, and off they went. My heart sank as I watched them drive away, but just as Sierra had to progress, so did I. I had to conquer my fears as well. One day, I would have to give her wings back and let her fly, and all these baby steps would get me there.

She knew tomorrow was Zo's birthday, and she had decided to sleep with her so they could wake up together. Zo couldn't have asked for a better gift for her birthday. She said the only thing she wanted for her birthday was for Auntie Sierra to be okay and get better. That was exactly what she got. Auntie was getting better and better all the time. Unfortunately, Sierra wouldn't be able to handle the stimulation of her birthday party, but she was okay with that because her Auntie was alive, and she got to spend the night with her and be there when she woke up on her birthday. We were all so grateful for that gift.

December 10, 2017

PM update on day 107 of Sierra's journey... She got to spend the night with her brother, and Zo was very happy to have her Auntie there for her birthday. She is afraid for the kids because she doesn't want them to see her like this. We explain that they are very happy to see her the way she is now because they have seen her much worse, she just doesn't remember. So Zo told her that she wasn't scared, she was happy to see her like she is now because it was very scary to see her in a coma. It calmed her for the moment but that is a constant fear. Whenever the children are around her, she is very concerned that if they see her like this, that it will mess them up.

Last night at her brother's, she asked Lee if they were okay, if they were fighting. Lee told her, "No way!" and her brother decided to joke with her and said, "No, she's not, but I am." And she broke down and cried hysterically. The thought of her brother being mad at her, was too much for her to handle. I scolded her brother and explained to him that she doesn't understand joking yet. He felt very bad and told her how sorry he is, held her and consoled her until she quit crying. Sometimes we forget. We look at her and most of her scratches, and scrapes have healed, but her face looks "normal" so when we talk to her, sometimes she's right on track. All of us have said something to set her off. It's a live and learn experience, and the only way we know it's something she can't handle, is to find out the hard way. Unfortunately that means we make her cry, then we learn more of what we can and can't say.

She had a very nice visit at home and she's is so looking forward to staying instead of visiting. We feel confident that we can continue the road to get her back while she's at home. We have learned enough that we feel pretty confident about her December 29 discharge date. As long as she doesn't digress for any reason, we are all ready to have her home and continue her journey in comfortable surroundings. We had dinner together for Zo's birthday since she couldn't tolerate the party, so we ate together before we left and she cried so bad leaving her family to go back to El Paso. We explain that she's almost there, and what she's got in front of her, doesn't compare to what she's got behind her that she has already overcome. Goodnight, and thank you, all. #TeamBdog

Trial and error; that is the only way we know how to handle each day. She told us she was better and she was ready to come home. We wanted to believe her, and sometimes we'd even forget how badly her brain was injured. When you looked at her, you couldn't tell that she was in such a terrible accident that took her life. She was fortunate that her face didn't get any scratches, scars, or gashes on it. But because of that, when you looked at her, she looked "fine." She wasn't fine, and all of her injuries were internal, mainly the brain. She didn't know how to joke or understand jokes. When her brother thought he would tease her, it backfired. She cried so hard at the thought of her brother being mad at her. They were so close, and she looked up to him for everything. I got very upset with him, and we all agreed we would hold off on joking about anything until she was healed more.

Zo picked a very quiet place to eat for her birthday so her Auntie could be with her as well. It was a very nice, quiet dinner with my children and grandchildren, more than I could have asked for. Until the end when we had to go, and Sierra was so sad she cried almost the whole way back to El Paso.

December 11, 2017

PM update on day 108 of Sierra's journey… Today was a very interesting day. She gets her mind stuck on something, like the cop ordeal, and she totally focuses on that one thing. With that said, today was Andrew. Actually it started last night. So she had told us that she died. We told her she never died, she almost died but she didn't. We assumed she was still in her altered state of illusion. Her brain "woke up" on October 5th, which is also Andrew's death date. So, through the course of her recovery, she has told us that she died on several occasions; we continued to tell her that she didn't die. Last night when we were at Anthony's she told him that when she died, she talked to Andrew and he told her that she had to go back. That she couldn't stay because Mom wouldn't make it. He told her that it was going to be a hard road, but he would be there with her and help her through it. I listened intently this time, but then she started going into detail that she could have never known. I mean we have talked about him through the years of course, but not the details that she described. It gave me chills for sure. Not only because of the story, but because I undeniably believed her for the first time that she actually died. Before today, I really wanted to believe it but I actually just went with it and didn't want to deny her beliefs.

Then today she reiterated the exact same story to me, with more detail that made me realize there is no denying what she is saying. Which makes us all the more thankful, incredibly thankful, that she is still with us. We *know* that we will get her back and we also know she's being guided from above. Goodnight and thank you all for your continued prayers. I see them working every day. #TeamBdog

She had told me multiple times that she died. It was an unimaginable thought for me. I couldn't accept it. I listened to her and just passed it off as one of her many stages that she had gone through since the accident. Sometimes, my heart would sink into my stomach at the thought of losing her as well, but I wouldn't let myself actually believe that she did die and her brother was there waiting for her. Today, on the other hand, she was adamant and precise with her details. She told us the exact same story with much more detail about her brother. She included details that she would have never known unless she definitely saw him and interacted with him. She gave much more detail about heaven and the feeling of being there with her brother. He told her he was happy that she chose the number eighteen for her softball career in memory of him, and he was aware of why she picked it. He lived for eighteen months and eighteen days, and the number eighteen had always been her favorite number since she learned her numbers. He told her that he had always had a connection with her and that he had been her biggest cheerleader her whole softball career. Now he would be her biggest cheerleader in her road to recovery.

While I was totally ecstatic that my baby girl actually got to meet her brother, the way in which she met him sunk my heart into my stomach and made my heart beat out of my chest. When I prayed myself to sleep, I thanked God with everything that I had that she was given the opportunity to come back to us.

December 12, 2017

PM update on day 109 of Sierra's journey... She started off her day with physical therapy. They actually let me be a part of it today. She wanted me to see how well she did the ladder walk. Wow! She rocked it; even with the weak leg, she rocked it.

She's got the app for Luminosity on her phone, so in her spare time she plays that and she's doing surprisingly well. She is so focused on getting out of here that she has been doing everything she possibly can to achieve that goal. She knows that we can call the insurance company to extend her stay if she's not at the point where we can feel comfortable bringing her into the outside world. She's been protected since the accident. As long as she continues the way she's been going, she will be fine. We will have to pay attention to the environments we take her in, and at this point, we need her to be able to tolerate more stimulation. She's really up and down on that, but that's better than not being able to tolerate eating in the dining room with more than three people in it. She is learning to breathe through it. When she starts to get overwhelmed she closes her eyes and takes some deep breaths to work herself through it. It's really impressive.

We had a Christmas party tonight and we didn't like it pretty quickly. It was hosted by a bunch of people who have had or are continuing to live with TBI. One woman came and sat with us; so it was Sierra, her dad, Mama Mimi, that woman, and I. This woman starts talking about her accident and what she went through and I could see Sierra start to cringe. I asked her politely not to talk about that because she is scaring my daughter. She continued with no compassion to any of the patients and their situations. I was getting very upset and I was keeping an eye on Sierra to see her reaction. Mama Mimi was also watching over her because that woman wouldn't stop talking and she told us she's been there so it's fine. I was getting ready to take Sierra back to her room because this woman refused to show any compassion to Sierra's fears when Mama Mimi laid into her. She told her that she needs to shut up or leave our table, that she is scaring Sierra and she doesn't even care so she needs to go sit somewhere else. That made us feel so much better and Sierra's Dad and I were laughing the whole time. If there is more than one conversation going on at the same time, she gets really confused, but tonight she did much better. She's been having really good days, we know the bad days are not over, but today and the last several days have been really good, and we are thankful. #TeamBdog

She was on a path of determination. She wanted to go home, and she was doing everything she possibly could to make that happen. After her meeting, she told her staff that she could walk on her own and that her abilities were further than they knew. She told them that they held her back, and she wanted them to let her do things on her own. This was the first time they let her do the ladder walk without the strap to hold her up. Her ability to handle stimulation was getting better all the time. When the staff brought a flier for the Christmas party, she told me that she didn't want to go because there were too many people. That was two weeks ago. Today, she said she was ready for the party tonight. It was being hosted by a group of TBI patients, so we hoped that she would find inspiration in them.

As the time for the party got closer and closer, she was more hesitant to go. Her dad came down to join us, so she was excited about that but less excited about joining the party. We told her that we would go down to the dining room where it was being hosted, and if it was too much for her, we would take her back to her room. I went down to the dining room early to help set up. When I got there, I immediately became concerned if she would be able to tolerate it. There were people with different degrees of injuries. I feared that when she saw some of them, she would not be able to handle it. There were people who couldn't talk or walk, people that needed a caregiver to do everything for them, and there were also people who looked "normal." It was somewhat overwhelming for me, and I had no idea how she would react to them. This was one of the situations that were trial and error. She may handle it very well, and she may freak out. I went back to the room and talked to her dad about what I saw, and we both agreed that we would let her try it, but we would watch her very closely to see if it affected her adversely.

When we brought her down there, she immediately got a look of fear on her face. Mama Mimi told her that we would sit together and she would watch over her. That seemed to ease her fear, so we all sat down together. Sierra's first question was, "Mommy, am I going to be like that forever?" as she pointed to one of the severely disabled people. I explained to her that she was already doing better than they were. They were already at their stopping points where they had to learn to live with their disabilities, and she was not. She was still getting better every day.

Then the woman with the big mouth came to sit with us, and even when we asked to her to be careful with her words, she justified what she was saying. Then Mama Mimi jumped in and told her flat out to be quiet or leave our table. She explained that Sierra couldn't handle it, and she didn't show any compassion toward her and her injury. The woman just sneered at her and got up and left our table. Although Sierra felt better about her leaving our table, the party proved to be too much for her, so we had to take her back to her room and talk her down, get her medications for the night, and rubbed her to sleep.

December 13, 2017

PM update on day 110 of Sierra's journey... Okay, so she's still stuck on Andrew and apparently she's still talking to him. I don't know, it's all so confusing. She seems more aware of everything, however, some of the things she comes up with makes me question so many unanswered questions about our brains. Since she has to make all new connections because of the shearing of her brain, parts of her new brain are connecting in parts of our brain that we don't use. I don't know how clear that is, but it's the best I can describe it. Today she said that her brain feels clear, that she's not clouded anymore. She continued with a very elaborate story of how she believes she is ready to go home because she understands things today that she didn't understand yesterday. She also earned Friday trips with the more advanced patients so she was really jazzed about that. She's not sure where they're going but she doesn't care, it's one more goal attained.

Morke made it safely to his family in Panama. We're very happy about that. She said she misses him, but it's very important for him to see his family because his Mom and Dad have not seen him since the accident and she can't imagine how hard it was on them. So she has the ability to look past her own feelings for the benefit of someone she loves very much. Her progress is amazing, I definitely was aware of her deeper thought today, now that she's out of the cloud. Yet another giant step forward. Yeah Bee! Thank you and goodnight. #TeamBdog

Many conversations today felt like I was talking to the old Sierra. She was able to articulate her thoughts and feelings better than she had since the accident. The staff noticed and awarded her Friday passes with the more independent patients. When her nurse came in and told her about her Friday passes, she had a great big smile on her face. She knew that she earned it by practicing safety, showing initiative toward hygiene, keeping her room clean, and doing her laundry without being told. It was a wonderful accomplishment for her, and she knew it.

The whole day, she repeated over and over, "Mommy, I'm so clear. I can remember things." It was a day that I had prayed for since August 24. Now when she talked to me about Andrew, I no longer got the feeling that it was just talk. I truly believed that not only did she see her brother when she went to heaven, but I also believed that she was still talking to her brother, and I envied her.

December 14, 2017

> PM update on day 112 of Sierra's journey... She started her day off on a really good path. On her good days she walks into the dining room and greets everyone. She says good morning and makes her rounds hugging everyone, asking them how they slept, how they're feeling, and tells them that she believes in them, and they can do it. She's an inspiration to so many of the patients here. They want to sit at 'the positive table.' She doesn't realize what an inspiration she is to all of us. People tell her all the time, but she doesn't believe it.
>
> Yesterday she said her head was clear. Her thoughts were clearer, like the cloud was gone, and today we were doing a puzzle and all of a sudden, she said she didn't feel good and wanted to go back to her room. When we got there, she said she's really confused about everything. She

was crying and telling me that she didn't understand what was going on. So we went over the
whole story…from the beginning. We started
with the accident, then Albuquerque, then Las
Cruces, and why she is here now. She absorbed
it as we were talking, and then she cried and said
she didn't know why she was crying, she just
didn't feel good. So we decided to go shopping.
I thought if we get her out of there for a while,
that would help. It worked. We ate and talked
about everything but the hospital, we were just
shopping like people do.

She thinks that everyone thinks she's a boy,
and wants me to put a sign on her back that she
has brain damage so people know why her hair
is short, why she doesn't understand sometimes,
and not to be rude to her. It's Christmas season,
which seems to bring out the worst in people
in the stores, and it's just something that we all
accept, but it's not so easy for her. She pushed
the cart through the whole store. She thought
she might need the electric wheelchair, but she
didn't, and we walked all around the store, it
was impressive for sure. When we got back, the
patients were going to see Christmas lights, and
she decided to go with them. That was a big step
for her. Also, she informed me that she can be
around people that wear red now.

She talked to a woman that was a cancer
survivor yesterday; she comes to the hospital for
her therapy. When she was telling Sierra about
her story of how she had a brain tumor and now
she is tumor free but has to work on her brain still
and she only cried once while they were talking.
She said she can talk about the accident, and
things that bother her because she can just cry

if she needs to and learn to accept it. She knows
people in the outside world talk about things that
scare her and she wants to go home so she isn't
getting away from conversations that scare her
now. She just looks at me, takes a breath, holds
my hand, and shakes her head letting me know
she's okay. She's just the biggest fighter I've ever
known. Goodnight and God bless. #TeamBdog

Today was an emotional roller coaster. She started off great,
greeted everyone in the dining room, told the cooks how much she
appreciated them, made her rounds to every table, and asked if she
could have a hug. She encouraged the other patients and told them
she believed in them. She stuck out like a diamond in the rough. She
was so young and so inspirational to everyone. When she got here,
we sat at the same table by ourselves. Now we all had to squeeze
together to fit at her "positive" table.

After breakfast, she wanted to work on a puzzle. Everything was
fine, and then it wasn't. She asked if she could go back to her room.
When we got there, she lay in her bed and started crying. Suddenly, she
was sad and couldn't stop crying. We went through the drill of telling
her how far she'd come and how amazing she was, but it didn't work.

We decided to go shopping, and that seemed to help for a little
while. Then she was scared and told me that she was not ready to live
in the outside world. Christmas season seems to bring out the worst in
people. They push and shove, and many people lack patience. It's the
usual hustle and bustle of the holiday season. But for her new brain,
it was just too much. Too much stimulation, too much impertinence,
too many conversations, and people bumping into each other as they
passed by, many times without even acknowledging that they did it.

December 15, 2017

PM update on day 113 of Sierra's journey... She
is extremely focused on getting out of here. She
is making her therapists push her so she can get

stronger. She knows that surgery on her knee is very possible even though she fears it. We will be taking her to the orthopedic doctor on Monday so we will know the next plan of action. Also they will x-ray her pelvis to see if it was put back together correctly. If she does have to have surgery, we want them both done at once. She said she doesn't want surgery, but if she doesn't get it, the way she has to walk will hurt other parts of her body because she compensates by twisting her body and it's very unnatural.

She earned another afternoon pass and wanted more socks, because she is the queen of socks, so we went to get her more socks, again. Then she wanted Peter Piper Pizza...on Friday night! I wondered if she could handle it but I figured I would just go with it and see what happens. When we got there, she looked at me and said, "I'll wait in the car!" I thought that might happen, but one day it won't. One day she will be okay with high stimulation.

So she was talking to me today about why she thinks she's a boy. She knows she's a girl, but why does she think she's a boy? I think that's progress because at least now she wonders about it. A couple weeks ago she thought she was a boy so I got her headbands and barrettes because she feels like her hair is too long to spike now, and when she looks in the mirror she can see she's a girl.

Tomorrow she gets to come home until Sunday evening, and she informed me that she doesn't care what her dad and I say, she is staying! She said she is not going back! I laughed at her and told her that she could stay here at the hospital instead if that's what she thinks. So she laughed and tells me, "Okay, I'll do what you and my dad tell me to." And, of course she ended her sentence with an eye roll. Her vocals cords are healing because her voice is definitely getting louder, especially when she laughs or cries. It's really funny or really sad. #TeamBdog

She was showing more interest in going out. She wanted to go shopping, go get an ice cream, and go on outings with the other patients. Her progress was staggering. Every day was something new. Some of her thoughts and actions were positive and enhanced her healing process, and others were almost debilitating to her. It was as the old adage says, "One step forward and two steps back!" The most important thing we had to remember was that even on her bad days, she was healing. So new fears, thoughts (even the bad ones), and anger, they were all progress for her. There were days when she cried all day long and she didn't know why, or she cried because she was beginning to understand that she had lost everything she worked for. She cried because she was starting to reason things out in her mind. All very sad yet very promising as far as the healing process goes.

December 16, 2017

PM update on day 114 of Sierra's journey... So she is home and very happy about that, of course. She loves visitors now. Her ability to handle more and more stimulation is increasing weekly, so she said that as many people want to come over at the same time is okay. That if she starts getting overwhelmed, she's learning how to deal with it. This is great and I've been pushing her to tolerate more stressful situations because I want her to be okay when she comes home. She's doing better and better every day. She handles stimulation and we can wear red now, she listens to conversations that used to scare her and says she can do it. Sometimes she has to cry, but she knows it will pass. She's been wondering about the accident and wants to find out specific details about it, so she text Leslie about it and they went through the whole thing again. I'm sure it was very hard for both of them, but we truly believe this is part of both of their healing process. She wants her to know that she doesn't blame her, that she loves her and knows that it was just a terrible accident. #TeamBdog

Lately, she had been asking me about the accident. I gave her as many details as possible, but that was only from the doctors. I knew about her injuries, her prognosis, and her medical condition, but I don't know much about the accident. I hadn't talked to Leslie, so my information was only from witnesses and Morke. Part of me was happy that her brain was healing enough to wonder what happened, but the biggest part of me hoped that she never remembers. Just the information that I do have makes my heart sink into my stomach.

I have dreams of her flying through the air and bouncing off the ground with a huge pile of blood around her and splatter marks where she bounced off the road. I have dreams of her crashing through the window as they are rolling. I have dreams of them rolling down into a gorge and all four of them dying. I wake up scared to death-heart pounding, shoulders so tight, and I can feel my heartbeat in my head. The only thing I can do to release the fear is cry. I cry and I pray, and I thank God for giving us our baby girl back.

Leslie had hardly seen her since the accident. I'm sure it was very hard on her as well, but Sierra didn't have the capacity to understand that. She only knew that she didn't come to see her, so I tried to explain to her that there were different perspectives to this accident.

December 17, 2017

Pm update on day 115 of Sierra's journey... She really enjoyed being home and she's getting more and more independent on a continuous uphill climb. We rarely help her get around anymore. Tomorrow after her orthopedic appointment, we'll have a solution for her knee, and the pelvis. If we could get those fixed, she wouldn't need help at all. She's understanding more why she has to stay at the rehab hospital in El Paso. In two weeks she will have much more control of her thoughts, less confusion, and we hope that she will have more understanding of each situation.

Actually she has shown us that the sky's the limit. She's courageous and she finds things that work for her to handle difficult situations, and that can change daily, or weekly. That's why we live one day at a time, or one situation at a time, whatever is appropriate at the time. She said she feels like she was a baby all over again. Anthony and I were talking about that very subject. We got her back as a newborn and have raised her again in fast motion. We are extremely grateful for the opportunity to do that again. Andrea, the passenger, came to see her today and they sat there and laughed and reminisced just like before the accident. Just a few girls talking and laughing. It was so great. #TeamBdog

It sounds so simple, and many people take that for granted, and I used to be one of those parents telling the girls to quiet down, turn the music down, and don't be so crazy. Funny, those are the things I missed the most when she was in her coma. I wanted her to be too loud and blast her music, and I yearned to hear the voices of her friends gathering in her room, driving me crazy. Listening to them talk to each other and laugh was so good to hear again. Oftentimes, it is the things that drive us crazy that we miss the most when they are gone. I wanted her to argue with me and tell me, "I know, Mom!" I wanted her to leave her dirty dishes in the sink and clothes all over her bedroom floor. But now I just appreciated her getting better all the time.

PM update on day 116 of Sierra's journey… Well, she's pissed! She wants out of here and will not hear anything we have to say about it. No matter how much we try to reason it out and tell her how much she has improved in the last two weeks. She has shown great improvement in these past two weeks, and we know that the next two weeks will show even more improvement. It's getting to where it's taking away her focus on everything else because she is so frustrated. She gets angry with me and argues many valid points, in her defense, but scattered thoughts as well. She said she wanted to do a puzzle, so we went out to the dining room, got all the pieces out, separated them, turned them right side up, and then she put her head down on the table. I asked her, "What's up?" and she said she wants out of this freakin' place! Then she got louder and louder about how she didn't need to be here, that these people don't even help her. She wants out and she wants out! So, we have to listen to her and do what we can do to get her home.

We will keep you posted on that when we know. Today we went to the orthopedic doctor and he doesn't want to do surgery yet. He doesn't think her brain is ready, and it's not hurting her, so he doesn't want to chance it right now. It makes her twist when she walks, which tweaks the pelvis. The pelvis was put back together correctly, but it's shifted. So he believes that as she builds muscle, it will work its way back into place. I appreciate the information people have given me to continue her progress once she gets home. I believe it will be very helpful. Thank you all… until tomorrow. #TeamBdog

We are at the point that we didn't know if having her here at the hospital was actually counterproductive. Her focus was on getting out of here more than her therapies. We believed it was starting to hinder her progress, so we had decided to fight for her to be released. We would ask for websites and specific exercises to help her continue her progress at home.

Almost every time we went to the dining room, she started yelling that this place sucks and the staff didn't care about the patients. In her defense, they had never shown near the compassion or knowledge that the Las Cruces rehab showed her and her dad and I. They continued to look at her like she was crazy when she did or said anything out of the "norm" and didn't seem to know how to pacify her or how to explain to us the stages she had gone through or was going through. To say we had been displeased with this place since she'd gotten here would be an understatement.

We were happy to know that her pelvis was put back together correctly the night of the accident, but if we didn't get her knee fixed soon, she would continue to have pain because she tried to compensate for the bad knee. So the way she walked had tilted her pelvis. More importantly, we had to wait until her brain could handle surgery.

December 19, 2017

> PM update on day 117 of Sierra's journey… She had a completely different outlook today. We went to breakfast and she talked about how peaceful and warm it is in the dining room. She said she feels really good and she's ready to work hard so she can get out of here. It was so nice because she's been pretty angry lately. We had our family meeting today and it went really well. They told her she's making tremendous strides, balancing, walking, safety awareness, independence, and self-awareness. Her ability to solve problems is increasing every day. Her dad talked to the insurance com-

pany and they told him that her discharge date is tomorrow. So when we went into the meeting Sierra stayed in the gym and I asked them if they thought she was ready because her dad and I feel that she is. They all agreed that I could take over from here on out so we came to a compromise, and her release date will be the 22nd.

She reads her posts so I will make the phone calls we need to make so she can have her homecoming after four months of being in hospitals. Alarms beeping constantly, people at all hours of the night talking and coming into her room to take vitals, to give medications, to tell her what she can and can't do. Having time limits and schedules for her entire day, not having choices over her own life. She is ready to take her life back! If I don't call you by tomorrow and you want to be there, please message me and I will give you the time and date. Thank you and goodnight. #TeamBdog

Today just goes to show how quickly her moods and her outlook changed so drastically. Yesterday, she was so angry, yelling at the staff that they sucked and she didn't need to be here. Then she proceeded to tell them that they were just here for the paycheck and that they don't even care about the patients. I just sat there, dumbfounded. She didn't have the ability to lie, and her lack of a filter made it so she said whatever was on her mind. I truly have to agree with her because everything she said was exactly what her dad and I felt.

I feel confident enough that I could take over her care from here on out. I was the one that had taken care of her since she got out of ICU in Albuquerque anyway. I was her security blanket, and she felt much more competent when I was with her. I still showered her and shaved her because of her balance issues, but she was getting dressed and using the restroom by herself now. She had started doing her own laundry here with very little help from me because she wanted to show them that she was ready to go home, and there is no better place to heal than home.

We didn't take her into the meeting because if they denied her this chance to go home, she may go off on them. Seeing as how she threw the "F" bomb every time she got irritated, I figured it would be best to let her sit outside while we conducted the meeting.

December 20, 2017

> PM update on day 118 of Sierra's journey… I had to tell her when she is coming home for good. She read the entire post, which she usually doesn't do, so I took a chance that she wouldn't read it. I was wrong, and she gave me the phone and asked what's going on? So I text her dad and we agreed we had to tell her. I told her that she's coming home for good on Friday the 22nd and I saw her light up, look up, and her favorite saying comes rolling out… "Thank God!" She's back on her rampage about how this place sucks; these people suck, but not the patients, just the staff, most of them anyways. #TeamBdog

I tried to be sneaky and post her homecoming without her knowing. We talked to the staff again, and we all came to the conclusion that she shouldn't have to wait until the twenty-ninth, that she should be home for Christmas. So, after our conversation, we all agreed on the 22nd. She was sneaky and read the whole post on her own. She showed it to me like she was my mom and I was in big trouble. It was quite funny; she looked at me and put the phone in my face, asking, "What is this?"

So I had to break down and tell her about the great news that she worked so hard that she got to come home for good. No more passes, no more doctors, nurses, and staff telling her what to do. She got to sleep when she wanted and wake up whatever time she wanted.

She was over the moon happy as was I! I actually started tearing up at the thought of our baby girl coming home after such an incredible fight to get her life back.

December 21, 2017

> PM update on day 119... Her spirits are definitely higher now that she knows tomorrow is her *freedom* day. The patients and staff are very sad, yet happy to see her go home. There is an older man here, he got here about a week ago, and he was not happy! He refused to talk to people when they talked to him, and he didn't like coming out to eat. Sierra, being the person she is, she smiles all the time at him and says good morning. At first she thought he was mad at her, but I just explained to her that he's just mad to be there. Anyways, she kept smiling at him and saying good morning, good afternoon, and goodnight. Well, he finally came around and he smiles now and tells her that he loves her smile, and now he sits at 'the positive table' with us and engages in conversation with us as well. They call her the rubber band over here and her tech can't talk about her leaving because she gets teary eyed. She has touched so many of the medical staff that has taken care of her through this entire journey, even the ones she doesn't remember.
>
> I can say it over and over, she is coming home! It just hasn't sunk in yet. There will be no more hospitals, staff, social workers, discharge staff, administrators, doctors, nurses, and everyone telling you what you can and can't do. We are looking forward to her homecoming more than words can say. To all of you who never quit pray-

ing for her and our family, we are forever grateful
to all of you. #TeamBdog

She was walking on a cloud today. She had made her rounds throughout the hospital, telling everyone that she was going home. Everyone was so happy for her yet very sad to see her go. Her personality added such an uplifting environment for all the patients. The staff that did care about the patients were very sad to know that she was leaving but very happy that she had worked so hard that she got to go home now.

I had made the necessary calls so that she could have a great homecoming after four months of being in hospitals. We were so excited that I'm sure tonight would bring no rest for any of us, but that's okay because she was not the only one that would be on their own schedule now. I had also been on the hospital's schedule, and I was definitely on the same page as she was. I just wanted to go home! I wanted our baby girl back home; I wanted to start our new life with so much gratefulness for every new day that we still had her with us.

December 22, 2017

PM update on day 120 of Sierra's journey...
Today is the day we hoped and prayed for, the day
that she has been fighting so hard for. Because of
her drive and determination, she made it home.
We have watched the most amazing phenomenon for the past 120 days. So many obstacles she
has overcome.

When I got the call that no parent ever
wants to get, she started in Albuquerque on life
support with tubes in her brain, in her lungs, in
her chest, towers of medications trying to keep
her alive, to giving a thumbs up and then signing, and writing and then swallowing, and sitting
up, and stages that were so unbearable that we
knew only God could have gotten us through,

re-teaching our baby everything, and thrilled and
blessed for the opportunity to do so. The tragedy
on top of tragedy that we have had to endure,
but through all the hard times and doubts, we
had all of you praying for her, for us. So many
people followed her journey; it just amazes us
the kindness people have shown us. We are very
grateful to everyone who had a part in her journey. It's not over by any means. We got her home
by the grace of God and every person who prayed
for her and believed in her. Thank you just isn't
enough. #TeamBdog

This is the day the Lord has made! We will rejoice and be glad in it!
She had a beautiful homecoming, so many people at her dad's house
to welcome her. Everyone clapped for her, and many people cried for
her. We had all seen the impossible happen with God's grace. Today
was the first day of her new life, and we knew it would be a beautiful
one.

December 30, 2017

PM update on day 128 of Sierra's journey…
Since she has been home, we have let her sleep
whenever she wants to, shower when she wants
to, eat when she wants to, and do pretty much
whatever she wants. We agreed that when she got
out, we would let her have some downtime where
no one is telling her what she can and can't do
and when she has to do it. So she has been taking
full advantage of it.

We got her set up with her outpatient therapies back at the Las Cruces Rehab. She will
continue Physical, Occupational, and Speech
Therapy, only now she will just be an outpatient, which she is thrilled about. She was very

happy that she gets to go back there, they work hard on her and push her and they actually care about her. We are in the process of setting her up with all new doctors, including a neurologist, a neuro-ophthalmologist, a PCP and psychologist. Her knee has been giving her problems so she may have to have surgery before the two months is up, but we have to go to the Neurologist to see if her brain can handle it yet.

Her boyfriend decided that he didn't want to be with her anymore. He text her on Christmas day and told her that he doesn't want to be with her, and for her not to text him anymore. She accepted it at that moment and asked him to remind her if she does text him because she might forget. He informed her that he has made his decision and for her to leave him alone. Of course this upset all of us very much, especially her.

We had a beautiful family Christmas celebration at Aunt Susan and Uncle Bob's, even though she just had a bomb dropped on her. The best gift we could all ask for was for her to be alive and home with us, and that is exactly what we got. She is now writing each day in her notebook. She writes what she did during the day, how she feels, what she thinks, and how she thinks.

I also want to take this time to thank so many of you. The people that have been here with us from the beginning, giving us care packages, making us food, offering us places to stay, money, the softballs tournaments, kickball tournaments, fundraisers, and most of all, your prayers. For my family not leaving me in the beginning, we all struggled through the hardest times together, and we made it this far. For our friends coming up to

Albuquerque to offer their help in any way they possibly could. For understanding the position we were in and sometimes just being there, not saying a word, just being there for us. For everyone who did everything they could to help us through our darkest hours, but mostly for your prayers for our baby girls healing. We all have made this journey together, and we continue this journey together. One day, my last post will be, *she did it*! She is 100%. That's our prayer anyways. This has been the scariest, life changing event our family has ever faced, and we did it together. We came out stronger and more appreciative of every minute we are given together. And with more faith in humanity because of the kindness all of you have shown us. Thank you. #TeamBdog

Now we start a new, completely different life, one that includes more appreciation, more gratitude, and more thankfulness. We have our baby girl home for good. We have to work on getting her doctors set up and her therapies so she can continue to soar.

Our Christmas was better than any Christmas than we have ever had. Aunt Susan was alive, Sierra was alive, and our family was more blessed than anything we could have hoped for. Not many families are given the opportunity we have been blessed with, and we all realize that this is better than any gift that can ever be bought. We have our family, and we are together again.

She still has a long road ahead of her, but we are very hopeful that she will continue to get better and reach 100%. She may not be the Sierra we used to know, but she is a new Sierra with a new brain, and she will soar. We have no doubt about that. We are so grateful for every person who has had a hand in getting her this far, beginning with the long list of doctors, nurses, and techs. All the softball parents and her longtime friend and catcher, Krystal, for putting fundraisers together, to my niece, Sarena, and my longtime friend, Becca, for setting up GoFundMe accounts to help us financially. To friends and strangers alike that have read every post and sent words of encouragement, and to my family who supported me and helped me through my worst days, days when I was sure I couldn't do it anymore. We all did this together, and I am proud of all of us, but mostly, I am proud of our baby girl for never giving up and fighting the biggest fight of her life.

March 12, 2018

Day 200 of Sierra's journey… Wow! Two hundred days ago our world was turned upside down. The exhilaration of knowing our baby girl was starting her second year of college. She was everything a parent could hope for. She worked her whole life to achieve her goals. Then, the call came in from Coach Lucas that she had been airlifted after being in a terrible accident. The rug was pulled out from under our feet in one instant. It felt like a robbery of the peace and security we had once known. We always prayed for her to be safe on the road and became more at complacent the more she came home. That dissipated immediately. That's how quickly our lives changed. Then tears and heartache replaced peace and security. We watched our baby girl, our sister, our niece, our auntie, and our friend have to fight for her life. And she did! She fought to regain her life back, and the fight was insurmountable. But she not only did it, she kicked its butt and didn't look back. She never let the "Why?" or "How comes?" or faults get her down. She never held a grudge or anger about what happened to her. She had a focus, and that was to get better. Because of her attitude, she has surpassed every obstacle, and every medical opinion that was in her path.

We are now blessed with the biggest fighter we have ever known, the miracle we have witnessed.

We watched an entire new brain forming, which, I have to say, has been the most incredible experience we could have imagined. We raised her not to go with the flow, to be strong, independent, and to work hard for everything she wants. Thank God for that because we know that not too many people could have survived that injury, but to overcome it as well as she has, is truly a miracle. She lost her independence; friends, well actually acquaintances, her scholarship, her ability to play softball, and her boyfriend. But through it all, she has not lost her drive, her passion, and her faith in God.

She is such an inspiration to us and to many people. We will be forever grateful to the people who supported her and us through this terribly awful period in our lives. Most of all, we are thankful for the beautiful young woman that we have raised. She is getting better every day in every way and refuses to accept medical opinions that only put obstacles in her way. She is walking, talking, eating, communicating, and starting to use reason to solve problems. She is well on her way to 100%. Friday she will be throwing the first pitch to start the softball tournament this weekend. Again one more obstacle that she was told would never happen. We, as her parents, her family, and her friends could not be more proud of our miracle. Thank you to everyone who helped her and us to get this far. #TeamBdog

She threw the First Pitch!

This has been two hundred of the longest days of our lives. We have watched her go through so much turmoil and come out on the other side with grace and integrity. She doesn't point her finger in blame; she doesn't hold grudges because she lost the life she once knew; she just works as hard as she can to regain her life back. She accepts what is in front of her and figures out a way to get past it and blow away any obstacle that is put in her path. She is my hero! I hope and pray that someday, I can be as great as she is. A miracle only touches the surface of what we have witnessed as she made all new connections in her new brain.

May 20, 2020

Day 1,000 of Sierra's journey... In one thousand days, she has relearned everything, including how to be an independent adult. She and Buster moved out into their own apartment last week, and they are doing great. I want to give a big thank you Lex and Krystal for doing most of the heavy lifting. She is happy and confident that she will succeed. Her dad and I are anxious, scared, and happy for her. My life has been "her" since the accident, and now it is also time for me to start my new life. Like her, I am somewhat unsure what tomorrow will bring, but I'm ready to conquer anything because I also learned from her how to be a warrior and accomplish whatever I set out to do.

She still has lingering affects including; memory issues, but has learned to write everything down in her planner. She has headaches, but she also has medication for when they get unbearable. When she gets sick or her schedule gets thrown off, it makes her confused and it affects her injured brain ten times as much as a healthy brain. So she knows how important it is to take care of herself and ask for help when she needs it. She still needs a nap every day to keep her on track. But this is her new normal and she continues to soar. Her main issue as of today is her vision. She doesn't see like we see, her brain is not connecting with her eyes correctly but she has learned to compensate. She does eye exercises every day to help her get her vision back and be able to drive again one day. She has an emotional support dog named Buster James Stallone Gonzalez to help her and he has brought more joy and security to her than we could have hoped for. Her softball career and her full ride are gone, but her life is not. She will find new passions and she will still do great things. Trauma nurse may still be in her future. Who knows? The sky is the limit. We gave her wings back so she can fly again. One of the most frightening experiences we have incurred but we feel sure we re-raised her well enough to succeed.

Her dad and I lost our baby girl that fateful day, but we were so blessed to get back a new and improved version of our baby girl. She also lost life as she knew it, but she is learning a new life and finding new interests. Her old brain and the old Sierra was an amazing young woman with dreams and goals she worked her whole life for. This Sierra is still a fighter, only now she has fought for her life back, and she has come out victorious. Our family is so blessed to have her, and life has new, better meaning with her in it. This will be the last post and I want to thank everyone who had a part in getting her here to this point. You people rock! #TeamBdog

She and Buster, the first day in their new home—*priceless!*

When all is said and done, our family has been blessed beyond comprehension. Sierra today is not the Sierra we once knew, but we call her the new and improved Sierra. When we have conversations of the past and present, we relate to her as her new brain and old brain. Because of her frontal lobe injury, she is more abrupt and less capable of holding her tongue. She is easily agitated and finds it harder to calm herself down in situations that upset her. Her tastes in food have changed—some foods that she used to like she no longer does. However, foods that she didn't used to like she does now. She

324

has taken on different interests such as sewing, cooking, and running. She has become quite the chef, exploring different recipes with more ingredients.

Naps have become an essential part of her life now. She tires easily, and any kind of stimulation, good or bad, really wears her out. Everyone in her life understands her new world. We all know that her old brain used to work full-time, go to school full-time, and play softball. Her days used to start at 5:00 a.m. and end about midnight. When she went to college, her days started with a five-mile run up a mountain, go to softball practice, go to her classes, go to softball practice again, and then go home and do homework. This was her life, and she handled it all very well.

Today she wakes up between 8:00 and 10:00 a.m., takes her best friend and ESA, Buster, for a walk, comes home and makes breakfast, then takes a nap. After her nap, she takes Buster for a walk, then comes home and either sews or starts planning what she will be cooking for dinner. Because of the COVID-19, she has not had any therapy or doctor's appointments. Although it's a pandemic that is affecting the world, it has actually given her a break from the continual doctor's appointments she has had since she got out of the hospital.

Our family has had the opportunity to watch an entire new brain form. Because our brains form in utero, not many people have been blessed enough to experience this miracle. When she came out of her coma, she was not able to do anything. We taught her everything again. We taught her how to keep a clean home and wash clothes, taught her manners, courtesy, how to manage her doctor's appointments, manage her money, and gave her a day planner so she can keep track of her appointments. She still struggles with compassion, patience, and memory, but she has all of our family to help her through her rough patches.

She has games on her phone that help increase her brain power and memory and relies on them to help improve all aspects of her brain.

She often argues with us, so we have to explain why it is that she needs to do these things; sometimes she gets it, and sometimes she refuses. We have had to teach her the dangers of the world we live in because she is a young woman living on her own, which can make her an easy target for the evil of the world. She doesn't have the capability to understand these things on her own, so unfortunately, we have to scare her enough to make her understand how important it is to pay attention to your surroundings, especially when she is going in and out of her home. She still can't drive because her eyes don't connect with her brain correctly, and her peripheral vision is nonexistent. Because of this, she doesn't go anywhere by herself, with the exception of her walks with Buster.

She lost the sparkle in her eyes, and she is no longer the social butterfly she used to be. She no longer goes out of her way to talk to people. She is more of a loner now, and she chooses to live by herself as opposed to getting a roommate. She knows that she is more intolerant and judgmental toward people now. She knows she shouldn't be, but she can't help it. This is something we continue to work on quite often. She is nice to people until she chooses not to be. She says they make her be mean to them. Most days, she is irritated and easily annoyed, so we talk about why she feels those feelings so that we can find the core of the problem, trying to find a solution that makes her feel better.

All in all, she has a new brain, and we have a new daughter. We are so grateful that we were given a second chance to raise our baby girl again. Not many people could have made it through the horrific accident and extreme trauma she has made it through. The doctors from the beginning of her journey gave very little hope for her to live, but like I told them, you don't know Sierra! Now they do! Every one of them tells her that she is truly a miracle, but we already knew that.

We have cried a river of tears and felt an ocean of heartache. We have witnessed our baby girl on the brink of death, watched her fight so hard to get her life back, live through unimaginable fears, watched her cry in pain, saw the terror in her eyes when she came out of her coma and couldn't communicate, watched her go through stages that scared us to the core, made us laugh and made us cry. We saw machines breathe for her and towers of medications to keep her alive. We watched every device and every medication dissipate as she fought to get better.

Our confident, driven, ambitious child has turned into an insecure, intolerant, and very impatient young woman. I always said that Sierra could go into a room of a hundred strangers and come out with ninety-nine friends, and now she chooses to be alone most of the time. She knows that her family accepts the new brain, but most of her old friends don't, but she is learning to understand that as well.

She is learning to live life on her own terms, has accepted who she is today, understands why her friends have dissipated, and continues to fight every day of her life. She doesn't remember some people yet does remember others. There is no rhyme or reason to it all. At some point, she has just had to accept things as they are and deal with the situation at hand.

We found her a new eye specialist in Phoenix, Arizona, and she is amazed that Sierra can even walk because of the way she sees. The doctor showed me a chart of how she actually sees, and all I could do was to break down and cry. Her eyes constantly jump up and down, and she sees everything like it is shaking. Somehow her brain has learned to compensate for how she sees. Although she wants nothing more than to drive at this point in her healing, she knows it is unsafe for her and for others on the road, so she is trying very hard to accept this fact and let the progress take care of itself as her brain continues to heal.

Good things have come out of this terrible tragedy, like the fact she and her dad have a stronger relationship than they did before the accident. She has learned who her true friends are, and she has also learned that she has more talents than just softball. Cooking has become a new passion, and she makes excellent dishes from scratch. She got a sewing machine and has taken up sewing and has become quite good at it.

Jeff and I went to Vegas to get married in September of 2019 while his mom took care of her. She is still impulsive and cannot follow a thought to its entirety. Having said that, when Jeff's mom had to run out for a bit, Sierra decided to take an uber to a tattoo parlor. Well, when we got back, we realized she got the 7 chakras down her entire back! Needless to say, I was not pleased at all. So, we agreed that she would not get anymore tattoos until her brain is healed enough to understand the consequences of her actions.

Unfortunately, we lost Aunt Susan two days before Sierra's twenty-second birthday. We thought that would stop her healing process because they were so close to each other, but it didn't. I insisted that she come with me to see Aunt Susan on a regular basis so she could see her deteriorating in the hopes that when she did pass on that Sierra would understand that she is no longer in pain. It worked; that is exactly how she saw it when she did pass on. We were all so very sad to lose Aunt Susan, but we all agree that she was too beautiful of a person to suffer so badly. Also, Sierra's time in heaven helped her be at peace with Aunt Susan's passing. She told us all that she knows where she is, that she is in "the peaceful place," where nothing bad can ever happen to her again, and she never has to feel pain again. She is right on all counts, but life will never be the same without Aunt Susan in it.

We were all so blessed to get Sierra back. I don't know why God chooses to spare some people and take others, but we believe in him and trust that his plan is more supreme than we can wrap our heads around. We are so incredibly thankful that he chose to spare our daughter from death, to let us experience every new day with our child here with us. She is not done with her healing, and neither is our family, but we can only feel gratefulness for the opportunity to see her grow, laugh, smile, and even cry. For all of it is part of life, and through it all, we continue to grow, and through pain comes strength, growth, wisdom, and healing. My one prayer in this life is that all of you may be as blessed as we have been.

About the Author

I was born in Mountain View, California, and lived in the Bay Area until I was a teenager. I moved to New Mexico and have made it my home ever since. I had twin boys in 1987 and unfortunately lost one of them eighteen months and eighteen days later. Sierra was born in 1998, and my childbearing years were through.

I met the most beautiful man I've ever known and married him in 2019. We had a beautiful life and were best friends. Unfortunately, he was one of the hundreds of thousands that COVID-19 took from us in October of 2021. Life has given me many challenges, but I've got God, and he's got me! So far, my track record for overcoming obstacles is 100%. I started this book as a healing process for me after she got out of the hospital. During the process I realized her story can inspire others and hopefully bring peace, hope, and faith to people suffering tragedy.